MOTHERING:
Toward a New Psychoanalytic Construction

❖

Mothering

TOWARD A NEW PSYCHOANALYTIC CONSTRUCTION

Silvia Vegetti Finzi

Translated from the Italian
by Kathrine Jason

THE GUILFORD PRESS
New York   London

© 1996 The Guilford Press
A Division of Guilford Publications, Inc.
72 Spring Street, New York, NY 10012

Printed in the United States of America

This book is printed on acid-free paper.

Last digit is print number: 9 8 7 6 5 4 3 2 1

Library of Congress Cataloging-in-Publication Data

Vegetti Finzi, Silvia, 1938–
   [Bambino della notte. English]
   Mothering : toward a new psychoanalytic construction / Silvia
Vegetti Finzi ; translated from the Italian by Kathrine Jason.
     p. cm. — (Feminism and psychoanalysis series)
   Includes bibliographical references and index.
   ISBN 0-89862-334-0
   1. Motherhood—Psychological aspects. 2. Psychoanalysis and
feminism. I. Title. II. Series.
HQ759.V3813 1996
306.874'3—dc20   95-38876
                                                CIP

❖

Acknowledgments

This book stands at the crossroads of two different types of experiences in my life that have converged: on the one hand, my psychotherapeutic work with little girls, and on the other, women's culture. In both of these contexts, the awareness—now taken for granted—that women must look at themselves through their own eyes (as Luce Irigarary teaches), and see themselves from the point of view of their sexual differences and specificity, has been decisive. In my research, I have relied to a great extent upon experience, reflection, and the cultural productions of other women.

The themes that I explore here have been discussed on numerous occasions in public. I would like to acknowledge the most memorable of those: l'Universita delle donne Virginia Woolf, in Rome; il Centro Documentazione Donna and l'Istituto Universitario, in Florence; I Centro Donna di Brescia, in Cagliari, Cosenza, Padua, and Leghorn; "Lo specchio di Alice," in Naples; "Melusine," in Milan; and l'Associazione "Livia Donini," in Turin. Among the most memorable conferences were the one on the culture of women that took place in Modena in 1986, and the one on bioethics, held in Rome at l'Istituto Gramsci, 1988. Oustide of Italy, I have tested my opinions in a series of seminars organized by the Universities of Valencia and Alicante, Spain, in 1986; at the International Conference of Bioethics, held in Montreal in 1987; and at the University "Paris VII," in 1989.

I would like to express my deep gratitude to the little girls who offered

v

me the inestimable wealth of their imaginations. I would also like to thank for their intelligent and involved cooperation to the English editing of this book: Professor Claudia Zanardi, Kitty Moore, Senior Editor at The Guilford Press, and Kathrine Jason, translator.

I thank my husband and my sons, Valentina and Matteo, for having shared the emotion of this work.

SILVIA VEGETTI FINZI

Note: The biographical details about the little girls whose clinical case studies are reported here, Anna and Paola, have been changed to guarantee their anonymity.

❖

Foreword

I am pleased to introduce Silvia Vegetti Finzi's work to American readers. It offers an important Italian perspective on the meaning of motherhood. The value of her work lies in her search for a new meaning of motherhood beyond the biological phenomenon of procreation. The Italian title of the book, *The Child of the Night*, represents a conceptualization of mothering which explores the creative dimension of a woman's body, a fantasized child belonging to all women.

Silvia Vegetti Finzi, a strong voice in the Italian feminist movement, is a professor of psychology at the University of Pavia, and the author of an influential textbook *The History of Psychoanalysis* (1986). She has written extensively on psychoanalysis and on women's issues, trying to integrate psychoanalytic theory with her feminist experience and her humanistic background. She utilizes history, anthropology, and mythology, as well as psychoanalysis, to trace the roots of women's identity in a new and interesting interdisciplinary approach to the understanding of women's psyche.

In this book Vegetti Finzi addresses women's historical identification with the social function of mothering, an invisible process internalized in the unconscious. This coercive mechanism transforms the maternal experience into a social role, changing woman's desire to be a mother to the necessity of being one. She analyzes how patriarchal values expressed through family structure and social expectation restrict the meaning of motherhood, forcing women into a constrained role.

Vegetti Finzi defines motherhood from a woman's perspective, attempting to trace its meaning in the "archaeology of the female imaginary"—the historically repressed women's unconscious. She utilizes a Lacanian framework to address the absence of the mother from the symbolic order, and demonstrates the need for women to search for their own definition of motherhood outside established discourse, in the archaic images preserved in children's unconscious and in ancient myths and rituals of fertility. In this ancient culture Vegetti Finzi finds a vestige of the conflict between the sexes over procreativity, a conflict which has ended with the supremacy of male desire.

Vegetti Finzi also finds evidence in her clinical practice with pre-adolescent girls of a desire and fantasy for spontaneous procreation of their own child—an imaginary child, a child of dreams, which she calls "the child of the night." This desire represents the girl's awareness of her womb's capacity to create, an awareness lost in the oedipal phase when she takes on the father's desire as her own. The author shows how ancient myths confirm this desire, in which innate spontaneous procreation is repressed by male figures who envision the womb as a container for their offspring: an appropriation of women's bodies, a paternal definition of mothering. As woman becomes mother, both idealized and imprisoned in a role of biological and social reproduction, she loses her identity, she loses contact with her body. Her womb becomes in her fantasy an empty space ready for the child of the man.

Vegetti Finzi suggests that the contemporary woman's struggle with motherhood is expressed in numerous ways including through psychosomatic disorders linked to reproductive functioning. She theorizes that psychosomatic infertility expresses woman's rejection of a constructed social role: the status of being a mother. She addresses the need to search for a conceptualization of motherhood that arises from the woman's body, a body that is capable of generating, and is not merely the container of the father's semen or of his baby. In mythology and anthropology, she traces memories of women's capacity to generate autonomously. These images of female creativity—a creativity which has been destroyed by patriarchal culture—remain a potentiality for all women: a complex of physical and psychic energies, of fantasies and attitudes which women can utilize in the birth experience as well as in other creative life projects. In Vegetti Finzi's view, mothering in the birth control era can no longer be seen as destiny, but as a potential that animates women's bodies and minds.

CLAUDIA ZANARDI, Ph.D.
New York University
July 1995

Introduction

"Where do babies comes from?" This is a question that every generation asks when it confronts the mysteries of life for the first time and feels the need to define itself. The simplest answer—"From women"—disturbs us somehow and is difficult to accept. In fact, what it means is that each of us must recognize that we are all dependent upon the female sex, and that little girls must connect with the mothers from whom they would rather separate.

Although psychoanalysis has brought sexuality into the realm of consciousness to a great degree, motherhood has remained obscured by repression; as such, it represents the most resistant obstacle that the analytic tool confronts in its probe of the unconscious. Furthermore, when women have looked at themselves in an effort to reclaim their particularity, they have been suspicious of the maternal role, which has been used historically to justify their exclusion from the spheres of economics and politics. Therefore, thinking about motherhood from a feminine point of view requires that we shatter a powerful tradition, which has made use of the apparent simplicity and naturalness of being a mother to conceal the laborious process that leads the little girl to become a mother in a world founded upon the priority and centrality of the male figure.

This book attempts to distinguish the disposition toward motherhood—the generative power that women carry within themselves, and the interactive attitude that this suggests—from its connection with its exclusive realization in filiation, which is to a large extent socially constructed. Since motherhood is both the most intimate aspect of being a woman and a woman's most common form of relationship, the view of it here consists of concentric circles: from the infantile imaginary realm to the mother–child bond; the symbolic forms elaborated by society and culture; and, finally, the potential for communication and ethics that is inherent in maternal competence.

In the effort to do justice to the complexity of the topic, I have used various codes of reading and different interpretive models. The observations that emerge never become organized in a conclusive system but are called upon when needed, at times offering confirmation, at times opening up unexpected inquiries. Given the vastness of the task, I hope that the reader feels involved in a process of research that is just beginning to delineate its field of inquiry and to apply its tools. Finally, I have often been tempted to do so, I have decided not to reconstruct the way in which men elaborate their fantasies of motherhood, so as not to fall back into the symmetrical schema that reserves for women a position of complementarity and shadow.

The book is divided into four chapters, which, although related, maintain a certain argumentative autonomy. The first, "Becoming a Woman: The Case of Anna," explores the clinical case of a little girl who is attempting to define her own sexual identity while struggling against the unconscious desire to be both male and female. This is a difficult choice, because it requires Anna to ally herself with the devalued sex and to accept a social position that has traditionally been subordinate.

The analysis (which relies upon Anna's drawings and dreams) progresses through a close comparison of infantile fantasies and age-old symbolic formulations, connected by deeply buried analogies. The interpretation of the infantile unconscious utilizes Freudian theory in regard to Anna's rejection of the masculine components of herself, but leaves it behind when an unforeseen psychic process presents itself: Anna's fantasy of making her own body image concave so that she can receive, from the outside, the baby that will be born. Evidently a powerful repression must have obliterated both her perception of the original maternal cavity and her own instinctive tendency—the prefigurations of gestation, of childbirth, and of her own generative product.

The questions raised by Anna's case history seem to be answered by another clinical story, Paola's, which opens the next chapter, "Who Holds the Power to Engender?: Reflections of Ancient Culture in Present-Day Fantasy." This chapter analyzes a distant feminine fantasy—that of the representation of a female body generating a "child of the night" on its own. This creative and autonomous fantasy is much like the one that animates the little girl's solitary game with her doll. A dream figure, the "child of the night" quickly vanishes from the sphere of thought, to be substituted by the conjugal concept of filiation that presumes the priority of the paternal function.

Only in the myths of the world's origins is the memory of this female desire for spontaneous procreation preserved. In actuality, they are "normalized" by male power, which has seized and kept for itself the capacity to give and form life, leaving women to function merely as inert containers of the male generative process. This is an opposition that is only confirmed by the punishment, expressed in other myths, for the fantasies of *giving* the mother a child and of *receiving* a child from the father.

The antinomy between male form and female matter, first presented in myth, has come via Aristotelian thought to influence the shaping of theoretical models of biology and medicine, and the impact of these models on social organization and ethical norms. The logical and argumentative power of cultural production makes it difficult for us even to glimpse this obliteration of the original feminine imaginary and its re-elaboration according to male desire. In this sense, the recovery of the female rites of initiation celebrated in classical Greece allows us to reconstruct the woman's process of adaptation to her social role, which has become invisible by now because it is internalized in the unconscious.

In the third chapter, "Becoming Mother," the most disturbing effects of the obliteration of the maternal imaginary is evoked in an extraordinary "birth story,"—the fruit of the self-awareness women have reached through consciousness raising. The amnesia that characterizes the human experience of maternity, in comparison to the innate competence of animals, hearkens back to a traumatic event that has been lost in the mists of time: the loss of estrus, which distinguishes the human female from all other mammalian females. Although the causes of this event are difficult to reconstruct, its effects can be analyzed. The sexual anarchy that it must have provoked was immediately countered by a system of social controls based on marriage and realized through underlying modalities of caring for the body and managing the feminine imaginary. The social regulation of fertility exploits a domestication of female sexuality that tends to make the woman coincide with the wife and the wife with the mother, and to contrast them with other female figures, which are considered marginal.

The position and function of the mother in the bosom of the family and in society constitute a historical constant of great duration, which has only been broken in the course of this century, when elements of emancipation and increasingly reliable and widespread methods of contraception have allowed women to practice nonprocreative sexuality. But while sexuality has found instruments of cultural expression, maternity, as I have said earlier, has remained unexpressed and unconsidered in our time. Therefore, it is no accident that the majority of psychosomatic disturbances in women are associated with reproductive functioning, because the symptoms represent elements that have been repressed from thought and return to find expression in the body. Among the symptoms of the present discomfort with maternity are unplanned pregnancies (and the recourse to voluntary abortions that often follows), which express women's difficulty in controlling an unconscious desire for motherhood. It is a desire that is inscribed as much in the individual's psychic economy as in the impersonal economy of the species; it forces us to reconsider our place in the sphere of nature. But it also forces us to find shared symbolic forms in an attempt to represent and incorporate this experience, which falls between conscious and unconscious, solitude and interaction, individual and society, past and future.

Traditionally, the figure of the mother has provided culture with a strong image in which to conceptualize the relationship of humankind with nature, the earth, and life. However, maternity as a process of feminine identity has remained without any sufficient representation. The last chapter, "Metaphors of Motherhood", takes its cues from these truths; it attempts to give expression to feminine generative capacity by applying the metaphors of manual and intellectual labor to gestation, of creativity to psychological birth, and of moral responsibility to the growth of the newborn. Here too, I do not attempt to define motherhood, but to reveal some of its unexpressed possibilities by tearing it away from the social regulation of its functions. What results is the figure of a woman who is reformulated in her own complexity—capable of alternating narcissistic and maternal stances, according to the goals she sets.

The creative dimension seems to prevail over every phase of the maternal process. I wonder how this could be transmitted beyond the original sphere of competence to become an intellectual and affective style, a modality of communication and comprehension. The maternal disposition has always been used for repetitive and subordinate helping and caring tasks, but its possibilities make it adaptable to social goals and types of cultural production that are much richer and more satisfying. I do not mean, of course, that the "making of babies" must necessarily be replaced by social and cultural achievements. I do mean that the capacity to give and preserve life can be translated into a particular existential quality that is syntonic with the feminine identity and its specific modality of being in the world and living in relation with others.

In the maternal undertaking, the mother continually limits the impulse to completely possess her child; in so doing, she translates domination into responsibility. We can find an ethical dimension in the sacrifice that is self-imposed in maternal omnipotence, but our culture has always denied it—preferring to exile the mother–child relationship to the realm of nature, at least until the father introduces social dictates and symbolic forms into it. But precisely now, when the field of bioethics presents society with dilemmas that appear to be unresolvable, motherhood—as a paradigm of our awareness of both the assumption and the limits of personal responsibility—can make a relevant contribution. In particular, it can contribute to finding forms of rational control to counter the omnipotence of the scientific imaginary and the uncontrolled proliferation of its technical applications.

In this sense, artificial reproduction is the last stage set on which the age-old struggle between the sexes over reproduction is being played out. It holds the last possibility that the historical defeat of women's creativity might be transformed into greater self-awareness, better uses of their own resources, and symmetrical reciprocity between the sexes.

CHAPTER 1

Becoming a Woman
The Case of Anna

THE THREEFOLD ENIGMA: ANNA'S FIRST DREAM

Anna comes to my office for a consultation, accompanied by her mother, after her medical doctors have reached the conclusion that her organic disturbances are psychosomatic and require psychotherapy. Thus begins a course of childhood therapy that will last two years (more or less, a session a week) and teach me many things about the female identity and the long process that leads from *being* female to *becoming* a woman. In this chapter, I retrace the stages of this complex journey that leads to sexual self-definition.

When she enters the consulting room, Anna hands me several drawing. "They're dreams," she says, as she squirms to get comfortable on the chair facing mine. It is an extremely harsh winter, and the little girl's smiling face, red with cold, peeks out of a large sweater. She is nine years old, and she still has a roundness to her body and the movements of a child. Her large teeth with their pearly edges give her round face an expression that is at once sweet and tenacious. In the course of our conversation, she defines herself as "a little violent," "an emotional tomboy," and "a strange type."

As I point toward the first drawing (Figure 1), Anna's gray, half-closed eyes stare up at me through her eyelashes with that air of challenge that initiates every childhood game. On an ordinary sheet of drawing paper, she has used Magic Markers to draw three figures that emerge in an arc from

Figure 1

the single base formed by a little girl's broad skirt. "I drew what I dreamed," she states with conviction. The drawing does not seem to have been made by a child, as it does not betray any infantile awkwardness or asymmetry.

Question marks appear above the heads of all three figures, raising the question "Who am I?" that inaugurates any search for identity. Anna's comment reveals her assumption that I know the truth about her and will reveal it to her immediately. But since events only gain meaning from the stories in which they are related, only listening to her will yield understanding. Thus, in a bare consulting room on the edge of the city, the analysis begins by pursuing the question of what preceded Anna's story. It will have to be inscribed in the inevitable coordinates of love and hate if it is to have meaning.

The central figure in Anna's drawing is the most elaborate of the three and looks fixedly ahead while seeming to approach us. The blond hair in loose curls and the long gown make it seem a regal figure, a fairy-tale princess. But, on closer examination, the compactness of the image seems split in two by the part that divides her hair, by the bangs that divide her face, by a kind of tie that extends all the way down the small body, and finally by the appearance of a yellow undergarment between lateral blue bands [drawings are reproduced here in black and white]. Also, the expression on the figure's face seems surprised, or even shocked.

In *The Interpretation of Dreams*, Freud stated that the figure of a prince or princess always represents the dreamer,[1] and we can certainly easily see that the main figure represents Anna herself. But what about the two other figures that flank her? Emerging from the central image, they immediately suggest a polar opposition. If we read the drawing from left to right, we see that the figure on the left has a clearly feminine silhouette, with a ribbon in her hair and modestly lowered eyes. The figure on the right, by contrast, appears to be an Asian with an enigmatic face and ironic smile beneath the characteristic pagoda-shaped hat; it also looks like an insect with antennae. Both figures are indefinite in appearance, almost protoplasmic, and appear to be linked to the central figure by arms that end in thread-like tentacles.

I give the drawing back to Anna and ask her to tell me about the dream that she has tried to visualize for me. Referring to the drawing, the little girl quickly begins a swift narration that I note down, using her exact words. This process seems to amuse her, and from that point on she tries to modulate her speech to the rhythm of my writing. The writing is my expression of engaged expectation.

> "This girl [the central figure] found herself in a really strange world, in a place she doesn't know. The first ghost, the female [the figure on the left], is surprised to see the other one, the male [the figure on the right]. The girl is even more surprised by those two beings than they are. Both are pulling to get her over to their side. And she's afraid . . . because she doesn't know this world, doesn't know these beings.
>
> "I tried to make the prince of ants [the figure on the right], and then I said to myself, 'Why should I copy?' I made it look strange because I don't like to copy. If I'm forced to do something, I can't do it. If I *have* to make a fly, it comes out like a crumb."

Anna's refusal to copy, which she equates with being forced to do something, severs her comments from any real referent, distances them from social expectations, and inaugurates the spectacle of figures and words that have no connection to anything but themselves and the latent meaning they hold. This gesture sets up the space in which an analytic effort, as opposed to a scholastic one, takes place; the analytic effort is characterized by pleasure rather than duty, by play rather than work, and by the imaginary rather than the symbolic (in Lacan's terminology).

When I point to the shocked protagonist in the drawing and ask Anna, "And what will she do now?", she replies: "I didn't think about that yet. I don't know what she'll do." Dreams are not messages from the gods concerning the future, as the ancients believed, but expressions of the present whose interpretation leads not to prophecy but to history. They lead not only to the history and biography of the individual, but also to an archeology of culture and the archive of its icons, which every representation reintroduces. According to Trevi, "The image penetrates where thought cannot reach and reflects that which thought must necessarily exclude from its field of vision in order to preserve its integrity. The image is an alternative to thought, but it nevertheless solicits thought and often precedes it."[2]

The myths that organize humanity's mnestic remains in constellations and the figures of the individual unconscious have a secret symmetry, which makes it possible to represent and share that which is most intimate and elusive in all of us. In the mythological atlas, the three-part figure occupies a central position that establishes our own self-representation. Plato stated in the *Symposium*:

> In the beginning . . . the race was divided into three; that is to say, besides the two sexes, male and female, which we have at present, there was a third which partook of the nature of both and for which we still have a name, although the creature itself is forgotten. For though "hermaphrodite" is only used now as a term of contempt, there really was a man–woman in those days, a being which was half male and half female.[3]

If Plato discovered the sexual trinity in myth, Artemidorus retraced it in dream: "A woman dreamed of seeing three images of herself in the moon. The images in fact represent her children, and a single sphere contains them."[4]

But the androgynous nature of the surprising figure in Anna's drawing—a being that is at once male and female, human and animal, Western and Eastern—recalls the Sphinx, which Oedipus encounters at the gates of Thebes. For Freud, the Sphinx is a symbol of the enigma of procreative sexuality, of the question "Where do babies come from?" that spurs our first "drive to know." This, according to Freud, "is the oldest and most burning question that confronts immature humanity." The little "perverse polymorph" can only represent its own sexuality in the plural and mixed form of its infantile libidinal organization, in which the mechanism of Oedipal prohibition has not yet taken over. The riddle of the Sphinx, whose solution forces the monster to kill herself and open the gates of the city to Oedipus, means that the order of time punctuates human life and that the simultaneity of opposites in the unconscious itself succumbs to the ordering force of the discourse.[5]

In any case, what is transmitted through the myth is a fantasy—a narrative construct that goes back to a previous three-part form, a primal phantom that we know only as a structuring mechanism. The number three, which dominates unconscious fantasy, also organizes models established by psychoanalytic theory, whose metapsychological aspect is so close to the products of the imagination. In this sense, the three drawn figures in Anna's drawing can refer, in a classic Freudian scheme, to the Oedipal triad of father, mother, and child; in a Kleinian model, they can refer to the splitting of the mother, in relation to the child, into a good and a bad figure. In yet another sense, they can represent the three functions of the psychic apparatus: the id (the animal), the superego (the contradictory image), and the ego (the intermediary figure). And, finally, it can recall the three Lacanian registers—the symbolic, the imaginary, and the real. In any case, we are looking at a fragmentation of the self, a spectral division of one's own image into its constituent parts.

Furthermore, from the vantage point of logical process, the number three takes on a special meaning for its ability to symbolize the dialectic of opposites. Freud stressed that the number three, marking the appearance of the female in dreams, in myths, and in fables (the three sisters, the three houris, the three fates), presents the problem of choice.[6] In the story of the events leading up to the Trojan War, Paris is called upon to choose among the three goddesses; in Shakespeare, Lear must choose among his three daughters, and Bassanio in *The Merchant of Venice* must choose among the three caskets. But in actuality the choice is not a real one because destiny has already decided the outcome, concealing the hard face of necessity behind the mask of possibility.

Commenting upon the three female characters who appear in the first and fundamental dream of the *traumdeutung* (Irma's), Lacan wrote, "we come to what lies behind the mystical trio. I use the word mystical because we know now what this means. Freud has shown us the meaning of the three women, the three sisters, the three caskets. The last term is quite simply death."[7]

The act of choosing, which evokes the limits of freedom and of will, establishes the psychological individual, but at the same time (and this explains the anxiety that every decision evokes) it confronts the individual with the suggestion of an impersonal destiny, in which choosing and being chosen coincide. The three women (the mother, the wife, and Mother Earth, who gathers all of us into herself) are disturbing because they present as possible what is actually necessary; they conceal the inexorability of individual death behind the promise of the eternal through sexual reproduction. From the moment of birth—and here I am speaking of psychological birth—we begin to move backward in time, to return to the state of original undifferentiation, whose certainty can only be denied by illusion.

The shock of the central figure in Anna's drawing reflects her own shock at seeing the imaginary identifications of her ego appear in the outside world, removed forever from the illusion of unity and forced to take form again through a game of mirrors that at once confirms and alienates them. In her comment, Anna does not hesitate to identify the alternatives (the lateral figures) as "female" and "male." And it is by following this initial antinomy that the work of psychoanalysis will continue, allowing the little girl to take the discussion where she will, following the clues from the beginning.

MALE OR FEMALE?: THE DILEMMA OF GENDER IDENTIFICATION

Although Bettelheim holds that nature gives the individual a single sex, he admits that a certain overlap must exist, given the fact that society requires a timely definition of self. In any case, Bettelheim continues, "the desire for the characteristics and the function of the other sex leads psychologically to a dead end: to become like the other (which the individual desires) implies the denial of one's own sex (which the individual fears). This factor is not taken into consideration as it should be in the construction of what we define as castration anxiety."[8]

The dilemma of omnipotence impels the child to deny the conflict and to put off the decision. On the surface, the choice appears to be between two alternatives, but there are always three options at work because it is always possible not to choose. At least it is necessary to believe this so that the player's freedom can be preserved. But in actuality, the third alternative is not a choice because it translates into a constraint to repeat the choice, to say "again." A story demonstrates this point:

> When an Arab nomad hesitated to make a decision, he took three arrows: on one he wrote, "My Lord orders me" and on the second "My Lord forbids me." The third had nothing written on it. He put the arrows back into the sheath, then chose one at random and followed its advice. If he happened to choose the one upon which nothing was written, he would begin the process all over again.[9]

This rite, with its ordered sequence of gestures, represents mental experiences that are difficult to comprehend, such as the coexistence of freedom and necessity. Crucial events occur in our developmental processes that we can only grasp in terms of their outcomes; for this very reason, they tend to appear inevitable and automatic, concealing the factors of intentionality (even if unconscious) that preside over them.[10]

Separation from the mother, gender identification, and Oedipal conflict are not only phases in a predetermined itinerary of maturation; they also constitute actual dilemmas—existential choices provoking conflicts that may be major or minor, but that cannot be evaded. These dilemmas should rather be thought of as part of a system composed of intention and possibility, a system within whose coordinates the child becomes an individual and makes herself the protagonist of her history.

In Anna's case, there is the option not only of being male or female, but also of choosing or not choosing. It seems that the superego, representing social expectations, is imposing a definition of self that the id, dominated by the desire for omnipotence, rejects. Anna is living the dilemma of gender identification, which carries with it the acceptance that one is partial, against a backdrop of nostalgia for an impossible wholeness (to be one, to be all) once experienced in the fused union with her mother. For Anna, it is a matter of reaching an accord between her desires and that indestructible original desire that contains all others. If it is true that every attempt to find the love object will always be modeled on that first unrepeatable experience, this accord is never fully reached.

Thus, we observe the coexistence of two contrary impulses: to distance oneself from the origin, and to return to it. For each step forward, as Freud observed, there is a step backward.[11] Contrary to every libidinal impulse, there is a movement toward the origin to which the soul would return "to be that which once was, when I was really happy," as Plato stated.[12] In fact, our unconscious desire never stops moving against time, pursuing the impossible recomposition of the fragmented parts of that lost unity. In this sense, Anna's dream seems to have accomplished its goal: to express the choice without making it, to delay any possible decision, to pull the nameless arrow from the sheath. Removed from any intentionality whatsoever, this weapon forces her to repeat the gesture of unresolved choice, presenting the blind economy of forced repetition under the guise of will. Repetition is the articulation of the symptom, the rhythmic rite that makes every neurotic an obsessive who obliterates time.[13]

But at this point, we must ask ourselves why a little girl of nine would find herself in the grips of the dilemma of gender identification that is normally confronted and resolved in early childhood—that is, during the Oedipal phase that appears at three years of age and is concluded by age five or six, making way for the period of latency. Now we must reconstruct Anna's case history, the life experience that has led her to put off these basic choices until well after the appropriate time for such events. The delay has allowed her to go through several stages of psychic evolution with an awareness of the stakes and a capacity for introspection and for representation of the psychic conflicts—capacities that never occur in the chronology of "normal" development. It is clear that we reap certain advantages from the therapy of neurosis; we gain knowledge of psychic apparatus and its processes. Yet the conflict that prompts neurosis has no particular quality. It merely appears "outside of time," causing the dynamics at work to be amplified and allowing us to "see" what would otherwise remain concealed by prejudice and habit. In any case, as Freud commented, "[Female sexual fantasy] is still wrapped up in an impenetrable darkness—firstly as a result of cultural atrophy and secondly of the silence and conventional insincerity of women . . ."[14] Women psychoanalysts have only recently managed to shed some light on this darkness.

THE STORY OF ANNA

Anna was brought to my attention by the medical team of the pediatric unit where I worked as an outside consultant in the mid-1970s. She was first admitted to the unit on an emergency basis with the diagnosis of "acute dyspnea" after her parents refused to take her into bed with them. On her second admission, two weeks later, Anna was given the diagnosis of "psychomotor disturbance" after an episode of violent itching of her feet caused an intense reaction. An electroencephalogram taken several days later showed "signs of an epileptic disorder," treatable with low doses of Gardenal. But the doctors still thought it advisable to combine pharmacological therapy with psychotherapy, particularly because the little girl was expressing a mysterious refusal to go to school. In this section, I summarize Anna's family background and the events leading up to her two psychiatric admissions, and I comment on various aspects of the case history. (Despite the fact that the case took place in the 1970s, I narrate the case history here in the present tense, for consistency with my description of Anna's analysis. Also, as I note in the Acknowledgments to this book, the biographical details of Anna's case have been altered here to protect her anonymity.)

Family Background

Anna was born and lives in Turin, in Northern Italy, where she is attending fourth grade. She is the second-born child in a middle-class family. Her father works as a typographer at a daily city newspaper, and her mother is a housewife. Both parents come from a town in Friuli. Anna's brother Marcello is five years older than she. A few years ago, the family moved to a comfortable apartment in a condominium belonging to the employees of the company for which her father works. Her father, who is intensely involved in his labor union, spends his free time drawing and painting;

Anna's mother is involved in the administration of Anna's school, as the representative of the parents' association. Both parents are people of great intellectual energy and participate fully in social causes, which allows them to connect their public and private spheres, and to overcome a sense of social isolation. Her mother, in particular, finds ways to go beyond her role as a housewife by being actively involved in social and cultural activities. At the same time, she experiences a growing sense of disappointment at the impossibility of having a real impact on institutions and changing the existing state of affairs, even minimally. "The bureaucrats are my prison," she once exclaimed after a series of school meetings.

(I should note parenthetically that the frustration produced by citizens' attempts to participate in institutions without gaining any real power has become a cause of growing social unrest in Italy during this period. As a result, the intellectual and emotional energies that have been mobilized in vain are often reinvested in the private sphere. Moreover, the family conflicts that were once traditionally assuaged by the existence of stereo-typical roles have become more acute, and the demand that they be recognized and resolved has become more pressing.)

Anna was born after a normal pregnancy and labor, and was breast-fed. However, she was born with a dislocation of both hip joints. She was treated in the hospital at seven months of age, at which point her lower limbs were spread apart and put in casts. Subsequently, she has undergone surgery three times. After recovering from the first operation, she developed insomnia. As a result of the repositioning of her legs, she has had difficulty sitting, and only began to walk after the age of three and a half. In contrast to this delay of motor skill development, her verbal development has been extremely precocious; she spoke her first words at seven months and her first full sentences at one year. Her lack of mobility has led her to devote much time to drawing and reading. Given an IQ test (Progressive Matrix 47) during her recovery in the hospital from her final operation, Anna was evaluated as an "individual of exceptional intelligence."

Events Leading to the Psychiatric Admissions

As I have stated earlier, the first of Anna's two recent psychiatric admissions occurred after Anna's mother forced her to sleep in her own bedroom one night and she developed difficulty breathing. For some time she has been demanding to sleep on her father's side of the double bed, next to her mother. On those occasions, the father has been forced to sleep in his daughter's bed. In addition, Anna does not want her father to touch her. One night when her mother was out at a school meeting, she actually had a hysterical fit when her father tried to help her put on her pajamas. Nevertheless, she has an intense intellectual relationship with him. She admires his drawings so much that she tries to copy them, and she enjoys her many talks with him.

All her life, until the day of her second psychiatric admission, Anna has followed the recommendation of the orthopedist she has been seeing for years—that is, not to run or tire out her legs. Walking has been limited or forbidden altogether. As a result, she was kept in a stroller for a long time; she has been prevented from playing in the courtyard; and her mother has accompanied her to school. Isolated from her peers, she is used to spending much of her day at the side of her mother, with whom she has established an intimate and dependent relationship that is much more intense and prolonged than usual for girls her age. As a result of this closeness, which has continued far beyond the attachment phase, she has become fixated on her mother—a condition that is still visible in their gestures.

I later find out that the day before the second crisis, the doctor who has been taking care of Anna's dislocated hips since she was born told her, "Now you're really cured! You can even run. Go on!," and gave her a little slap on the cheek. This exhortation has proven to have unexpected consequences; the optimistic physical diagnosis has unleashed a pathological psychological reaction. We must keep in mind the recency of Anna's first psychiatric admission, brought on by a violent crying fit after she was forbidden to sleep next to her mother in her parents' bed. We can hypothesize that her increased capacity to walk has already caused her to anticipate and fear the risks of distance. In the face of such a possibility, which feels catastrophic to her, Anna has reacted by regressing to an infantile state of infancy. On one recent occasion when she was in bed with her mother, she asked whether she could nurse at her breast as she had when she was little. Her mother's joking response to this last request has finally led her to regress to the earliest phases of the mother–child bond—that is, to a fetal phase, as the fit of dyspnea demonstrates. The symptom typifies an infant's inability to survive outside the maternal womb.

Comments on Anna's Relationship with Her Mother

Anna's illness also brings her secondary advantages: It has divided the parental couple and prompted the parents to neglect their son. Despite her normal—indeed, superior—progress on an intellectual plane, Anna still has an affective fixation on her mother, which is usually overcome (at least in this intense and exclusive form) by the age of two. Anna's fixation has lingered beyond the allotted time into the period that Freud called the pre-Oedipal stage, which in little girls precedes the development of love for the father and the consequent rivalry with the mother.

Anna has based her own identity, or at least that nucleus of self that precedes the formation of an articulated identity (which can only be

reached through a "dialectic" alternation between autonomy and dependence), on the continuation of that primary relationship. The obstacles she
has experienced in walking have limited her centrifugal tendencies, both
motor and mental; they have kept her, in some senses, in an original state
of undifferentiation.

As is true for every child, Anna's first love object is her mother—"object" in the true sense of the word, because the survival instinct, for which
sexuality provides a support, can only find satisfaction in the mother. But
for a little girl the mother is also a narcissistic object, because the little girl
recognizes a mirror image of herself, of gender identity in the mother. In
this phase, which we can call "original sisterhood," the little girl's identity
is feminine but not sexual. It is feminine because mother and child feel
alike; they have a perception of anatomical similarity, although they are
still not differentiated from each other or differentiated in their way of
relating to each other. As long as they remain undifferentiated, one cannot
speak of sexuality in any real sense, because sexuality requires an acceptance
of incompleteness and the recognition of the other's complementarity. For
this reason, original bisexuality, which Freud always maintained in spite of
lack of theoretical support, should actually be understood as a mixture, as
the coexistence of two potential sexual definitions of self.

In the model of normal development, as Freud construed it and Lacan
confirmed, the primary identity with the mother is finally shattered by the
introduction of the paternal prohibition into the dyad. In representing the
social law that prohibits incest, the father prevents the mother from
prolonging her hold on her offspring beyond the physiological limit, and
thus allows for the newborn's definition of individual identity. In my view,
this is a partial schema; as we will see, it disregards the centrifugal dynamics
that operate autonomously within the mother–child relationship.

In this case, however, Anna's illness has inhibited the process of
separation, which therefore seems to come about in response to an external
injunction. The orthopedist's diagnosis, representative of paternal authority, has forbidden Anna to live from now on as an attachment of her mother,
forcing her "to walk on her own two feet."But in what direction? For the
child, as we will see, it is a question of going from her mother to her mother,
by a path leading from the connectedness of primary identification (being
the mother) to the similarity of secondary identification (being like the
mother).

Anna's Itching Feet: Multiple Meanings of a Physical Symptom

In Anna's case, the connection to the mother already seems to be broken
by a movement toward the father, which is evidenced by the barrier of the
phobia the child experiences in his presence. To accept the father's love, to

become his object, would mean that Anna recognizes herself as feminine and identifies with her mother. But there is also the opposite desire—to be the father, to replace him, as the fantasy of sleeping next to her mother in the couple's bed reveals. This uncertainty has been effectively expressed by the symptom leading to Anna's second psychiatric admission: the episode of psychomotor disturbance, expressed in an intense itching of her feet, causing her to kick and scream. In hysterical crises the schema of the body comes apart, and one part, invested with intense meaning, becomes separated and exalted. It is known that the foot constitutes an infantile representation of the phallus (which the analytic work with Anna will attempt to confirm). As such, it also occupies a central role in the myth of Oedipus, which in fact means "he who is endowed with a large foot," "a bigfoot."

A myth also collected by Sophocles tells that the newborn Oedipus was brought up to Mount Citerone by a servant who has been given the father's order to kill him. The boy's feet are pierced and tied so that he may be carried over the shoulder like a lamb. Many interpreters agree in attributing a sexual meaning to Oedipus's deformed feet. Vernant sees in them a sign of Laius's perversion, maintaining that his homosexuality is what causes his son's fate.[15]

In any case, fetishism demonstrates how frequently the foot is compared to the sexual organ[16]—in particular, to the phantasmic phallus (an unconscious representation) that children also attribute to females in their attempts to deny castration and to avoid the consequent anxiety, which will appear more clearly in Anna's case later. Along with the itch that children often liken to autoerotic pleasure, Anna has manifested a phallic type of sexual pleasure. Female sexuality, which is centered in the clitoral area of the genitals, is seen as masculine and at a certain point is experienced as an obstacle to femininization, as a shortcoming; it is eventually denied and rejected along with the images that it evokes. In everyday usage, the word "itch" alludes both to the specific sensory experience and to an urgent and inopportune erotic desire.

Kicking, then, represents an attempt to give value to and to display the foot as the signifier of infantile phallic femininity, but also to distance it as the representation of the self's phantasmic masculine component, which Anna wishes to reject. Through condensation, the foot is thus called upon to express both a feminine and a masculine sexual fantasy, based on that imaginary bisexuality that Freud saw as the basis of every attack of hysteria. In order to resolve the symptom, he believed, it is necessary to go back to "*two* sexual phantasies, of which one has a masculine and the other a feminine character."[17]

In Anna's case, the organic symptom is linked to the drawing of her dream, indicating an indecision about her own sexual self-definition. Anna does not know whether to be male, female, or both, as infantile omnipotence suggests. But, on closer inspection, the by-products of the unconscious (dreams and symptoms) already point in the direction in which she should proceed. In her first drawing, in fact, Anna attributes an animal constitution ("the prince of ants")—one that is ambiguous and disturbing—to the male component. As much as the insect-like figure is exalted by nobility, it demonstrates a devaluation of masculinity, a degradation of its nature that foreshadows its repression in the archive of the unconscious. That is where unacceptable mental images survive—those elements of the "not me" that have been severed, in the process of self-definition, from the sense of original omnipotence.

Anna's discomfort reveals that a definite sexual priority has not yet been established, and that the three parts of the self (the male, the female, and the indefinite self) are engaged in a conflict that does not find any viable solution in the present. Still, the organic symptom expresses her cry for help. The question that this implies, however, can only become a question if the response directs it to another dimension, the dimension of language. "The language of the organs" returns to its source, like a riddle that must be translated in order to be solved.

This does not take away from the fact that the somatic symptom maintains a functional economy of its own—that the itching of the feet is, for example, also an epileptic symptom, as Freud himself recognized.[18] In this case, for reasons we do not yet understand, the psyche avails itself of the soma's expressive potential to say what it does not yet know on the conscious level; thus, it finds somatic satisfaction in the weakest organs, and prompts the gestural expression that was once experienced before verbal ability was acquired.

Anna's self-therapy has already made progress in this sense: from the body to the drawing, from the drawing to language. What is asked of me is to only to listen to her and follow the path she has taken. Nevertheless, these three expressive forms will remain operative for her as long as she does not overcome the obstacle that is causing her to hestitate rather than choose. Having chosen the nameless arrow up until now, the only thing she can do is take another from the quiver of the unconscious.

SEPARATION AND CATASTROPHE

The breach that has been produced in the unity of the daughter–mother dyad seems to have aroused anxiety in both Anna and her mother. The mother has tried to question the orthopedist's diagnosis of cure, insisting that the little girl is still quite fragile and in need of attention and care. Anna, for her part, refuses to go to school. She does not know why, but she is afraid. Afraid of working in groups, she says, but mainly afraid of her friend Antonella, with whom she has shared some homework questions and who is in the habit of bossing her around. It seems that Anna once turned to Antonella point-blank, asking polemically, "And who are we?" To which Antonella responded, "You are a beast, and I'm the teacher's favorite."

"As soon as someone gives in to her," Anna notes, "as soon as someone trusts her, she blackmails them by threatening to tell their secrets." And she adds, "I don't trust her because she has the same last name as another friend of mine, from the school where I lived before. There nobody ever argued. Everything was as it should be. I understand in my head and heart that this girl is not worth much."

Fear of and diffidence toward the outside world reveal unexpected elements of paranoia. At the end of his analytical exploration of the female mind, Freud pointed to elements such as hysteria, considering them the inevitable effects of the little girl's intense, passionate, and exclusive attachment to her mother during the pre-Oedipal stage. He elevated them, as such, to characteristics defining femininity.[19]

Anna's world is bifurcated: the good world, already lost along with her childhood home, and the bad world, over which the terrible Antonella presides. This child is presented as a replica who goes under the name of another child who lived elsewhere, in another time and place. The dimension evoked by the disturbing re-presentation of absence has all the characteristics of a paradise lost. The house "where we lived before" is described as full of flowers and sun-filled, inhabited only by good children. It is a place of lost happiness, in contrast to a fearful present. The memory brings about the reappearance of a past that is, in itself, irrevocable and mute; as a consequence, the reaction to it is irremediably transformed into suffering, into "an experience of what is no more and can no longer count as experience."[20]

The evocation of the two polarities—"before–now" and "else-where/here"—constitutes an attempt to control the catastrophic anxiety that characterizes the separation from the original body and to delineate temporal boundaries. The chronology of paternal order takes the place of the static and eternal dimension of maternal space. Since nothing is more painful than free-floating anxiety, which lacks any representation one can grab hold of, we must consider Anna's fantasies a spontaneous form of therapy, directed at opposing the sudden collapse of the most validated points of reference that she has.

Directed away from the maternal vessel, Anna confronts the hostility of the world, and above all the rivalry of her friend, who is contending for the common love object (represented now by the teacher). Rivalry suggests a difference within parity, a situation that Anna, privileged by the exclusiveness of her mother's love, has never experienced. The "secret" that

Antonella is threatening to tell may be precisely the fact that each of us comes from a primal undifferentiation, and that the "bestial" component of our sexuality—which Anna has identified with the masculine, and from which she cannot separate—persists in us all.

In the opposition between past and present, Anna's prior situation is idealized and forever set apart from the flow of experience (there is no possibility of returning to the childhood home). This constitutes the condition that precedes the emergence of nostalgia, defined by Freud as the "principal characteristic of hysteria." It is such a fundamental feeling because the recognition that loss is inevitable and that the past cannot be repeated organizes the background against which identity emerges, with all its unavoidable connotations of solitude and abandonment. This identification always implies at least a partial rejection of the love object, and the consequent creation of a "no-man's-land" between the ego and the other, which the fantasy and the symptoms attempt to animate with their substitute creations. In this sense, as Freud claimed in connection with the mother, "Attacks of dizziness and crying fits are all directed towards the other, in fact, towards that unforgettable prehistoric other that will never again be equaled by anyone else."[21]

The moment that any child separates from the object that has contained him or her, he or she falls into the irreversibility of time. The past, previously manifested by the child's omnipotence, is internalized in memory and made history in biography (to a large extent elaborated in the stories told by relatives), so that childhood constitutes a background that is inaccessible and fixed.[22] One's personal history, therefore, seems to take an inflexible shape that is resistant to the manipulations of autobiography; its egocentric narcissism is counted by the inevitable dependence on the stories of others.

Freud defined the first attachment of the little girl to her mother thus: "elusive, lost in the past so dim and shadowy, so hard to resuscitate that it seemed as if it had undergone some special inexorable repression."[23] In this instance he was so perplexed—which was a rare occurrence for him—that he acknowledged the limits that being male imposes on the analytical exploration of the female unconscious. He then entrusted himself to the evocative power of metaphor and compared his astonishment at the existence of a specific pre-Oedipal phase in women that "comes to us as a surprise, like the discovery, in another field, of the Minoan-Mycenaean civilization behind that of Greece."[24] The image is even more surprising, given that we now know that the end of Minoan civilization might have been brought about by a terrible earthquake that shook Crete during the fifteenth century B.C., leaving few traces of the island's greatness. It is also significant that the Mycenaean civilization crumbled under the invasion of Dorian "men of war" toward the end of the second millennium. Although

Freud was surely not aware of it, this is a strange analogy of metaphorical constructs, because the pre-Oedipal bond also often comes to an end with a catastrophic experience. In Anna's imaginary, this is evidenced by a dream of the world's destruction, which is then elaborated through its opposite: fantasies of a second creation.

In the dream, Anna describes the world sunk with all its inhabitants, the people of Atlantis, who were buried forever by a great tidal wave, following an all-out nuclear war. Then later that day she fantasizes about what would have happened after this event, and about the "metamorphoses" that would have come about afterwards.

The fantasy of the "end of the world" constitutes the mnestic residue of an internal occurrence, of a "silent catastrophe," provoked by a conflictual situation that cannot be eluded. Freud discovered an analogous fantasy in the autobiography of President Schreber and commented: "The sick man has withdrawn the libidinal investment he had once directed onto the people in his world and onto the outside world in general; as a result, he is indifferent to everything, and he loses all relation to it."[25]

At the moment of distancing from her mother, Anna prefers to destroy the world to salvage her ego—to recall all affect onto herself in order to protect herself from annihilation. In some sense, she has regressed to the primary narcissism that knows no object. However, the anxiety produced by the loss of objective reality sets off a spontaneous remedial process, constituted by the fantasy of the world's second creation. Her libidinal energies are once again extroverted; the preceding attack is repressed; and "that which had once been abolished within us," as Freud said, "returns to us from the outside." Then the construct of reality takes the place of the absence of the great maternal body; on the empty screen of the "not mother" the things of the world are projected, animated by the inexhaustible resources of creativity, the secret "work of the spirit." Nevertheless, the recreated universe will never again be the one that was known before, which, as we have seen, remains isolated, much like a "lost paradise."

In this phase, Anna's mythopoetic powers seem to be engaged in the struggle "to recreate the world"—a struggle that empowers her expressive abilities.

GENDER IDENTITY
AND THE RECONSTRUCTION OF THE WORLD

Three disturbing drawings further illustrate Anna's visions. In the first (Figure 2), two newborns have been abandoned nude in a field beneath the

Figure 2

red sphere of a distant sun. The genitals attest to the different sexual identities, which are emphasized by the placement of the infants facing each other, with their fists raised in opposition to each other. "Here we're in the future," Anna comments. "The mother abandoned them here so that they wouldn't suffer in the smog of the city. These babies won't die, they won't die, but I don't know why. They'll become teenagers."

The image of the smog suggests breathing difficulty, and thus can be related to maternal attachment, which becomes unbearable, stifling, at a certain point in childhood development. Anna's frequent nightmares of suffocation and fits of dyspnea and asthma attest to this. The two infants represent the unconscious bisexuality that has already been experienced in the internal conflict.

The next drawing (Figure 3) depicts two adolescents, who differ in terms of their specific primary and secondary sexual characteristics. The girl, unlike the boy, is still prepubescent. The field is filled with flowers; two butterflies, one red and one blue, are joined; and a large black and white bird flies toward them. Anna says about the drawing: "They're adolescents. They are friends of nature. They're undressed. Maybe because I don't see anybody with clothes on, I mean . . . naked." She has drawn two bubbles above the figures' heads, in which the girl responds "Let's go" to the boy's invitation; Anna adds, "They want to play." Nevertheless, the girl's hands,

Figure 3

which she holds behind her back, contradict the willingness she expresses verbally. The sexual relationship is clearly suggested and the complementarity of the sexes is recognized, but the reticence about contact remains. In accordance with the characteristic time frame of the latency phase, sexual contact will be delayed until "later," "when we're grown up."

The union of the two butterflies suggests the existence of a universal natural law that neutralizes human sexuality, purifies it of the components of passion, and relieves it of the combination of desire and prohibition that characterizes it. The large bird that streaks across the sky symbolizes a protective and normative paternal presence and its internal representative, the superego function, to which sexuality must yield in order to free itself from infantile egocentricity.[26]

The third drawing (Figure 4) represents the attainment of maturity. The two young people holding hands, both pubescent, stand in a natural setting much richer and more articulated than the preceding ones: The sun (the final symbol of the superego) is setting behind the mountains, as if to signify an attenuation of its power and influence. The mountains that block the horizon seem to constitute a barrier to the return of what has been repressed, to the disturbing reappearance of the pre-Oedipal mother. Anna says, "They'll grow up. Through a strange wish, they grew out of the mountains. Now they love each other. They will have children. I don't

Figure 4

know how. I'll know when I grow up. I don't care. I know they have to put something into the woman's body. An arm, maybe."

In this dream, Anna exercises the creative aspect of her thought—her capacity to evoke an intermediate dimension between archaic omnipotence and the objectivity of things. The reality she creates is characterized by the presence of human bodies that are marked by sexual difference, united in their reproductive complementarity, but engaged in a broader process in which the enactment of the self is carried out simultaneously with the enactment of the world.

Anna has received complete and precise sexual instruction, but as is often the case, she prefers to repress her knowledge and elaborate it into other forms that are closer to her own affective experiences. The discrepancy between the anatomical precision with which she depicts the sexual development of the two figures in her drawings, and her rudimentary explanations of the manner of their sexual union (which she has volunteered; they have not been elicited), permits us to discern the contrast between the thought of fantasy and the thought of logic. This will be taken up again and thematized during the third session, in the next week. There will begin the process—fundamental to the process of gender identification—that moves from recognition of the presence of the two genders in the world to the acceptance of one's own specific sexuality, and finally to its inscription in one's own body.

SEXUAL IDENTITY AND FAMILY ORDER

For everyone, the acquisition of a sexual identity means giving up the omnipotence of the imaginary; seeing oneself as lacking; and opening oneself up to the desire for the other, who holds what can make one whole. For a little girl, this is particularly difficult because in our civilization, the phallus represents essence and narcissistic unity. To be deprived of it precipitates her into the most radical sense of privation. In the unconscious, castration represents a most anxiety-producing threat, but it is a paradoxical one for a little girl because it suggests removing something she does not have. Nevertheless, as we will see, our culture forces the girl to represent herself, above all, as a negation of the male. This is a definition that Anna tries her best to avoid, but that at the same time she stubbornly imposes upon herself, because she feels that she is no longer supposed to linger in infantile undifferentiation.

Children grasp sexual difference at an early age, but if asked to represent it, they attribute it mainly to clothing, along with social functions and roles. It is difficult for them to admit that anatomical differences exist and that some human beings, like their mothers, lack an organ they consider fundamental. The fact that half of humanity seems to be "castrated" is felt, in fact, as threatening to males and devaluing of females. The latter oppose their membership in the ranks of the "lacking sex" with particular vigor, waging what Adler calls the "virile protest." But family structure, together with the endogenous impulse for development, pushes a little girl to abandon the illusion of virility and presents her with the rather difficult task of feminizing her own self-image, so that it conforms to the identity that anatomy and society have always attributed to her. Anna lingers in uncertainty and tries to put off choosing, attempting in every way she can to maintain her infantile omnipotence.

Relating a dream, she states:

> "I was a boy from the very beginning. That's the thing that bothers me: being a boy. I'm a Ferrari Testarossa [a sports car] and a girl wants to marry me. It's infuriating! It makes me nervous. Do I really have to be a boy? In the dream I have no family. We go home to the girl's house and her father doesn't want me there. Am I the brother-in-law in that case? Who am I? The son-in-law, the brother-in-law? I only know about my brother (unfortunately!), Papa, Mama, cousins, uncles and aunts, grandparents, great-great grandparents! That's it. I don't know anything any more."

Anna seems to be thinking that if she holds narcissistically onto a masculine identity, she is excluded from matrimonial relationships, from the alliance pacts that establish acquired kinship. Virility is as valuable as a Ferrari Testarossa, but the father and his internal representative, the superego (expressed in the words "Do I really have to be a boy?"), decide that it would be more suitable for Anna to fill another position. In comparison to the promiscuity of the unconscious and its indulgence in coexisting opposites—the omnivorous demands of desire—gender identification is like a rigorous ethical exercise. The accomplishment of gender identification means that the categorical devices of kinship, which assign a place to each individual, must be inscribed upon one's original undifferentiation, thus shattering one's centrality and ubiquity. The combined logic of family relationships, based upon the incest prohibition, imposes the greatest distance precisely where the greatest proximity exists, according to a rigorous geometry of positions. In fact, only the prohibition of being and having the parents permits the introjection of the formal components of the love objects without being engulfed by them. The all-encompassing mother of the infantile imagination must die, so that a part of her can be recovered in the daughter's identity—that is, recognized as a part of herself in their shared membership in the same sex (which is nevertheless not the only one because it stipulates another, reciprocal sex).

For the child to acquire a personal identity, it is also necessary for her to become integrated into the web of family relationships, to practice relating there, and to be recognized. The most intimate attributions of identity do not take hold unless they are confirmed from outside, so that paradoxically, as Lacan stated, "The I is another." The question "Who am I?", which has initiated Anna's therapy, now prompts a myriad of characters to appear on stage and brings the family theatre to life, establishing order in the promiscuity of unconscious desire. Once a child is assimilated into the family group, he or she occupies a position that belongs to him or her alone. The child recognizes the positions of the others and progressively internalizes the scheme that orders the economy of his or her drives. As we have seen, however, this occurs neither immediately nor without resistance, but after a laborious and never-ending rejection of infantile omnipotence.

Gender identity, inscribed in the cultural order, does not necessarily coincide with natural sexuality, the expression of the biological body. Instead, it involves the acquisition of social position, of a preordained role that sets in motion all interfamily dynamics and the currents of love and hate that animate them. The desire of the infantile economy "to be everywhere and everyone" comes up against the command "to take one's place and one's rank" in the law of the superego. We can see how these two imperatives confront each other in this fragment of Anna's dream:

> "There was a strange machine, the machine of wishes. It wasn't actually a machine; it was a piece of material, of brown material, a kind

of sackcloth that's made of many threads. And there was some carbon paper underneath this material, and if I inserted an eraser underneath it and said, 'Oh, I'd really like a ballpoint pen,' the pen would appear and the eraser would disappear. I was a grown-up man and I did all of that."

Commenting on the dream, Anna states: "The machine of wishes would let you put something female under it, like the eraser, and something male, like the ballpoint pen, would come out." The dream expresses the wish for a masculine identity and reveals that Anna's narcissistic masculinity has had to be repressed. In fact, she wishes for the only thing she does not possess. Yet the waking thought that this chubby-faced little girl expresses—"Do I realy have to be a boy?"—represents the frustration that denies the wish.

"I don't want to be a female," Anna insists, "because I'd have to obey boys. Females are timid. Being all male is strong, brutal!" It is meaningful that the feminine is represented by the function of removing writing (the eraser) and the masculine by that of writing (the pen). Femaleness, in that it involves the banishing of narcissistic virility, represents a loss of an aspect of the self that is highly valued, and that provokes a sense of disqualification when it is lacking. In fact, the female part cannot make itself as powerful as the male part.

We know that this impossibility is predetermined by a long cultural history that still interferes with women's self-image. The inferiority of the female gender goes back to Greek culture, where it was part of the contemporary understanding of biology and was sanctioned by society. As Aristotle saw it, man and woman pertain to the same species but to opposite genders, in which everything negative is drawn to the female. In Aristotle's view of reproduction, as Chapter 2 will show more clearly, the woman need only provide the raw material; the man provides the vital form.[27]

The dream metaphor of the "machine of wishes" reduced to an inert "brown material"[28] reveals the difficulty of envisioning female generation as active and formative. Cultural stereotypes aggravate and rigidify the difference of gender, to the extent that occupying the lacking and inferior position becomes an ontological position for women. One should not be surprised, therefore, that female identity is seen as a characteristic that is far from desirable and that adopting it is accompanied by an intense reaction.

Playing with puppets, Anna invents the story of a king who guillotines all his subjects. One puppet opposes the will of the sovereign, but the little girl beheads him, exclaiming in exasperation: "No, sweetheart, you deserved it. What happened to me is happening to you." It is easy for us to see the analogy between the symmetrical logic of the dream and that of the unconscious. But who ends up being beheaded? In some sense, everybody—that is, women and men together. Castration, which is opposed to an omnipotent totality, makes no exceptions, and for that reason takes on the absolute and impersonal nature of moral laws. But as Freud emphasized over and over, this is particularly unbearable for females.

When Freud asked himself about the incomplete nature of all analysis, he came up against what he calls the "denial of femininity." "At no other point in analytical work," he commented, disheartened, "do we have such a painful and oppressive sense of the futility of our repeated efforts, never do we have such strong suspicions of 'preaching to the wind' as when we try to get women to renounce their wish for a penis, based on the fact that it is impossible."[29] This wish, in fact, repressed from the conscious mind, remains preserved in the unconscious. When we have crossed all psychological layers, concluded Freud, there we come upon the "bedrock"—an element in the great enigma of sex that puts an end to our endeavor.

If female resistance to femininity can be frustrating for therapists (especially if the therapists are holding onto omnipotent desires), in reality it serves the essential functions of preserving a nucleus of the ego that is protected both from biological determination and from social injunction, and of maintaining a living demand for completeness. Since society drives sexual identity toward a rigid and absolute stereotype, the individual must defend the traits of the opposite sex so that they can survive in him/her. Nevertheless, until a certain stability between the two components is established and the definitive predominance of one sex is reached, the neurotic conflict provokes immobility and suffering. We see this in Anna's refusal to go out and insistence on having her mother at her side at all times.

At this time, Anna's mother has moved out of the parental bed and sleeps on a cot next to her daughter's bed. At Anna's insistence, she recounts the minute details of her day as she lies next to Anna; the story can go on for two or three hours until the mother falls asleep. The child appears sad and listless. She complains that nobody understands or loves her. She makes up religious fantasies and ends up in tears, remembering that "God, who is so good, sacrificed his son Jesus for us!" Her depression, sublimated in mysticism, reveals that an elaborate mourning is in process—that one part of her must die so that the other can live. Her obsessive discourse represents her attempt to create some reparation in the void that has been produced. As in the tale of Scheherazade, the time taken up by the mother's story suspends action. But the omnipotence gradually loses the boldness it had in early childhood and is recognized as immobilizing. In the meditative state caused by the depression, the conflict between the two sexual components is internalized: from the furthest exteriority of the personal myth of the world's recreation, to the intimacy of the mind's scenery.

AN ANCIENT DIATRIBE, A PRESENT-DAY CONFLICT: HEART OR HEAD?

When Anna returns after a few weeks, she has gone back to school, but she is still complaining of sporadic itching of her feet. This time she has brought a sheet of paper folded in quarters. The following sentence appears in large childish letters: "My heart causes me to have doubts, and then my head chases them away, but my heart convinces me again to spy on my parents and my brother."

The drawing that illustrates this (Figure 5) represents a naked human figure that lacks definite sex or age, a gaunt mannequin. A large red heart is drawn on the left side of its chest, and it wears a purple beret on its head. On the side, two little figures with gangster hats—one red, one purple—face off, their guns pointed. As the legend at the far right-hand corner specifies, the red figure represents the heart, the purple one the head. Underneath them, a sentence that has been partially erased and interspersed with graphics states: "It's war, but fortunately, the head hasn't struck the heart."

The capacity of the unconscious to utilize material from the archives of culture in its representations is revealed here in a question that has long been debated in the history of science: that is, which organ plays the dominant role in the organism, the head or the heart? Heart-centered and brain-centered theories, which are closely linked to the particular require-ments of self-representation and to the anthropological definition of a human being, have been argued for centuries. The brain-centered model was first claimed by Hippocrates and his school in the Athens of Pericles, and later found a scientific foundation in the works of the great Alexandrian anatomists and of Galen (second century A.D.), to whom we owe the definitive refutation of the Aristotelian heart-centered theory. The central-ity of the brain is connected to the predominance of rational components over emotional ones, of inductive over intuitive reasoning, of science over poetry. From the history of this controversy, we learn that the emergence of the brain-centered paradigm has provoked a double fundamental break:

> On one hand, [there is] the schism between man and nature, no longer connected by a relationship of the part to the whole, by a sympathetic homogeneity: man places himself before nature in his perceptions, in his knowledge as if it were the subject of his inquiry, of his sensation, of his research and he thus reduces it to the status of an object. . . . The other schism . . . between men and gods comes into being, distancing them irreparably. . . . The man represented by this culture is a maker of his own destiny.[30]

In spite of this rationalistic triumph, in the imagination the heart maintains the capacity to represent the individual's vital unity, his or her desire, and

Figure 5

the direct and immediate relationship between the individual and the world. For children especially, given the connection between the heartbeat and emotion, there is an intuitive link between psychic functioning and the "warm" heart, rather than the "cold" brain. Finally, it is interesting to observe how individuals who are less cultured and closer to the residue of a distant peasant civilization still attribute psychosomatic disturbances to the heart, and how the attribution of symptomatology to the head occurs simultaneously with the process of urban assimilation and of cultural homology.

In Anna's case, the heart seems to represent the desire that pushes her toward her origins, where the imaginary unity with her mother is connected to a particular way of knowing and feeling—a sharing and participating relationship to things—that must be sacrificed to the formation of the individuality and subjectivity. "It could be," wrote Klein, "that the prenatal physical tie with the mother contributes to the formation of that sense that is innate in the child that something exists outside of himself that can satisfy his every need and desire."[31] With separation, a magical perception of the world and of a connection to the sacred ceases, although it does remain operant in the imagination.

Anna's drawings are created out of the desire for unity, nonseparation, nondifference; they stand in opposition to another imperative, which is based instead on articulation, diversity, rejection, division, delineation. The logic of analogy, of resemblance, of immediate relationship, of natural expressivity, of the icon, is separated from that of articulation, of hierarchy, of time, of predication, of language. But what the dreams, in the immediacy of their symbols, demonstrate is that Anna as an individual has become cut off and that the renunciation of original unity separates her from herself as well.

The history of thought, reconsidered in the light of the unconscious, helps us to understand that—beyond the fundamental connection between infantile intellectual development and the history of science, which Piaget always supported[32]—there also exists a parallel between the events of the individual imagination and those of science. In both cases, these events do not proceed simply as results of improvements or accumulation, but also as the outcomes of crises and subsequent restructuring. The catastrophes and conflicts whose evidence is preserved in dreams represent not only progressions but losses—of life choices, of cognitive and imaginary possibilities, and of unrealized potential.

In Anna's oneiric thought, her doubt, which is an expression of her heart, manifests a will to know that pushes against Oedipal barriers, disturbing the spatial order of her family and her house in its transgressive intrusion. Her parents' room, where the scopic impulse to look attempts to come into being, represents mature genital sexuality, the eroticism ordained by marriage. In this realm, which is bounded and protected by intimacy and restraint, Foucault has recognized two major systems of rules at work, conceived of by Western cultures to regulate sex: "the law of marriage and the order of desires."[33] In comparison to this realm of reproductive and legitimized sexuality, other peripheral forms come to be seen as disturbances, acts against nature, perversions. As a consequence, infantile autoeroticism, with its solitary and sterile pleasure, becomes a prohibited behavior, an unmentionable and secret guilt. Moral norms can then be brought to bear on the child's body and the economy of his or her drives, thus introducing the system of prohibitions and exhortations that governs social economy. Reconstructing the dynamics of social repression that act upon the libidinal microeconomy, Freud wrote:

> The development of the sexual instinct then proceeds from auto-erotism to object-love and from the autonomy of the erotogenic zones to their subordination under the primacy of the genitals, which are put at the service of reproduction. The forces that can be employed for cultural activities are thus to a great extent obtained through the repression of what are known as the *perverse* elements of sexual excitation.[34]

Sacrificing the "*perverse* elements" means that the elements of the opposite sex are destined to fall under the yoke of repression. In the case of a little girl, this is a question of giving herself over to a process of socialization in which she must, paradoxically, reject the masculine characteristics that are particularly in tune with dominant social values and exchanges. This requires her to be flexible and resistant at the same time—to adhere to social expectation while maintaining a center of opposition. But this is only possible if the relationship with the mother has allowed for an unconditional basis of self-confidence, a sense of security that survives the experience of abandonment. To give up social approval, even partially, requires that one be able to feel alone, to withstand hostility and blame, and to re-establish broken bonds.

In the prevailing model of female sexual development, distancing from the mother and rejecting infantile masculine identity are two opposing but converging operations that proceed at the same time. If at this point in a girl's development, a substitute for the love object of the opposite sex (the father or his external representation) is lacking, she runs the risk of rejecting femininity without inscribing herself in the ranks of masculinity. As a result, she remains suspended in a sort of limbo that destines many women to an angry or resentful search for an impossible sexual orientation.

In any case, acquiring a female identity is a highly risky undertaking, because—unlike the boy, who always maintains the same polarity—the girl must abandon her initial love object, a female one represented by the mother, so that she can take on one of the opposite sex; at the same time, she must emerge from sexual undifferentiation by internalizing the very female characteristics that her mother represents. We must thus assume that the primary mother–daughter dyad is in itself undifferentiated—that a sort of mirroring effect functions within it that does not allow for hierarchical positions. Thus, the term "sisterhood" might be more accurate than "filiation." In this sense, Jung's oracular statement becomes clearer: "Every woman holds within herself her own mother and her own daughter."[35] The differentiation between the two cannot be understood as a distancing of the daughter from the mother, but as the simultaneous defining of two positions of femininity that are both opposed and overlapping.

Given the high level of conflict in the unfolding of infantile female sexuality, developmental and regressive tendencies conflict with each other and mediate between each other. On this occasion, however, we see them no longer projected outward but isolated in an inner theatre where reason, as opposed to desire, can impose its law directly.

AN IMPOSSIBLE KNOWLEDGE:
ANNA AND THE OEDIPAL SCHEME

Asked to explain her statement about "spying" on her parents and brother, Anna says:

> "I began to suspect that they were very rich and that they're making me learn everything over again the wrong way. So I go to check to see if my parents speak another language between themselves, what they say, what they do. I think they may have taught my brother the right things and me the wrong things. My brother is in cahoots with them in this. Maybe it's because I'm a very jealous type. My heart makes me have doubts and my head rejects them. They are fighting, and that hurts me too. They make me so afraid, my whole body hurts. My eyes hurt. They are fighting inside of me and making me itch. They're not outside at all. I'm not wearing my brain on my forehead."

On the left-hand side of the "head and heart" drawing (Figure 5), she now writes: "This hurts the body. The eyes (an arrow points), the heart, on the right (an arrow points), legs, etc. Everything inside too." This is followed by her signature: "Anna Piedali."

Anna's attempt at expression is aimed at giving voice to an internal conflict that is expressed in her symptom of itching feet. This conflict, as the "Testarossa" dream has revealed, is the little girl's confrontation with an already articulated family scene (represented by the scheme being plotted at her expense) in which she must find her rightful place. But this is only possible if a concomitant reorganization of the interior scene occurs. In fact, there is a reciprocal relationship between family structure and psychic structure. Whereas the dream of her family members alludes to the formation of social relationships, the heart–head conflict goes back to the intrapsychic structure, to the functional organization of its demands.

Up until now, Anna's privileged position beside her mother has kept her apart from the network of relationships, protected from the system of prohibitions. Now, however, she too is called upon to take her place in the

Oedipal triangle. This is why she experiences jealousy toward her brother, with whom she finds she must share the filial vertex in respect to the married couple.

This feeling shows that Anna has moved out of the dyadic relationship with her mother, where the conflict hinges upon possessiveness, and into the triadic structure, where only jealousy thrives.[36] The suspicion that parents speak a secret language to each other appears frequently in the course of children's therapy. Analysis demonstrates that the mysterious language that unites the parents and alienates the child is nothing other than the sexual relationship, which is neutralized in the metaphor of verbal communication. The "secret" alludes to the forbidden and unrepresentable aspect of what Freud called the "primal scene."

In the face of parental coitus, the child, in all his or her infantile omnipotence, must admit that neither sex is adequate in and of itself. The parents, who find completion in a reciprocal relationship, demonstrate that mature sexuality belongs to the symbol of castration—that is, to the "not all." The primal scene, independent of the facts of experience, is a categorical structure of the unconscious that represents both the child's involvement with and exclusion from the couple who generated him or her. The individual who "sees" this scene, either in dream or in fantasy, feels simultaneously present in and absent from the event; its dimension, which is oblique in relation to thought, is analogous to the oneiric experience in which the subject is present as the dreamer but is not part of the dream and does not see himself or herself among the others. The fact that the primal scene is an inborn figment of the imagination excludes the fact that it comes to be experienced later by the child—that its empty categorical structure is later filled by experiential facts.[37]

In any case, whether the primal scene belongs to reality or the imagination, it has structuring effects. In fact, in the face of the primal scene, a sort of exile from the place of origin occurs: The child is pushed toward the vertex of familial triangulation, equidistant from the parental figures. This is expected of children, in reality as well as in unconscious representation. Once internalized, the Oedipal topology functions as a shield against the primitive dyadic bond with the mother, which is placed definitively out of reach. As Freud might say, the unity of mother and father hides the natural mother–child couple as Greek civilization did the Minoan–Mycenaean cultures.

Thus it comes to pass that gender identification, initially represented by the impersonality of myth, is being transformed into subjective experience through the successive rearrangements of family scenarios and of the individual imaginary. In the enactment of the Oedipal scheme, a redistribution of affective and aggressive forces is accomplished in conformity with the individual's sexual orientation. In the case of a little girl, she must turn love toward the father and hate toward the mother, but in a less obvious manner she must accomplish the opposite operation as well; in other words, she must both love and hate her mother, allowing her father to play an ancillary role.[38]

In any case, the libidinal economy is strongly conditioned. In fact, the love objects are internalized—they are elements of the ego—and any sort of damage to them becomes an injury to the self. Inevitably, the internal conflict elicits an anxiety about fragmentation, which refocuses the energies that were invested in others back onto the self again in a defensive gesture. So the Oedipal conflict, the prototype for every other relationship, terminates (at least the first time) by activating those egocentric and narcissistic elements that characterize puberty.

According to this hypothesis, the signature "Anna Piedali" at the bottom of Anna's commentary on her drawing constitutes an attempt to restore to herself the affective intensity lost with the maternal totality. The signature, which simultaneously signifies her symptom (the itching feet), her autobiography, and the family history, expresses the complexity of the various dimensions involved in the process of identity. Anna can no longer "be the mother," nor can she "have the mother." Now she can only have her near or far and experience affective ambivalence, gratitude, and rancor.

If the daughter was part of the mother before, now the mother must become part of her. This necessity sets off both amorous and aggressive forces. Up to this point, Anna has avoided hostility by projecting it onto her friend Antonella, who (Anna anticipates) will retaliate forcefully. Similarly, she has transferred her love for her father onto the figure of her teacher, with whom she claims she is madly in love, eliciting an unforeseen jealous reaction from Antonella. The Oedipal conflict is thus directed outward, keeping the good family figures intact. Anna is fairly close to puberty, when the libidinal forces, after taking a narcissistic turn, tend to be projected onto intermediate figures (e.g., teachers and peers).[39] Nevertheless, the displacement of aggressive components outside of the family sphere renders the outside world hostile and fundamentally dangerous; it only reconfirms the regressive tendencies that oppose the accomplishment of autonomy and independence. The process of individuation thus occurs in a constant weaving back and forth between "moving out" and "going back in."

In the course of successive sessions, Anna draws the map of her apartment again and again, sketching lines to show the paths she takes from her bedroom to her parents' double bed in her attempts to place herself between her mother and father—attempts that, in their intrusiveness, end up separating her from them. Although her intentional plan pushes her toward the margins of the family, her fantasy carries her back in the ancient direction of infantile love.

We are witnessing here the paradox of human desire, in which one must replace the parents with a partner, and look toward the future for what one yearns for in the past—a past that is manifested by desire and precluded by desire. The anxiety that unleashes the pressure to reunite with the mother is a signal that suggests the proximity of birth and death. This is why infantile sexuality, which is inseparable from sex, appears to have an element of estrangement. Anna will try to reconstruct her parents' secret language over and over again, but in such a way that it will never be revealed. She tells me:

> "I suspect that my mother is very rich and that she has a language that she keeps secret from me. For example, 'si' means 'is.' My mother taught this language to everybody but me, to confuse me when I grow up. My mother pays everybody for this, even you [alluding to me]. The only ones she didn't teach it to are the people in the old house. There they speak the right language. They're the only ones I have faith in. There, at home, at school, I was happy. Now my only chance for happiness is by climbing the walls of my imagination. It makes me nostalgic to think about it. . . . What does my mother want? . . . For me to learn everything backward so that I'll be bungled when I grow up. So that my mother can abandon me, and everybody else—even the blacks—can learn the language I don't know."

It is interesting to observe how Anna contradicts herself when she attributes to her mother the desire to teach her "everything backward." That is, she believes her mother will see to it that she alone will never inherit the language and the treasure of her mother's enviable secret. Paradoxically, Anna appears to have learned a code from her mother that nevertheless keeps her in a state of ignorance. It seems that the female line is blocked by an insuperable obstacle, and that what does actually pass between one generation of women and the next is a message whose meaning cannot be grasped by anyone or remains mysterious.

Anna is envious of maternal sexuality and of the libidinal power that her mother derives from her privileged relationship to Anna's father. Anna would like to be like her mother but cannot. Such is the conflictual nature of the Oedipal triangle for a daughter: It simultaneously commands the daughter "Be like your mother" and "You cannot be like her" (i.e., "You cannot take her place beside the father"). The law that opposes desire and subjects it to a principle of order provokes the separation between intelligence and affect that is responsible for the distinctive trait of our anthropology. A price must be paid if the ego is to separate from the id in order to assume control (but never in a final sense) over one's self and the subjectivity of one's own life. "To adopt a popular mode of speaking," said Freud, "we might say that the ego stands for reason and good sense while the id stands for the untamed passions."[40]

In subsequent sessions, Anna alternates between relating pleasant fantasies of moving away from her family (represented by trips, adventures with American Indians, and memories of vacations in her grandparents' house) and describing her fears of the outside world, which is felt as hostile and threatening. In Italy, the years of Anna's therapy are years of great political massacres, assassination attempts, kidnappings, and underground struggle, but also of grassroots activism and militant culture. Anna puts this material from daily life to use in expressing her agoraphobia, her difficulty with peers, her anxiety about reprisal for her feelings toward her parents, her psychic conflicts, and their solutions. It is as if the struggle of society has become a great metaphor for her internal work and her own struggle for identity and individuation. The people generically referred to in Italy as the "Red Brigades" (a terrorist group) stand in opposition to the great social body, just as she stands in opposition to her mother; both are parts that are trying to free themselves from the whole, to cut the bonds with their own historical connections. The musical group Inti Illimani,[41] on the other hand, represent an ideal of the cohesion of internal elements and of the process of mourning for the exiled "motherland."

For Christmas she brings me a large drawing to wish me well, showing an old man with a long white beard. "Is it Santa Claus?" I ask her. "No, it's Ho Chi Minh."

THE MOUSE UNDER THE SNOW: REJECTING THE IMAGINARY PHALLUS

Our work recommences after a long Christmas break. Anna enters warily, closes the door, and starts off by saying: "I have to tell you something. You said to me that I have to be male or female. Okay. I've decided."

"What?"

"I'm male."

"Maybe I gave you that impression," I answer, "but I certainly don't know what being female is."

Then in silence she shows me a drawing of two villages. The first, in color, animated by people, animals, and flowers, is where she lived before. The second, composed of a row of gray, deserted houses, is where she lives now. As she comments at length about the abandonment of the earth, she becomes sadder, in contrast to her initial boldness. Sadness seems to be

Figure 6

taking the place of nostalgia, as it appears that nostalgia cannot defend the psychic apparatus from mourning.

In fact, nostalgia is an attempt to project onto the outside a loss that has taken place in the inner world—to distance it and control it in an intermediate dimension of mythopoetic creativity, where presence and absence coexist.[42] The process of gender identification, on the other hand, requires that absence become inscribed in the bodily self and its psychic representation. This brings one face to face with the inevitable experience of mourning, without mediation.

Naturally, the injunction that Anna attributes to me has never been spoken, at least in such explicit and definitive terms. Nevertheless, her apparent conviction shows how acutely she has grasped the direction and meaning of the therapeutic work—except that she attributes a preordained intention to it, with the risk of compromising it and giving it the inflexibility of orthopedic control. The verb "*have* to" reveals that the superego has entered the scene, with its ability to resolve conflicts "by the sword"; soon after this, in fact, its effects become visible, turning the scene of the unconscious bloody.

During the following session, Anna displays an overwhelming desire to tell me about her dream of the night before: "I only remember these images. . . . I dreamed there was snow up to here [she points to a point just above her knee], since I always want snow. . . . It came in through the windows, it came in through all the cracks. I tried to grab it, to play with it, but they were all mollusks. Disgusting, living things." She asks to draw the mollusks, but in color because the dream was in color. She becomes quite embarrassed in choosing a marker; first she takes an orange one, next a beige one, then a brown one, and finally, a yellow one. She draws a kind of snail (Figure 6) and comments to herself: "I never touched those things, because they revolt me, even in a dream. I've never even seen such things."

At my request that she free-associate in order to find words for the images, she says, "Snow." A long, unusual pause follows; then she closes her

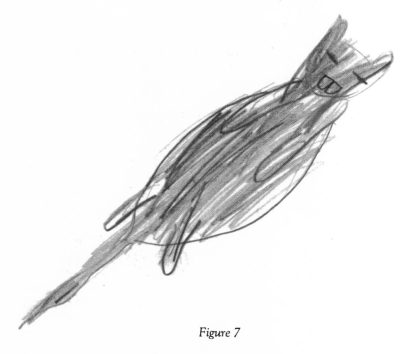

Figure 7

eyes with both hands and continues, "Dark, green, mouse," which her brain must have told her. She then adds: "Because I have to say something. When I woke up, a little snow had really fallen. Then I went to the nuns' field to play. I went to make a snowball, and underneath the snow there was a dead mouse, gray, black, rigid. A sewer mouse." She takes a big black marker and quickly makes a large drawing that crosses the sheet of paper diagonally (Figure 7). "The mouse had a wound." With a red marker, she draws, tracing a line of blood [descending on the right]. And adding, "Here," she marks the throat just below the chin. She raises her head, and I glimpse her white, taut skin lacerated by a deep, open scratch that is raw inside. She says that she scratched herself without realizing it with her fingernails. Then she quickly intuits my association with the wound of the mouse and corrects herself: "But I did this much later—Monday, I think, though I can never keep days straight." Note that Anna claims first that the episode of the mouse discovered under the snow really happened; then she admits that it is something she only imagined—a fantasy.

Then she begins to free-associate again spontaneously: "Snow, house, pen, eyes, eyelashes, nail polish, blue, steel, red, blood, mouse blood, disgust." She is silent. "Nothing's coming to me." But then she begins again. "Drawing: snail, drool, mollusk, disgust, yes. I'm thinking of something that—Ugh!" She gestures as if to vomit. "That's it. I don't know what to say any more!"

I prefer to comment on both drawings, which were produced in the same sitting and refer to one experience. Anna is rejecting the imaginary phallus, the masculine part of herself, which in her first drawing (of the triad; see Figure 1) was instead united with the whole through the syncretism of infantile omnipotence. Her gender identity is passing, as it must, through loss—that is, the taking away of what does not belong to her own sex. This is the only way for her psychic identification to come into alignment with her anatomical sex, which from this point onward will "fulfill its destiny" (i.e., the parameters of social identity). The phallic component—which, as we have already seen in the minimizing configuration of the "prince of ants" (see Figure 1), was ready to to be rejected—has finally been devalued, as the comparison to a mollusk (or the snail in the drawing) shows. Anna assumes two kinds of distance in relation to it: Emotionally, she opposes it with disgust; intellectually, with feigned ignorance ("I've never even seen such things.")

It is important at this point to observe how the process of gender identification involves a global restructuring of the infantile psyche. Almost simultaneously, Anna has overcome her confusion with her mother, her confused bisexuality, and the intrusiveness of the id; she has confronted the partiality of a single sex, her exclusion from the parental couple, the otherness of the other, and the limits of desire. In short, although it is delayed, she has made a leap from the protected world of childhood toward the harsh world of puberty. It has not been an easy process, because it has progressed through a series of dislocations and mutilations, and not only in a metaphorical sense. (In another case of a four-year-old girl who was in therapy with me, the same experience was elaborated through a dream; this was then carried out in daydreams, in which she imagined her body cut into pieces on a butcher's counter.)

According to Freud, the emergence from childhood is accomplished by raising a system of barriers against the proximity to animals, the pleasure of handling excrement, incestuous desires, the conviction that only one sex (the male) exists, and the anarchy of pregenital sexuality.[43] Anna seems to have accomplished this difficult task of self-regulation, but this has required an introversion of psychic energies, which has reinforced narcissism and the autoerotic economy. The itching of her feet has been replaced in the meantime, by the admission of masturbatory pleasure. As is well known, masturbation requires the activation of two fantasies—a passive feminine type and an active masculine type. Furthermore, both sadism and masochism, the pleasure of watching and being watched, coexist within it. All this is directed exclusively toward the unconditional search for pleasure that in the woman finds a special representation in the clitoris, the only organ in the human body meant exclusively for pleasure. In this way, what once was—the unifying infantile sexual modality—is re-evoked. But the supremacy of rationality (represented by the brain as opposed to the heart), carried out by the superego, transforms autoerotic pleasure into guilt feelings during the course of the latency period (six to ten years of age). Corporeal phantoms (connected to masturbatory pleasure) are banished, and their energy is transformed and utilized to counter drives. The inhibition against autoeroticism and the repression of fantasies confirms the separation of mind and soma, which we have already seen in progress, with consequences in structuring the opposition of brain and heart. Thus silenced, the body can only be represented in unconscious fantasies or take on meaning in the symptom.

At this point, perhaps we can better understand Anna's second terrible image, that of the dead mouse. For women, the mouse is a disturbing symbol of repression, in that it symbolizes the phallic components of the opposite sex that have been displaced outside of the self. The image of the mouse seems to have aroused not only the disgust produced by the dream about the mollusks, but a further sense of revulsion. The most intense rejection that Anna knows raises a final barrier against the eventual recurrence of the repression—not only in connection to the mouse, but in connection to the violence of its wounding, the mutilating act, which is only evident in its consequences. In order to defend herself from its proximity, the child acts out a physical rejection (vomiting), with the purpose of casting out that which she feels to be intrusive within. While she acts out the distancing of this nocturnal imagination, however, the lesion on her throat (which is like the mouse's) emphasizes an existential similarity. It is interesting to note that in this phase of feminization, Anna expresses herself on more levels than she ever did before—reality, dream, fantasy, symptom, words, and drawing—in accordance with the plurality of elements at play and with the need for coordination among them.

THE CUT THROAT: CREATING THE SYMBOLIC WOUND

A cutting wound to a throat recalls the ritual sacrifice of females in ancient cultures, the most memorable symbolic instance being Agamemnon's sacrificial killing of his virgin daughter, Iphigenia. Agamemnon is, in turn, a victim of divine coercion: Artemis will not grant the favor of winds in carrying the Greeks to Troy unless the king sacrifices his daughter. Iphigenia is slaughtered "like a goat" in the name of war. Her death, in its excess—represented in the tragic dramas of Aeschylus and Euripides—is meant to confirm the prohibition against homicide and the substitution of the

human victim for the sacrificial animal.[44] But it reveals the violence
inherent in every killing and in the very aspect of sacrifice.[45]

As Nicole Loraux observes, there is a further, deeply buried analogy
between murder and marriage. Iphigenia is forced to reach the Greek army
on the promise of marriage to Achilles, but in the end marries Hades. It is
therefore an infernal marriage, like the one that rips Kore (Persephone)
from the love of her mother, Demeter. In the common representations of
Athenian social life, "death is the metaphor for marriage, given that in the
course of the nuptial procession, the girl dies as a girl."[46]

The equivalence between marriage and death established by the
sacrificial rite reveals the element of coercion inherent in the marriage pact.
However, in every sacrifice the acquiescence of the victim is required, for
without it the rite becomes a bloody murder. Analogously, in marriage,
every aspect of imposition and abuse is veiled by the consent of the bride,
who transforms destiny into choice. Marriage as a rite of passage for the
woman celebrates maturity and domesticity, the end of the freedom of
childhood, and enclosure within the walls of the conjugal household. But
the sacrificial blood also alludes to the loss of virginal integrity, to the
laceration of the female body caused by coitus, as if slaughter could be
connected to being deflowered. Furthermore, the throat represents the most
delicate and precious part of the woman, where intimacy, fragility, and
beauty converge. It is also the throat that is lacerated with the fingernails
in the excess of mourning because the pulses of life beat there, and in
sacrifice death enters the body there. As Loraux points out, perhaps some
secret order that regulates the feminine body is hidden in the throat, as if
"beyond ritual practices and their imperatives, a woman's throat suggests
death . . ."[47]

To return to Anna's case, what the myth represents as an external,
divine, and social constraint is instead revealed here as a violent internal
demand[48] that requires the submission of infantile desire to invisible social
impositions based upon predetermined sexual destiny. In this process, the
imagination seems to emerge from the sphere of unreality to which we
relegate it, and to reveal its transformative power and acute abilities. One
is reminded of the mysterious links that connect the psyche and the culture
to the body in psychosomatic illnesses. Anna's wound, however, appears to
be closer to symbol than to symptom, in the sense that Bettelheim intends
when he speaks of "symbolic wounds" to indicate rites of initiation.[49] The
self-inflicted laceration attests to a desire that the law be inscribed within
the body, in a "graphic" imposition of its edicts; we are familiar with this in
the form of the ritual mutilations inflicted on initiates in so-called primitive
societies. But even in our presumably more highly evolved culture, numerous operations for appendicitis in adolescents (fortunately, these are rare
now) also constituted an unconscious rite of initiation. Abortions among

young women—a more recent phenomenon that has become surprisingly widespread—may serve a similar function. Given the general lack of symbolic recognition in our culture, in many cases these procedudres take on the symbolic value of the "rite of passage" into the period of fertility.

According to Freud, the loss of the phallic component is what renders the little girl psychologically adapted to her biological identity. To be a female, corroborated Lacan, gender identification means being one without having one (a phallus), while for the male it means having one without being one. The phallus takes on the meaning of what is missing, what is whole—the impossible completion.

In this regard, psychoanalysis seems to assimilate a biological model that is inscribed in our self-representation, although its source is remote. Aristotle wrote in *De Gereratione Animauium:* "There is also a resemblance between the forms of a boy and a woman, and the woman is like a sterile man. The female is, in fact, distinguished by a kind of impotence."[50] Paradoxically, the female sex, which bears the major responsibility for the reproductive task, is considered to be sterile and impotent. This denial of reality, which is transformed into its opposite, is still visible in Freudian theory when it identifies femininity with passivity.

But therapeutic work with little girls (when it pays particular attention to the specifics of femininity) has confronted me with a final process, which in some sense is linked to and overlaps the one I have just described, without being identical to it. It seems as if the mere denial of the narcissistic virility of infantile sexuality is not sufficient to ensure that the process of feminization takes place in the woman, as specular male thought claims. The lack of a penis and the submission to clitoral autoeroticism do, in fact, create a "non-male," but this does not necessarily guarantee the identification with the other gender, a female sexual identity. For this to occur, a final work of fantasy—one that Freud did not anticipate—must take place.

A first indication of this symptom can be seen in Anna's self-inflicted wound, which transforms the distancing of an imaginary external organ, such as the phallus (which is seen as separable from the body), into a cut that reaches within to reveal another dimension of the gendered body. Like all children, Anna first experienced her body as contained within the maternal vessel (belly, arms, clothes, cradle, environment), whereas now she must herself be a vessel—in other words, must maternalize herself. The cut may serve to represent the vagina—a patency that opens toward the "insides" of the body, that designates the body as female.

The criticism that the early women psychoanalysts addressed to Freud hinged correctly on the demand for a female imagination, based on female sexual anatomy and on the recognition of an early vaginal autoeroticism.[51] It is also true that the little girl passes through a certain phase as if she had a phallus, but this does not equate her with a male. Her male component—

evoked by the omnipotence of her desires, by the negation of being incomplete—is sustained by dominant social values; yet it remains ancillary in view of her similarity to her mother, which arises from a mutual identification with the female.

Although Freud valued the contribution of women psychoanalysts, he never recognized that a sexual representation might correspond to anatomical sexuality, that psychic identity might be determined by biological identity. In reality, no one claims that a linear causality exists between body and psyche, or that homosexuality involves being untrue to oneself. Rather, in the fusion phase there is no sexual determination at all. The question only comes about at the moment of separation between daughter and mother, which corresponds to their mutual recognition. In separating, the daughter "enters" into her own body and grasps the specific messages of drive, but this does not mean that she is now a little woman.

Prefigurations of womanhood do exist in the similarities that the mother transmits to the daughter (symbolic functions, social expectations). Nevertheless, these still do not necessarily determine a female identity, because there remains a margin of decision in the matter. Anna has depicted this state of affairs in her first drawing (see Figure 1), particularly in the three question marks. The choice, whatever it may be, is not limited to the gesture of favoring one alternative over another; it begins a process that necessarily involves indecision, conflict, regressions, and progressions, and therefore one that can never be considered complete. Clinical experience shows us that there is no absolute correspondence between the actual body and the phantasmic body. Rather, the two levels are bound together in a dynamic that remains unstable and provisional. Although Freud ends the process of feminization with the rejection of the phantasmic penis—that is, with symbolic castration—my work with little girls has led me to view that paradigm as partial and to suggest that it be integrated with the one I describe here.

If we can view Anna's dream of the mollusks and her fantasy of the mouse within the context of confirmed psychoanalysis and the normality of its paradigms where femininity and castration coincide, we enter into unexplored territory with the cut throat. Freud based his model of female gender identity on that of the male, and as much as he may have examined its particularities, he was never aware of the maternal component and its interaction with the sexual component. For that reason, he viewed the woman as journeying from original bisexuality to genitality, which was seen as a total receptivity to reproductive coitus; genitality was thought to introduce the specificity of the reproductive task and of its related psychic representations. He did not recognize that maternity involves a time frame that does not coincide with male development. The interpretation of the products of Anna's imagination demonstrates that the distancing of the phallic appendage is not sufficient for the process of feminization to occur; a final elaboration is required, one that inscribes reproductive sexuality upon a psychic body designed for this task. To that end, the sexual impulses change direction, are introjected, and turn in on the self to produce an internalization of mind and soma.

As far as the wound under the chin is concerned, we can note, as Freud suggested, that it is usual in hysteria to observe a displacement of representations that actually refer to the "lower organs" or genital zones in an upward direction, usually toward the head.[52] This higher anatomical placement involves the attempt to desexualize and to intellectualize the symptom. In Anna's case, the scratch on her throat represents the female cut, the actual vaginal slit, which cannot be represented. In this phase, this is experienced in the negative, as privation—as "a-penia," so to speak. But the "female eunuch" possesses within herself the resources to transform the mutilation into a vital process—to evoke a fullness that through the recognition of her own creative potential will lend a positive value to what she lacks.

THE PIERCED FOOT: CONFRONTING EMPTINESS AND SEXUAL COMPLEMENTARITY

Anna's mother advises me anxiously that something has happened since the last session. But the little girl interrupts her, saying, "Don't talk. I have to tell her my dreams." She then relates the following:

"The first one began like this: with my foot . . . no, that's wrong. First I should tell you that drops were falling from my foot, it was dripping. Then I went to the doctor in the old house where I lived before, and he told me to go to the hospital. I don't know which one. I went, and they put a small silver plate right in the middle of the sole of my foot. Then a metamorphosis occurred. I was completely changed, even my sex. I became Edmondo, a really lively nurse in San Gervaso [Hospital]. Whenever I ate, he would always say, 'Today it must be snowing red'—because I never used to eat. Then I made him a beautiful drawing of red snow, and when he came to take my tray away he stayed like that—happy and shocked.

"I went to a room in the hospital where people were waiting to be operated on; I *walked* there. There were two girls there. The doctor said, 'Whoever needs an operation, step forward.' Then one of the girls disappeared from my dream. The other one remained. That one had the same illness as me: Her foot was dripping. Then I made a date with her. I said, 'See you later,' because I had to leave with my parents. I

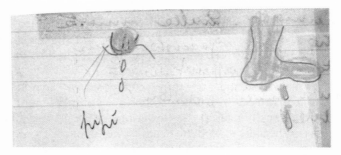

Figure 8

woke up just during the best part! The second girl [the girl who stayed] had blond cascading curls and red lips, even without lipstick."

I ask Anna to provide associations for some of the images in the dream: She replies:

"Foot: The tap in the old house that always dripped, the rain. Garden: Daisies, violets, sweet violets; the old house where I lived before; the doctor's apartment that was like mine. Silver plate: A song that goes 'Oro e argento, che fanno cinquecento, centocinquanta, la gallina canta, canta il gallo.'* Foot: Every time I said 'foot,' it itched there. So that's the plate! The last operation I had was to remove the plates. They put them there to support my bones. Now I feel the itching on my foot, but only a hint of it. Red snow: Red pen, the hen's feathers. But my brain came up with that, it led me to it. The metamorphosis: I became the nurse! Who knows how somebody could become someone else and then turn back into herself again? I don't know. But you can't know everything!"

Then she draws a vulva and a foot, both dripping, and states: "It reminds me of that thing there for making pee. The penis or the vagina."

Perhaps Anna's last words, so crudely desymbolized, recapitulate the meaning of the dream: How is she to correlate penis and vagina, masculine and feminine? How is she to wrench them out of the polar opposition that forces an exclusive choice? The vaginal opening, taking form as the scratch across the neck, introduces a dimension of emptiness, confirmed by Anna's not eating, the pierced foot, the surgery—all of which suggest the complementary fullness. The silver plate (which in Anna's initial account of the

---

*Gold and silver, which make five hundred, five hundred and fifty, the hen sings, the rooster sings.

dream is used to suture the hole in the foot and in her commentary is removed), in its dual functions, represents a possible coexistence of opposites; this has already been prefigured in the theme of metamorphosis, in which the desire for a reversibility of sexual choice is expressed. In the logic of the dream (in which opposites do not necessarily imply contradiction), "to close" can mean "to open." Thus, the act of "applying the plate" can be interpreted as the desire to be opened, made accessible to the insertion of the male genital organ, but also as the desire to be virginally sealed and protected.

In fact, once the phallus is removed/distanced from the narcissistic self-image, it is transformed into a object of the sexual drive (penis and boy); as such, it is anticipated as a means of reattaining lost wholeness.[53] However, Anna both desires and fears a psychic image of her own body, which, because it is characterized in terms of lack, suspends her in the expectation of the other. Inner emptiness will be experienced as a mere deprivation if it is not transformed by a possible presence—that is, if it does not become receptive.

Women's tendency to plunge into depression is rooted precisely in the difficulty of transforming lack into anticipation, emptiness into receptivity, the absent element into a guest. Whereas the expectation of completeness takes place outside of the self for a man, it can only occur within for a woman. Ginevra Bompiani writes in this regard: "Expectation is the space where an arrow shot from any point homes in on a target. The target is in the heart of the expectant one."[54] Whenever emptiness does not evoke fullness, it generates the anxiety of deprivation, which is then amplified because it resonates with the series of losses characterizing individuation—from birth to weaning, from the giving up of feces to imagined castration.

Three female figures, analogous to the triad in Anna's first drawing (see Figure 1), reappear in this dream in a kind of oneiric regression. Now, however, they no longer elicit the same sense of shock and perplexity. The anonymity that made them so disturbing at first has been replaced by a precise identification: They are Anna and two other girls under treatment. Significantly, one of them disappears after refusing to be operated on. We can assume (as the next dream confirms; see below) that she represents the phallic identity that Anna has devalued and rejected. The other two, on the other hand, must be sutured—a process that alludes to a previous incision that has not stopped draining. On one hand, the drops, a metaphor for tears, express the ongoing mourning over the loss of a narcissistic component of the self. On the other hand, it evokes (in its association with the rain) a diffuse atmosphere of melancholy. The melancholy arises as the inevitable affective connotation of Anna's nostalgia for the house she lived in before.

Once again, the flowering garden symbolizes the lost paradise that precedes separation, loss, the process of gender identification, and the recognition of limits ("you can't know everything!") We know that the foot symbolizes—in the dream, in the drawing, and in Anna's symptoms—the coexistence of opposites: both the narcissistic, infantile, phallic sexuality and the subsequent feminized one. But, now in the drawing, the female genital is represented directly without any need for the foot to substitute for it. In a certain sense, Anna refuses to undergo the feminization of the body and objects to an inscription of lack, but at the same time she accepts it and tries to restructure her identity on the basis of this very specificity. For while the girls in the dream are suffering patients (it is not insignificant that in the eighteenth century the female sex was known as the "the sick sex"), the male figures (the nurse, Edmondo, and the doctor) are happy and healthy.

At this point, the disturbing image of the "prince of ants" is quite distant. The mollusks and mice are now replaced by more pleasant phallic symbols (the hen, the pen), and Anna is now able to express sexuality directly in a graphic representation and to name the sexual organs.

If defense mechanisms remain in place, they lie mainly in the splitting of the genitals from the scheme of bodily unity; in the confusion among the urethra, penis, and vagina; and in the abrupt interruption of the dream. However, during this phase of Anna's oneiric work, we can see an initial recognition of sexual complementarity, even if it is accompanied by a proud enclosure in virginity—in the self-assuring affirmation that perhaps one sex is sufficient unto itself. In some way this conservative attitude makes the recognition of the reciprocity of two genders more obscure and slow. Yet it also represents an emancipation from social conditioning; a claim for completeness and autonomy; an enrichment of the self through the conservation of the masculine components that give it value.

I ask Anna to free-associate further to the word "silver" as it refers to the plate. She responds: "It certainly makes you think of something valuable, but not of a piece of jewelry. My 'little sparrow' needs no jewels; it's beautiful just as it is. It's a prize, a trophy, like they give champions. I pee standing up, but for cleanliness, not because I like to. I love my 'little sparrow' so much that I always touch it." She demonstrates the pleasure of rubbing her genitals through her pants and states, blushing, that "girls' caresses are much better than boys', who only have a little mushroom." She caresses her "little sparrow" when she has an itch. I point out to her that she is using the same word she used to describe her attacks—"itch." In fact, Anna now admits that the two sensations are the same, only that in the first case she enjoys it, while in the second case something compels her to stretch, to shake, to get rid of it. I ask her how a pleasant experience can be the same as an unpleasant one. She answers that one is the right amount, whereas the other is too much—"an itch goes all over like crazy." Then she remembers how afraid she was one day when nobody could turn off the shower and the water flooded the entire bathroom. Anna's final comments introduce the problem of energy in infantile development.

In representing the development of drives, Freud himself used the metaphor of a flow of water that must be channeled so that its force can be checked. Whenever it reaches the sea without having come up against any obstacles, it will be repelled by an opposing wave, and thus will flood the surrounding land. Anna's libidinal energies, which have been released in the phase of affective detachment from her mother, have not found any timely, adequate investment; instead, they have overflowed, provoking the anxiety that is expressed in her symptoms. They are not qualitatively different from the energies regulating those processes that are considered normal; only the quantity and the regulation of libido vary. These have overburdened the phallic investment and the associated homosexual identity, to which the little girl responds by setting off a process of feminization that propels her dangerously back toward her mother. In the face of this eventuality, which she both longs for and fears, Anna evokes the parental couple and is thus subjected to the efficacy of their law. From this moment on, she is able to assume her sexual identity without feeling obligated to occupy the position of mother or father, or to interfere in their reciprocal relationship. The incest prohibition functions indirectly, through the exclusive relationship that the conjugal couple maintains and that, as a consequence, restores Anna's desire to her.

But since no sex is sufficient unto itself, Anna now confronts the complementarity of the other. In the face of this evidence, she engages in an elaborate celebration of her own specific sexuality, in contrast to her earlier penis envy, manifested by her habit of urinating standing up like her brother. Childish competitiveness spurs her to establish a priority. Just as she placed a value upon the male sex during the phallic phase, now she attempts to give a similar preference to the female (the trophy to the victor).[55] At the same time she elaborates a defense against the fear of being deflowered through two fantasies: first, closing and fortifying the vaginal opening; second, devaluing the male phallus and rendering it innocuous (the comparison with a mushroom).

It is clear here how the same unconscious processes can be put to the service of different demands. In this case the oneiric work strives to feminize the body image, to subject it to sexual complementarity; at the same time, however, it attempts to defend it from passivity, to overcome devaluation, to make the other sex less threatening, and to maintain a link of a continuity with Anna's previous identity. We can see over and over again that becoming a woman involves a complex redefinition of the self and of relationships with others. Every progression in the spiral process of infantile evolution is accompanied by a partial regression, so that no stage is ever really completed.

What her mother wanted to tell me at the beginning of the session is that Anna sometimes seems to be a baby again. She clings to her, even physically; refuses the company of her peers; and amuses herself by talking in babble, the private lexicon of her early infancy. The suspension of Anna's social life appears to serve the interior elaboration of affective dynamics on two levels: the structuring of the self, and the elaboration of new relationships with others. The second dream Anna describes during the session, which I call "the dream of the walled-up boy," can be read this way too. It occupies a decisive place in Anna's imaginative work because it introduces the theme of the concavity of the body, where sexuality and maternity become connected.

THE WALLED-UP BOY: CONCAVITY, THE DOUBLE, AND COMPLEMENTARITY AGAIN

Anna relates the dream as follows:

> "A boy has kidnapped a girl and is going to force her to marry him. The girl convinces him that it's not fair, because he would not be happy if the shoe were on the other foot—if he were being forced to marry another girl. Then the boy lets her go, but cannot stand the solitude and kidnaps a second girl, the first one's cousin. This other girl is a bit—I don't know how to put it—sneaky, shrewd. She makes him give her the address. She calls the police and has him arrested. Then she has the boy turned over to her and puts him in a block of cement, with only his head sticking out. . . . Then she calls the first girl and tells her to guard the boy. The first girl approaches the block of cement and asks him: 'But why, why did you want to kidnap me?' "

Anna quickly picks up a pen. Tracing the outline of a boy within a square, she comments, "I can't draw him well because what's left of him is only an imprint, a pit in the cement" (Figure 9). The graphic gesture that turns the male into a void is the last act in the work of Anna's self-feminization, the final transformation of the phallic component of the self. What remains now in the place of infantile wholeness is a pit, an empty casing. The feminine body has only taken that shape following a complex transformation of its original form—a fully rounded form that the infantile imagination wishes to be filled with itself, but that evolutional, biological, and social forces have replaced with a concavity that can serve as a recipient. In this way, infantile narcissism has repudiated the celebration of the male component and, in some sense, has become "maternalized."

The little girl becomes a woman by renouncing the sufficiency of the self, recognizing herself as "not whole" and therefore open to the desire of the other, and taking the love object into herself. In sexual economy, this self-limitation of the omnipotent infantile imagination helps her to take

Figure 9

on a seductive and receptive position—to desire and anticipate the phallus and the child, which seem at this point to meld into a single figure in the unconscious. Freud observed that a typical fantasy of a young bride is to hold the husband's penis inside her own womb like a prefiguration of the awaited child.[56] In the Freudian model, the penis–child equivalent represents the end of the girl's sexual evolution, which finds its outlet "in what is known as the normal sexual life of the adult, in which the pursuit of pleasure comes under the sway of the reproductive functions."[57]

Thus narcissistic love becomes object love. The condensation of the figure of the penis into that of the child promotes a feeling of tenderness, which diminishes the fearful aspects of coitus. To counter the male imagination, which transforms the erection into a display of warrior-like power, the woman evokes, in an ironic guise, the infantilization of the phallus—its diminishment into something "little," as in the German word *klein*, which refers to the child and to the penis alike. The Freudian model, which makes the child a substitute for the penis, clearly expresses male desire and its presumption of precedence. But for the little girl, this model mainly involves an adjustment to the male imagination, an acquiescence to the phantasms of the other, and a denial of the limits both of her own libidinal autonomy and of her own gender-specific imagery.

Making the self concave and giving up omnipotent totality occur when the girl forgets her own fullness and when the phantasm of the child takes precedence over that of the phallus, as the case of Paola (see Chapter 2) will show. The repression of the phantasmic events of the infantile female is such that these become inscribed in the unconscious in the one language that is legitimate—that of the male imagination. Elements of autonomous femininity persist mainly in the resistance against social expectations, in the transfiguration of their codes, in the objections to their aims. It is interesting to observe that the maternal function appears (at least initially) in the negative statute of absence, of death, and of burial. The third of the three female figures in the unconscious, with its disturbing combination of love and death, reveals here the connection I have noted at the beginning of this chapter between the mother who gives life and the Mother Earth, who takes us all in. This is a connection that ancient Mediterranean civilization formalized in the funerary cult of the Great Mother. What the male culture represents as the projection of the other (part) of itself, which the woman represents, we can see operating in Anna in the context of the feminine unconscious. Determined as it is by a long historic tradition, it cannot be symbolized in the context of its own perspective. The very process of feminization, accomplished by the feminine components of the self, conceals the conflict and asymmetry between the sexes that control it; it thus appears in the form of an inevitable maturation. This is why the maternal attitude, when it is construed as "natural," remains devoid of meaning. It is an emptiness that must wait for something from the outside to give it value and meaning.

With the boy gone, the two young girls from the original set of three remain. Using the colored pencils (which she has previously refused), Anna draws two almost identical heads (Figure 10) and remarks:

> "These are the first girl and the second girl in the dream of the boy who was walled up alive. I'm not making them blond, though I'd prefer to, because the girls in my other dream [the one about the clinic] were blond. They are part of a fantasy I can't tell anybody, or I won't be able to have it any more. These girls don't have names, because the names I like best I already used for the other fantasy, the one I can't talk about."

This anonymity reveals that the feminine components, which assert themselves in intrapsychic conflict, are now being repressed. In fact, this repres-

Figure 10

sion serves to obliterate not only the unacceptable contents of the unconscious but also the mechanisms that are antagonistic to them, so that the process of repression itself disappears, as if it had never happened. If any traces remain, we must search for them (as in this case) in the by-products of the unconscious, in its nocturnal residue.

Now that the boy is gone from the scene, the two girls remain, one the double of the other. Their presence evokes the theme of the double, which inevitably appears in every dynamic of identification in which traces of primary narcissism persist.[58] It is necessary for the ego to split off from itself and be duplicated in the self, so that the body can gain distance from its phantasmic experiences; only then can interior and exterior psychic and social life be split. Once the totality with the mother is lost and narcissistic unity is broken, the individual can only gain integrity again by overcoming the anxiety of annihilation and attempting a provisional reconstitution of the self. The actual body, which in the experience of the double appears in the place of the other, reveals the narcissistic component of every relationship—the autoerotic modulation that persists in heterosexual desire. The disturbance produced by the theme of the double is such that Anna must protect a part of herself, as the secret fantasy of the blond girls whose names she cannot mention demonstrates.

The secret alludes to what Winnicott calls the "real self," a kind of sanctuary of the personality in which the subject shuts the meaning of his or her own uniqueness and intimacy.[59] In therapy with children, I have often encountered the claim of a secret. I consider this fantasy a positive defense in the face of the therapist's intrusion and his latent voyeurism, and a partial neutralization of the violation inherent in any interpretation. The affirmation of the secret confirms that the children do not wish to lie; they are remaining faithful to the pact that psychotherapy implicitly makes with truth—which still does not mean that everything can be said.

Also in this dream, the specification of Anna's sexual identity involves a re-elaboration of body image; however, as a consequence, this involves a redefinition of social relationships. We can re-examine the dream from this perspective.

At the moment that Anna completes the process of feminization, she comes up against relational problems, which the process of gender identification produces. In fact, determination of gender does not exist without the concomitant complementarity; identity does not exist without the recognition that comes from the glance of the other. The little girl feels truly feminine only when masculine desire confirms her sexual identity, and only then can she also acknowledge herself as desiring. In fact, in the dream, amorous desire is initially attributed to the boy. The girls passively submit to his attacks, each responding with a particular strategy. The first girl uses reason and invites her male companion to behave according to an ethic of reciprocity. But such an ethic is rendered impossible by the erratic desire of the male, who turns suddenly to another girl. In order to escape his clutches, the latter uses a tactic that is closer to Metis than to Logos—that is, closer to animal instinct than to rational norms. Once she has the boy in her possession, she sets out to wall him up alive much as he planned to kidnap her, thus following the rules of retaliation that dominate the unconscious. It is interesting to observe that the first girl, who has adopted an ethical attitude, is later the one who re-establishes contact (however feeble) with the then-disappearing boy, and who expresses an amorous question, an expectation. Here differing tendencies confront and conflict with each other: action and passivity, ethical behavior and cunning, domination and submission, conflict and reconciliation. The dream seems to express a diagram of the evolutional lines of femininity—a task so all-involving that it has pushed Anna back into a regressive position. She asked her mother— as she has before in the previous months—whether she could look at her and caress her breasts. This time, sitting on her mother's knees, she announced: "I'm not sitting on your knees; I'm on your vagina."

ANNA AND OTHERS:
REGRESSION AND PROGRESSION

Because the interior elaboration has pushed Anna out of childhood too quickly, regressive mechanisms are set into motion to slow down the growth process, to synchronize reality and fantasy, and to modulate the external world so that it conforms to the internal world. In this sense, the following dream appears to be projected further into the future than the previous ones, in terms of its amorous strategies. It is also closer to Anna's daily life and her situation as a child, in terms of its setting.

"Me and my friend Mattia Roversi became partners. Angela had done the same thing with another boy. We had all arranged to have a wedding performed by the priest of the class. But when I wanted to do this, this wedding for our partnerships, everybody made fun of me: my teacher, my schoolmates, the parish priest. Instead of a marriage bed we'd bought a marriage table. Then, since we didn't know what to do with our time, I asked for a ping-pong table: 20,000 lire from me, 20,000 from Mattia. When I left school, I went to the old house, but the caretaker wouldn't open the door and I couldn't get in, and then I woke up."

Once again the regression finds the threshold of infancy barred, there is no way to go back. There is nothing to be done, then, but to gestate one's desire in the present for the future. The transformations of the marriage bed into a table and of the sexual relationship into a ping-pong game reveal Anna's capacity to wittily sublimate sexual needs into a game. The little girl shows that she is capable of setting up an interior laboratory in which the most disturbing contents of the unconscious can be tamed by the imagination, re-experienced as a game, and defused by irony.

Nevertheless, a discrepancy between the psychic and the social economy remains: Family conflicts have not yet been resolved. Anna is still trying everything she can to keep her mother at her side, to keep her from going out, to maintain their old physical intimacy. "I want to enter a body, which body?" she asks. She then answers her own question: "My mother's." One of the greatest difficulties in the mother–daughter bond lies in finding the limits of the relationship, establishing equal distance between what is too close and too far. We can assume that the mother too experiences the desire to take the daughter back into herself, to blot out the loss of her maternal complement.

By now (we are in the second year of therapy), Anna has turned ten and has had her first menstrual period. When she tells me this, I look at her body and see that it has taken on a new roundness, which could almost go unnoticed under her comfortable childlike clothes. Only now do I realize that her menarche has been prefigured by the dream of the pierced foot— that the red snow, the dripping foot and vulva were her body's messages, although I could not read them at the time.

Menstruation demands new work of the psyche. It asks the psyche, in fact, to incorporate an occurrence that to the child's eye appears to be dirty, obscene, and violent into the bodily identity (which up until now has delimited itself by raising barriers of disgust, modesty, and morality against infantile sexuality). In a certain sense, menstruation reactivates anal drives (to manipulate, to dirty), their related anxieties, and the consequent defense mechanisms. However, the emotional investment is now increased by the aggressive nature of blood—by its connection to sexuality and death. Menstruation provokes an eruption of irrationality in the well-ordered world of male laws; within the code of civilization, its "laws" appear disorderly. The body is suddenly felt to be sick and impure, as the history of female medicine demonstrates.[60] But it is through these anxieties that menstruation confirms the little girl's place in her femininity; it demonstrates the power of her body and its productive capacities.

The attainment of fertility reactivates the procreative phantasms of early childhood, the desire to have a baby. Yet the incest prohibition obliges the little girl to displace her erotic desires outside of the home, to connect them to the desires of others who people the external space around the family; at this age, this means at school. For this reason, amorous fantasies are often transferred onto the teacher, the first substitute for Oedipal objects.

But, as we all know, love cannot be reciprocated in this case either, and Anna finds herself caught between dual impossibilities that push her toward dangerous experiences. In fact, she tells me that one afternoon, unseen by anybody, she went to the ruins of an old house nearby, in order to spy on an old exhibitionist who is well known around the neighborhood. She searched for him, and when she spotted him, she ran without a word and hid amidst the remains of a wall and surrounding undergrowth, while the old man struggled to follow her. As she tells it to me, she enjoyed the fear, the pounding of her heart, confronting the risk and the unknown. The old man slowly prowled the neighborhood in a blue Cadet (a car), and when he found her, "he stared at me with those eyes of his!"

I doubt that all of this actually happened, but the imagination and the game demonstrate Anna's difficulty in mastering the erotic impulses of puberty, which are at once voyeuristic and exhibitionistic. Her fantasies about the dead mouse and now about the exhibitionist express the typical infantile desire (so often represented in fairy tales) to leave the family by being violently away taken by an adult who serves to exempt the child from all responsibility; the child thus tries to attain autonomy in a protected form of subjection and obedience.[61] But what Anna really wishes to affirm here is the passage from a passive to an active position: In her fantasy, it is she who seduces the old man, attracts him to her.[62] This is exactly the opposite of what must happen in the course of early childhood, when the child is seduced by its mother—that is, drawn to move toward her, to love her, to shatter the protection of narcissistic barriers. In this sense, Anna's fantasy inverts the position of the initial trauma, which is provoked by the erotic love that is invested in the newborn; it forces the infant to confront an adult sexuality that he or she knows nothing of and cannot control, but that attracts and overwhelms him or her.[63] From the analytic literature, the first adult–child relationship appears to be imprinted by violent seduction—characterized by a reciprocal excitement that never finds adequate representation in the little one and that remains bottled up in the body, ready to set off an hysterical attack whenever the pathogenic conditions re-present themselves.

Freud considered it impossible to determine whether the seduction of early childhood, which shows up in every female analysis, is a fantasy or a fact. However, he believed that hysterical symptoms, with their specifically corporeal nature, are rooted in this experience. There is an erotic complicity between adult and child that is rather difficult to seize upon or to analyze, because a particularly severe censure opposes it. Nevertheless, Anna wants to be the one to lead the amorous game, to look and to seduce, thus making herself a participant in maternal activity.

There begins at this moment an elaboration of the feminine erotic position, in which the passive component (which Freud considered the psychic equivalent of femininity) takes on strong masochistic tendencies. As in an earlier phase of Anna's therapy, the "Red Brigades" enter upon the scene. Now, however, they enter the house at night, unhinging the front door, and rob her of valuable objects and jewelry. We know that in the symbolism of the unconscious, jewelry signifies female genitals, while the theft refers to the sexual relationship. On other occasions, bands of vandals or fascists come to beat her. The following dreams are typical of this phase of the therapy:

> "Once I was in a glass room with slides and swings. I was attacked by a gang of kids who beat me up, and then I ran away. Then I got punched and kicked while I was on the swing.
>
> "Once I was in the house, and a man came up and made me write everything I knew about different countries (China, etc.). He beat me and threatened me with a pistol. . . . he punched me in the back to make me do it faster. Then when I told him the police were coming he tried to escape, but I got in front of the door so he'd be arrested. . . . Afterwards the police brought us to a class where there were other kids I didn't know. And that man was sitting down in a chair, studying too. When he sat down in the chair, all of a sudden he turned little again. He became a schoolboy."

In some sense, the second dream represents the anxieties connected to the sexual relationship from the female point of view (fear of being looked at, wounded, incompetent, alone), but it also acknowledges the pleasure of the power that a woman holds over an infantilized man. This modality of overcoming her sense of inferiority and weakness in the face of the male consists precisely of locating the infantile aspects in him, in putting him in the place of the child. Therefore the male's manifest feeling of superiority is checked by the female's hidden feeling of superiority.

In accordance with the strong social contract and the demands for self-affirmation characterizing the women's movement of those years, Anna battles to regain those aspects of masculinity that can correct the deprived and mournful elements of maternalized femininity. Her favorite interlocutor is the female teacher who has replaced the male teacher of the previous year. Anna enjoys frustrating her expectations of traditional and reactionary attitudes, of stereotypical femininity, of ideological conformity:

> "She wants me to be a little lady. She always says that girls shouldn't say bad words, shouldn't be messy. Stay at home and cook, that's what we should do, according to her. But I told her that cooks are always men. She gets angry and starts shrieking like a shrew. Yesterday she read an elegy for Franco [the Spanish dictator] that was saying he was a great strategist, and she started to cry. But me and my friend Mattia were whispering to each other, 'We're better strategists than him.' And when the teacher asked us what Mussolini's and Hitler's greatest mistakes were, I answered loudly: 'Being born.' "

Then Anna confesses that she has not been able to express her feelings openly because her parents have forbidden her to speak badly of her teacher. But now that she has done this, she feels really good; saying this, she begins to dance and jump around the room, expressing pleasure that I am her ally. In fact, I have allowed myself to whisper the word "Fascist!" when she was speaking of her teacher's opinion of France. Anna immediately grasps the liberating potential in this and begins to chant, debating her parents indirectly: "Then we can give her that label."

Her opposition to her teacher is also an indirect way for her to confront her mother without having to invest any direct aggression. In fact, she confides to me, "Now I think my mother is attached to me like a sucker, and I'm afraid she'll leave me suddenly. My mother is neither this or that. She's as close to me as I want, but when I grow up? When I'm grown up and I go to talk to her, will she speak in another language?"

At the same time, Anna's view of both her teacher and her mother refer back to me—to my progressive detachment, in which she intuits the end of therapeutic work. "The other language" could mean, then, the end of a dialogue that is not like any other.

THE SHAMEFUL SECRET: MENSTRUATION AND REPRODUCTIVE POTENTIAL

The dreams Anna describes in the next few sessions are characterized by the anxiety provoked by her menstruation as social behavior. By a tacit convention among young girls, this physiological event must be handled with the utmost secrecy, since male peers must not know of it. The very existence of this inconvenient and shameful phenomenon within oneself provokes a whole series of persecutory experiences. The eyes of companions, which one cannot escape, recreates the vigilant function of the infantile superego, with its voyeuristic and intrusive nature. Anna's fragile sexual identity is put to a series of imaginary tests. Seizing a red bold-tip marker, she describes a bad dream in big letters: "Marco rapes me. What a nightmare!" And on another day: "I dreamed that Marco was pulling up my skirt and raping me. At school a while ago, they opened the bathroom door on me. And Franco said, 'They saw you, they saw you!' I woke up all sweaty, thinking I couldn't go back to school again because everybody knew." And then: "I had this impulse to immerse my hands in color, imaginary color, and to leave handprints on the yellow walls of the school." And finally: "Another dream and another nightmare: I have my period, and everybody comes into the little room where I'm changing my underwear. I'm afraid of staining them"; "I had my period, and while I was changing my underwear, guards came to watch me."

As we have seen, the autonomy attained in respect to the family provokes an investment of sexuality in external relationships with adults and children. Menstruation plays a determining role in this dynamic, as does the development of the breasts; both distance young girls from their male peers, who are seen as infantile. The delay between female and male puberty, which happens later, produces a dissimilarity that is difficult to overcome. The pubescent girl then withdraws into herself to elaborate the embarrassing transformations occurring in her body, either in her private fantasies or with close friends, and to integrate them into idealized aspects of maternity. However, they are closely connected in the unconscious to fears about sterility, as the following dream and its real-life aftermath reveal:

"A while ago I dreamed I had two hens. One hen laid nice eggs. One every minute, one every thirty seconds—pretty, oval eggs. Chicks came out of her eggs: black, yellow, and white chicks. The other hen was pushing—'Eh . . . Eh . . . Eh'—but nothing happened. Then she sat down and pushed again; she got up; but nothing! Finally, there was only one solid egg, faceted, hexagonal, but there was no chick, nothing came out. . . . A few days ago, I had my period. Yesterday, there was just spotting. My mother said to me, 'The little egg broke apart.' And I said, 'The little egg? A real little egg? Then I can go 'cluck, cluck, cluck.' "

Gradually, as menstruation becomes a habitual occurrence, its traumatic aspects are attenuated and it becomes connected to the recognition of the body's reproductive potential. The monthly blood is no longer considered an absurd soiling, but is transformed into a vital process—except for the fact that this carries with it the shadow of its opposite, the infertility that the little girl uses as a defense against the task of acknowledging the terrible reproductive power that she holds within. Her body, which is still a child's, appears inadequate to the physiological task of maternity. The cyclic repetition of her periods will gradually confirm that a different economy has taken over the organic processes, and that another temporality has taken over the regulation of biological rhythms. The menstrual flow, because it is uncontrollable, constitutes a difficult test of self-mastery; it threatens the sublimation and idealization of the self-image, upon which women base a great deal of their value. The "baser" aspects of female corporeality thus provoke a schism between sexuality and conjugality. The image of the prostitute, which is rather common in the fantasies of female adolescents, now appears in Anna's dreams. The following is a confused dream based on the feats of Che Guevara:

> "The whole story is related to Che Guevara. Do you know who he is? But it has no meaning. He meets a girl and together they have some adventures . . . . and then when they come back, while they're coming back, there's an army of fascist soldiers that—where there's a sergeant who this girl likes a lot. She was some kind of prostitute. [The dream continues with Che meeting a blond girl.] After the marriage, though, this girl goes back to black hair and shows that she's the prostitute from before."

The dream tends to distinguish sexuality from love, the prostitute from the wife. However, in mistaking one for the other Anna is forced to confront once again the very thing she has formerly found intolerable: sexuality in conjugality. The erotic relationship is only clearly distinct from pornography when the woman unconsciously connects it to a fantasy of engendering, in which the impersonal dimension of life transcends the bodily circumstances and creativity sublimates pleasure, removing it from the transience of infantile onanism.

THE ANIMAL CHILD: MATERNALIZATION, THE LOST SELF, AND CREATIVE POTENTIAL

As we have seen through the various stages of Anna's analysis, the transformation of a little girl into a woman does not happen by itself. It requires a long and complex elaboration, in the course of which we can distinguish four fundamental moments up to this point: the disappearance of the imaginary phallus; the image of the full body's becoming concave; the recognition of complementarity; and the integration of the reproductive process into the body image. Each of these phases has had precursors in early childhood. We have seen that, in a certain sense, phallic castration repeats earlier experiences of loss, such as birth and weaning. Similarly, the body has already been experienced as concave in the form of the hungry mouth. Complementarity characterizes the relationship with the mother on an existential level, in the sense that one cannot be without the other. Finally, the reproductive capability has already been manifested in the fantasies connected to the first transitional objects (blanket, teddy bear, doll).

The child who finally emerges from this process synthesizes within the self all the elements that have gradually been distanced from the body: the placenta, the nipples, feces, the mother, the imaginary phallus, the favorite toy. And yet the child will be found in an external space, far from the body and its phantasms. It is from this encounter that the child "goes home again."

Up until now, Anna's narcissistic investment has been such that she has been the protagonist of her dreams and daydreams. But suddenly, and almost furtively, another character is introduced: the little boy. In the first dream, he appears as detritus, forgotten, after an attack of the Red Brigades: "When they heard the police siren, they escaped through the window, leaving lots of things broken—even Inti Illimani records and the picture of Che Guevara with the words 'Long live freedom!' I began to collect everything, and a certain point I realized that a little, frightened boy was left in a corner of the room, who reminds me of the little cat that I want."

In another dream the little boy drowns in a pond, like the little child who escapes from the arms of Ottilia in the waters of the lake that graces the ideal space of Goethe's *Elective Affinities*. Often an animal, such as a ladybug or a cat, appears in the place of the little boy. Anna notes: "Now, before anything else, I have to explain . . . that I am waiting for a cat, a pretty little male cat, who I'm going to name Yuri, like Gagarin [the Soviet cosmonaut]."

Anna's mother eventually allows her to keep a female cat in the house, and Anna remarks: "I treat him [sic] like a child, a male child." What Anna has lost in the process of feminization is recaptured in maternalization; the cat or child then represents the "not self"—its valid aspects that have been repressed, but remain in the unconscious and reappear in the world, to be internalized again.

One night Anna has an analogous dream to the now-distant one about the "machine of wishes," and comments: "It could be me who gives birth to a male! . . . People have always mistaken me for a male, but actually the male might not be me, but my son." At the same time, her own "pretense of virility" remains unchanged: "I want to be a man–woman," she claims.

"I don't want to be like my mother, a housewife, or even worse, a fool like my teacher. I want to be something new." One night she has a fertility dream:

> "One day I was in front of school when I saw my friend/enemy Federica coming toward me. She is whining (she's always such a phony!), and as I listen to her, my belly begins to swell. At that point the front door of the school opens wide and all my companions come out, among them Marco, Nicola, and Mattia. I inform them all that I'm pregnant, and they're all happy. My belly, meanwhile, keeps growing, and Federica says to me, very sweetly: 'But how could you be expecting a baby?' I don't understand the question, and she insists: 'But have you ever done it?' At this point my belly begins to go down; it becomes flat, skinny—I don't like it a bit."

Commenting on the dream, Anna relates that her cat is now going to have kittens and that she is awaiting this event impatiently. But she's afraid that her mother won't let her keep them—that she'll put them out on the street. Other themes are connected in this dream: the connection between sexuality and maternity, the rivalry between women, and the need to put off the desire for generative fullness. It is interesting that two female figures oppose Anna's reproductive imagination: her "friend–enemy" Federica in her nocturnal reality, and her mother in her daily reality. Her male companions, on the other hand, are enthusiastic.

On other occasions, too, I have found that pregnant women fear female envy, especially maternal envy. One young woman refused to tell her mother the unborn baby's chosen name, because she felt that, magically, "it would have been dangerous." A young girl's fantasies of maternity remain even more secret than her erotic fantasies, for in them the daughter takes the place of the mother and therefore no longer acknowledges her as such. It is only when the mother is able to rise above the aggressive phantasms at play without being overly disturbed that the girl will feel that her attacks of anger, dread, and envy are not truly destructive, and thus will overcome the resulting feelings of guilt and depression. Federica's envy represents maternal envy that is attributed to a less emotionally conflictual object. Federica still manages, however, to damage Anna's manifestation of fertility and creativity: Anna's shrinking belly becomes "skinny" and she loses pleasure. In the absolute logic of the unconscious, the female body is subjected to the alternatives of fullness and emptiness, of swelling and of withering. In its static atemporality, the infertile womb is sterile, without remedy, and without the future possibility. This explains the difficulty that the little girl has in delaying the realization of motherhood, her continuing dread of the inability to procreate. On the other hand, the chorus of Anna's male companions, in its expression of recognition and gratification, represents the promise and social expectation of maternity.

It is true that early pregnancies, which are often terminated in abortions, are frequently brought about by young women's very need to affirm that their power to procreate has not been jeopardized by attacks of maternal jealousy, or else to prove to themselves that their guilt, provoked by the jealousy that they once felt toward their mothers, has not brought a punishment of sterility upon them. These dynamics are particularly intense for young women, their comparison with their mothers being direct.

Whereas for the male, as we have seen, achieving sexual maturity is a matter of displacing his love for his mother onto other women, leaving female polarity intact, a woman is required to abandon her mother as a love object and to replace her with a male partner.[64] This abandonment involves the loss of affective investment and value. But, at the same time, the little girl must be "like the mother"—that is, must occupy the very role that she once impoverished by withdrawing affective investment and symbolic recognition. Sometimes the solution of the conflict involves taking the place of the father, sharing his sexual prestige and the mother's love with him; at other times it involves maintaining the subordinate position of the daughter. Most often, however, the little girl recovers the mother in herself, containing her within as she was once contained in her. She receives in exchange, through a secret metabolism, an inheritance of generative power.

There is no passing of banners, no symbolic exchange, no social recognition in this generational exchange. It all occurs within the context of a sex that knows no hierarchies, only penetration. The satisfaction derived from the exchange defuses jealousy and allows the daughter to experience a gratitude that will become the expectation of the other and the pleasure of sharing herself. The psychological attainment of maternity often brings a resolution of the relationship with the mother, a truce in relation to earlier conflicts.

But the fear Anna displays about her own procreative capacity also expresses her anxiety about the imminent end of therapy. Since I must leave the city where I work, Anna and I agree that her present pediatrician, who is also a capable psychologist, will see her in therapy for the time being. Anna's symptoms have not recurred for a long time; her refusal to go to school is now a distant memory; and her electroencephalogram is normal now.

Some time later, Anna brings the following dream to the doctor: She is keeping a little male Siamese kitten in her room. She keeps it hidden from her mother's sight. But her mother finds out and forces her to get rid of it, even if she has to "kill or drown it" to get it out of the house. Then the mother takes it and puts it out on the street. The kitten runs away and is hit by a car, which is also heading for a cocker spaniel puppy; the puppy, however, manages to escape. Anna carries the puppy home and begs her mother to let her keep it. "The dog food will only cost forty cents a day," she says. "It only eats forty cents' worth of meat a day!" Actually, the puppy is so small that it is still only drinking milk. Her mother agrees. But there is another cat on the street; this one is not dead, though its spine is broken. Anna brings it home and bandages it. The cat heals and lives forever alongside the spaniel. At this point, her mother is no longer there.

This last dream represents additional unconscious dynamics. First, it contains the exogamous components of the Oedipal interdiction. Her mother's order to get rid of the kitten means that filiation must occur outside of the family—that children are not made with the mother or the father. The fantasy recapitulates the myth of Laius, who gave the newborn Oedipus to a slave to be killed. It also echoes the fairy-tale theme of the child abandoned in the woods, thrown to the mercy of ferocious animals, witches, and ogres. The little cat that dies on the street represents the end of the unconscious phantasm of the child. This is the "child of the night," about whom more will be said later—a condensed imaginary representation of all the parts of the self that are lost along with infantile omnipotence; a plaything among all the others from one's childhood room. Sacrificing it, however, allows Anna to bring into the house the puppy from the street, which was miraculously saved from the automobile that crushed the cat.

The dog appears in the dream as a metamorphosis of the cat—a kind of *revenant*, whose infantile state is symbolized by milk, maternal nourishment that "doesn't cost anything." The dog takes the role of the newborn, establishing a maternal genealogy in which Anna for the first time finds her own place. The bodily contact with her mother, which has characterized the acquisition of her sexual identity, dissolves. The cat with the broken spine simultaneously represents Anna, who has survived the loss of infantile omnipotence, and her cat/child, which has had to be sacrificed to the demands of exogamy. The cat can return, healed, to life in the house, because Anna has accepted a partial image of herself. She has pacified and integrated the components of her ego, recognizing that the mother, although separated, can welcome and wants to welcome her and her "children" in the parental home.

At this point, the mother, who at the beginning of therapy unified every possibility in her threefold figure, can even disappear, without denoting the annihilation of self or the end of the world. Through a ideational and emotional struggle that is difficult to reconstruct in its complexity, Anna has succeeded in abandoning infantile self-sufficiency and has become part of the universe of social exchange, in whose network sexual relationships are entwined.

The accomplishment of maturity has involved a sacrifice of self to which only a recovery of the infantile imagination can attest. Its first creative potential, the challenge to "bring into the world," has been transformed into the expectation of the other (both husband and child). Nevertheless, it is important that the maternal cavity not be filled exclusively by the child, but that the woman become open to other life plans as well and that the capacity to procreate biologically be amplified into a symbolic creativity. Anna seems to be potentially capable of this. The depth with which she has conducted her therapy, the vividness of her pre-Oedipal imagination, the strength of her resistance, and her criticisms of societal injunctions all reveal that normality has not become normalization.

Whereas the hysteric of the past expressed her discomfort in the contortions of the body, like a butterfly on a pin, the woman of today attempts to free herself from the immobilizing hold of the "female position" with a myriad of identities. To this end, she makes a double movement in respect to her figures of reference (as Anna has done with her mother, her teacher, and her friends): She approaches and distances, identifies with and opposes. By evading every possible identification, she interweaves autonomy and authenticity, and recaptures a sense of possible wholeness.

EPILOGUE: ANNA'S FINAL DRAWING

Anna's final act is to send me a gift—a beautiful self-portrait that shows her in the center of a multicolored and festive world. She is a splendid blond princess who is holding a little bird up on the palm of her hand, like the *Madonna del cardellino.* Behind her are the words "To Mama and Papa from Anna." There is no better expression of a feminine identity; she has succeeded in giving up the male components of the self while accepting and integrating them. The pictured girl's regal aspect, her command and mastery of the world, the gratitude she expresses—all constitute the representation of perfect femininity, as it might be construed by a little girl.

However, the drawing does not represent reality, but the idealization of the end of therapy. We know that the incompleteness of every analysis and the never-ending nature of its task can be attributed precisely to the impossibility of placing oneself in the feminine position, and of eluding its determinants.[65] In this sense, the "cure" is always provisional, and its certainty is written in sand. But the elements of harmony, beauty, and truth that emerge at given points, as well as the faith that one can still be loved and (sometimes) understood, represent an inalienable gift. Finally, the figures of the unconscious, crystallized in the atemporality of personal myth, distill their enigmatic meanings in the narrative understanding of self. The dialectic of constitutive desires that has come to light in Anna's analysis has given her the thread of her history and the direction of her intentionality. And it gives us the knowledge that if we begin even from the most fleeting existential condition, that of a little girl, we can see into the

Figure 11

struggle—in all its specificity—that leads her from being female to becoming a woman.

The path that has led Anna to a feminine definition of self appears to be unique, not reproducible, utterly original, and inscribed in her singular identity. At the same time, it is obviously constructed upon the tracks left by our culture, having utilized symbolic figures taken from centuries-old archives. Words already formulated and images already visualized allow for a great expressive articulation, but also enact invisible interdictions. Among these are the prohibition against a woman's thinking of her own body as hollow, which simultaneously evokes the complementary fullness. A sort of amnesia of the self suppresses any representation of the power to engender that springs from within, or of its vital product, the child that will be born. What takes its place is an image of the self as an empty recipient for a substance that will come from the outside. To reconstruct how and why this elaboration of the feminine unconscious comes into being requires further digging into a little girl's imagination, as well as an examination of the most distant figures in our anthropology—the gods and animals.

CHAPTER 2

Who Holds the Power to Engender?

Reflections of Ancient Culture in Present-Day Fantasy

BEYOND FREUD

To a great extent, Anna's case falls within the boundaries of Freudian theory: It can be described in its lexicon, can be understood in terms of its categories. But, as I have pointed out, in certain regards it exceeds the limits of Freud's theory. It is precisely this excess of experience and of meaning that I wish to explore now.

Through Anna's story, a sort of psychoanalytic "novel of formation," it is possible to follow the process of constructing a gendered identity, beginning with the condition of undifferentiation from the mother. Separating from this original unity, Anna constructs an autonomous self that by definition must face the dilemma of sexual identity—whether to be male or female. The two alternatives have different connotations and implications: For one, social esteem (appraisal) prevails; for the other, biological determination and the injunctions of the family prevail. Beyond both choices, however, there is a nostalgia for an undivided totality that seems to fulfill the unconscious desire for omnipotence and its demand to give up nothing, to be simultaneously male and female. Only a very strong push to "become oneself" forces the child to abandon his or her original unity—to relinquish maternal security in order to confront the enigmas of the world, of which, the child, too, is a part.

A sexual identity is attributed to every newborn child (this can now be done even before birth). But this gesture does not necessarily mean that this identity will be assumed, made the child's own, shared. As we have seen in Anna's case, a long process of self-awareness, of self-representation, and of inscription in social roles is required for the imposition of an authentic sexual identity to take hold. Becoming a woman is a complex undertaking and is never finished if it is true that the hysteric never stops asking herself, "Am I really feminine?" In saying that, she tries to construct an image of femininity to which she can adapt. As Anna's expressive struggle has shown, the young girl undertakes this task by assembling the materials of experience from pre-established symbolic forms: the process in unconsciously mediated by age-old cultural patterns. As the philosopher Enzo Paci writes, "The genesis that led me to be who I am is a kind of internalization of the history of the world."[1]

There is a fundamental correspondence among the figures of the unconscious that emerge during the course of therapeutic work, the interpretations that clarify their meaning, and the visions of the world that have been historically transmitted. In fact, analyst and analysand communicate within a single tradition of knowledge and meaning whose common basis is the history of the culture. This history is regulated by categories, such as Aristotelian logic and its consequent organization of the world, which though invisible are nonetheless pervasive. Roland Barthes writes: "There's a sort of persistent accord between Aristotle and so-called mass culture, as if Aristotelianism, which has been dead as a philosophy since the Renaissance, survived in a degraded and inarticulate state, in the widespread cultural practices of Western society. "[2] In some respects, the Aristotelian tradition constitutes the matrix of common sense—of a way of thinking that has become so obvious that it seems to coincide with the natural order of things.

When we reconstruct Anna's gender identification in the terms of castration, we activate Freud, but behind him the archeology of Occidental thought and the repertory of its metaphors unfold. Freud himself was aware of this when he wrote: I should like you to notice, too, that the analysis of dreams has shown us that the unconscious makes use of a particular symbolism, especially for representing sexual complexes. This symbolism varies partly from individual to individual; but partly it is laid down in a typical form and seems to coincide with the symbolism which, as we suspect, underlies our myths and fairy tales. It seems not impossible that these creations of the popular mind might find an explanation through the help of dreams.[3]

In this sense, the little girl who dreams, the therapist who interprets, and the theorist who teaches all formulate a single discourse, even if they express it in different codes and in various settings. This discourse has already taken shape in a single cultural imagination, and a single cultural context contains them and gives them order and meaning.

But no context is ever comprehensive, just as no map is coextensive with of what exists, able to represent it on a scale of 1 to *n*. There is always a surplus of experience and meaning that requires us to "reopen the case." In Anna's case, the fantasy of the dead mouse, the dream of the walled-up boy, and the dream of the rescued animals go beyond the interpretive capacities of classical psychoanalysis—the model that equates femininity with castration. Anna suggests another process, a task of "maternalization," which interferes with the sexual process but does not coincide with it. We have glimpsed two phases of this process thus far: The first makes the representation of the female body hollow, and the second evokes its generative product, the baby it will contain.

The figures that express the maternalization process are not unheard of; what changes is the questioning invested in them. Recent developments in women's culture may have produced conditions that erode what appears to be obvious and that foster the emergence of new interpretive hypotheses. We must marvel that Anna must work to "hollow out" a body image that is already anatomically hollow, and that after a dream sends her the message that the self-fertilized womb will remain sterile, she finds the child she wants outside of herself. Making the self concave and internalizing the generative product seem to allude to two opposing fantasies: a body that is too full before and too empty later.[4] Nevertheless, they allude to a conflict within the imagination and to a problematic maternity[5] that the traditional theoretical models seem incapable of explaining.

Before advancing any interpretive hypotheses that go beyond this particular case, I would prefer to entrust myself once again to a child's own words and to her ability to express what has been blocked in adult thought by repression and replaced by the evidence of shared reality. For this purpose, I describe the case of Paola. (As I have done with regard to Anna in Chapter 1, I describe the case in the present tense, although I saw Paola some years ago. Also as in Anna's case, and as I note in the Acknowledgments to this book, the biographical details of Paola's case have been altered here to protect her anonymity.)

GAMES INSIDE THE HEAD: THE CASE OF PAOLA

Paola's Case History

Paola is seven years old when she comes to my office, accompanied by her mother, for an initial consultation. She is a large, strong child, with a serious and intense face. Although she responds to my questions honestly, she sticks to the bare essentials. She appears to be quite wise and mature for her age. She lives in a residential neighborhood with her parents, upper-middle-class professionals, and a younger sister aged four. She is in her first year of elementary school and is benefiting from it.

Paola was delivered late by Caesarian section, was bottle-fed, and has never had any major illnesses. Her development has been normal except for several regressive episodes related to the birth of her sister. During her nursery school years she devoted herself to physical exercise with great pleasure, using the gymnastics facilities at the nearby playing field; she often spent hours on the swings or on the parallel bars.

But the beginning of elementary school coincided with a change of attitude: Paola's games became more mental and fantasy-based, while a single close friend, Betta, replaced her old group of peers. Paola got into the habit of watching afternoon television programs with Betta and her younger sister. One night her mother, while trying to convince her to leave her toys and go to bed, told her: "In bed you can play games in your head." From that moment on, the little girl has called her daydreams "games in my head." At the same time, she has developed a liking for table games: puzzles, dominoes, games of skill and patience.

At the age of one, Paola chose an old brown woolen blanket as a "transitional object,"[6] which she clutched to herself during moments of introversion, only to drop it indifferently all over the house later. Since the age of four, however, she has only reverted to this "affective prosthesis" when she is watching television and when she goes to bed. She has never shown this kind of attachment to any doll, nor is she particularly demonstrative with her parents or her sister, for that matter.

Her mother's concern has to do with Paola's behavior during the last month. Every night at dusk, the little girl slides into an inexplicable melancholy. She lies down on her bed and abandons herself to fantasy, clutching her beloved blanket between her legs and sucking her lowr lip. In response to her mother's concerned questions, she says, "My stomach hurts," and vaguely indicates her abdomen. Then she eats normally at dinner and seems to forget her discomfort until the following evening. Since the pediatrician has excluded an organic cause, her mother does not know whether or not to oppose her daughter's behavior.

When I meet Paola, I ask her to draw whatever she wants. The little girl sets about the task with great concentration; outlining a little house with a chimney, a path, a tree, a cloud, and the sun, she colors these objects according to didactic conventions. It is a diligent and impersonal composition, demonstrating that she has displaced her expressive abilities into other areas. It often happens that the acquisition of writing—which corresponds with the beginning of latency—is accompanied by an eclipse of graphic creativity. Whereas children's drawings are almost always free, original, and surprising during nursery school, they are often characterized by stereotypical conformity by the beginning of elementary school. Psychic processes (which from the ages of six to ten are subjected to the dominance of rational components over emotional ones) contribute to the sudden flattening of spontaneity, as do the pressures resulting from scholastic instruction.

While Paola colors the sheet of paper before her, head bent, I ask her to tell me about one of the "games in her head." She does not hesitate to confide that before she goes to sleep, she imagines many little animals in her belly. During these years in Italy there are vast advertising campaigns against hunting, disseminating an ecological sensibility that can easily strike a chord in infantile fantasy. Paola maintains that these little animals have sought refuge inside her to escape pollution and poachers.

Inside her belly, there are green valleys, woods, little lakes, and a playground where everyone can live happily together. There are puppies, cats, serpents, lions, turtles, and little parrots. Then Paola entertains herself imagining other animals that come to her tired, wounded, and sick; she takes them in, comforts them, and heals them until they are able to play, laugh, and turn somersaults in the field. Then she prepares a great picnic: She spreads colored sheets out on the grass and invites all to eat cookies, ice cream, and peanut butter. Paola's fantasy world constitutes an alternative to external reality, in which the relationship between adults and children seems to be inverted; that is, in her world she occupies the position of the mother rather than the daughter. This is a common fantasy in girls.

In Paola's class, she and her peers who attend the after-school program have been sharing a secret game for some time. Each one carries in the pocket of her smock a little colored cotton ball (the kind used to remove makeup), which she considers her own child. Around this nucleus of fantasy, a whole transmutation of ordinary objects is organized: An eyeglass case becomes a little carriage, a Kleenex a sheet, a pencil sharpener a child's chair, an eraser a piece of cake, and so on. The little cotton-ball children become the objects of fantastic conversations, related to scholastic success or failures, trips, artistic performances, or victories in sports. Every ball has a name of its own and individual adventures, which take place in a fantasized dimension that is evoked by the common desire for maternity. These submerged ludic expressions are characterized by the miniaturization of the toys themselves and the things that surround them. Whereas in early childhood the largeness of a toy increases the enjoyment it gives, in the latency period there is an overall reduction in the dimension of toys. A Lilliputian universe seems to be particularly suited to the internalization of reality—the transformation of games into fantasies—in accordance with a progression that is the inverse of the better-known movement from imagining to acting out. In the evolution of infantile logic, too, the shrinking of objects represents a way to symbolize them.

Many years ago, I had in my care an aphasic five-year-old boy who could recognize and name a chair and even a baby seat, but could not make out the same object if it was reduced to a model of five or six inches, and was even less successful if the object was pictured in a drawing. His deficit was located in the transition from concrete and operative thought to formal thought, and his inability to hold onto the identity of tiny objects consti-tuted an insuperable obstacle for him in symbolizing the world. Similarly, the imagination shrinks things in order to inscribe them in the internal world—to subject them to the elaboration of fantasy, which in game playing can more flexibly carry out the orders of desire.

Paola comes to the following session with two sheets of writing done in "pretty script." "I wrote a story," she tells me, confessing that it is one of the "games in my head" that she plays at night when she goes to bed. Since our meetings never go beyond the diagnostic stage and end with a consult-ation with her mother, I will limit myself to a discussion of this piece of writing and the fantasy that it illustrates. I believe that these provide important evidence for the present endeavor—to reconstruct the archives of the female imagination.

The Inner Theater: Paola's Writing and Fantasy

Paola has written her story on both sides of two sheets of wide-lined notebook paper, using nine different colors (red, green, yellow, pink, violet, orange, brown, blue, and black). Her recourse to multicolored repre-sentation of words is not casual; it expresses the complex range of emotional resonance. But there is something else too: The density of color adds a material quality to the text that gives it the quality of weaving or embroi-dery, like the stitched patchwork and piecework of female artisans that filled the intermediate space between body and house for centuries.

The calligraphy, in its chromatic resonances, suggests the "amphibi-ous" nature of the imaginary, which extends between the concreteness of the body and the abstraction of thought, between life and form.

Even before they evoke a meaning, Paola's polychromatic graphemes function as a ritual gesture to evoke the magical space where the uncon-scious can make itself known. They evoke the anticipation of a phantasm that words attempt to translate in her story, to locate within narrative time, but that nevertheless remains an extratextual substratum. Their effect can only be glimpsed in their impact when the imagination produces something surprisingly new that echoes something ancient.

What Paola shows me is a transgressive fragment, because, as we will see, it represents a desire that we are forced not to speak of. For this reason, she has had to invent a new means of expression in which drawing, painting, and writing are combined, with the effect of both representing and concealing. Her story expresses daydreams—fantasies that aim, like all fantasies, to "cover up the auto-erotic activity of the first years of childhood, to embellish it and raise it to a higher plane." As Freud observed, the entire sexual life of the child lies behind these fantasies.[7] In fact, as noted earlier, Paola is in the habit of fantasizing while she presses her blanket between her legs and sucks on her lower lip. "Sensual sucking," wrote Freud, "involves a complete absorption of the attention and leads either to sleep or even to a motor reaction in the nature of an orgasm."[8] The pleasure is always accompanied by a component of irritability. The pain characterizes excess, the expenditure of energy that runs counter to the homeostatic economy of pleasure, which tends instead toward the elimination of all pleasure.

In latency, the abandonment of infantile autoerotic sexuality brings the eclipse of fantasies connected with this, or at least a re-elaboration of them. Autoerotic pleasure, which is ego-syntonic during childhood, becomes uncomfortable during the latency period; this may be a result of education, which connects it to guilt feelings, or to the child's own interior management. It is the very nature of pregenital sexuality, the anarchy of its drives, that makes it intolerable.

We can suggest that the pain of which Paola complains expresses both sexual enjoyment and the punishment for this self-induced satisfaction. In this way, the drive pursues its goal: Freud maintained that "we have every reason to believe that sensations of pain, like other unpleasurable sensations, trench upon sexual excitation and produce a pleasurable condition."[9] Paola's stomachache conforms to the hysterical symptom in which two contrasting tendencies coexist: the first aimed at realizing the drive, the second at inhibiting it. The inhibiting impulse leads to the repression of the content of the fantasy and to its replacement with compromised representations. Paradoxically, repression finds its possibility in sexual pleasure.

Freud noted that during orgasm, there is a fleeting loss of consciousness that functions as the prototype of every successive act of repression.[10] Fantasy rushes into the "emptiness" that is produced in this twilight state of mind, invading in the body, which at that moment finds itself at the height of stimulation and receptivity. The "falling" of representation from the psychic to the organic level seems therefore to be based upon the absence that comes over one at the height of erotic pleasure, when an eclipse of consciousness accompanies the zenith of sensation. All this is no more than an intuition that allows us to glimpse how and where it might be possible to link the mind to the body, the repressed image to its somatic conversion.

In this sense, Paola's abdominal pain would be the translation of an unacceptable autoerotic pleasure into an "organic language." On the other hand, the story of the "game in the head" would constitute the inverse process—an attempt to retranslate the bodily perception into mental content. But the "hysterical discourse" is not easy, because in order to remain faithful to the phantasmic referents, one must simultaneously express desire and the prohibitions against it, the concreteness of the body and the immateriality of thought, the subjectivity of feeling and the objectivity of its phantasmagoria. The difficulty of such a compromise is obvious.

Paola's writing can be translated as follows (some punctuation has been added for clarity):

> "Marianna is expecting [a baby]. At six months she has her first stomach pains. She doesn't feel well at all. She complains all the time of a bad stomachache. [In the] ninth month she is about to give birth, but Sandokan doesn't want her to. Ianez insists that he let her give birth. Marianna feels sick and says, 'Let me give birth.' 'No and then DON'T,' Sandokan says. Marianna is beside herself. Sandokan's servants don't know anything about it, because Marianna has not gone out since she has been expecting, because she is ashamed to have such a big belly. Sandokan is finally persuaded and a beautiful baby boy is born."

The word "baby" is always written in pink Magic Marker, as if to evoke the phantasm of "flesh" that is intended by it. In fact, such fantasies belong to an intermediate dimension between bodily sensations and mental representations, between the "thing" and the "word"; they emerge from what Breuer called "crepuscular states," in which consciousness fades and time seems to stand still. They are rarely shared, because, as Freud observed, "These day-dreams are cathected with a large amount of interest; they are carefully cherished by the subject and usually concealed with a great deal of sensitivity, as though they were among the most intimate possessions of his personality."[11]

The daytime material that feeds Paola's fantasy comes from the film *Sandokan*, shown on children's afternoon television in Italy during this period. But Paola's re-elaboration removes it from its context. She transforms it into a sort of rite whose contents might be called an "elaboration of childbirth," analogous to the "elaboration of mourning" that Freud discussed in the context of melancholy. In this case too, the little girl manifests a melancholic mood, and her dilemma is represented by the need to confront a loss.

In the text, time is configured as a mythic duration, a fluid continuity in which the two temporal specifications related to pregnancy attempt to introduce a chronology, although in vain. The protagonist, Marianna, with whom the narrator evidently identifies, is in the grips of intense pain. But we know that this masks an autoerotic pleasure, which the needs of the superego condemn and reject. Marianna is expecting a baby, and this causes her months and months of stomach pain—a pain that is coextensive with narrative infinity. In the ninth month she finally wants to give birth, but Sandokan is opposed. The emotion that is awakened in Paola by this is such that she makes an error in writing and erases it (" *'No e poi NON,' dice Sandokan*"; this can be translated as " 'No and then DON'T,' says Sandokan").

How is this fantasy transgressive? As I see it, it is transgressive in imagining a child who comes from within—a child whom the woman keeps inside herself, and whom the "father," excluded from its conception, can only allow or not allow to be born. Usually in young girls' fantasies (as we have seen in Anna's case) the girls "become pregnant" from the outside; they retrieve a little one from the outside world and internalize it. Instead, Marianna seems to have conceived on her own. The story does not even say that Sandokan is the father. It only goes so far to evoke two male figures at Marianna's bedside: one who inhibits and another who favors the expulsion of the baby.

There are strong analogies between these endogenous fantasies and playing with dolls. Although the majority of little girls live with married parents, and all grow up in a society based on father–mother couples, the first game with the doll does not provide for the existence of a father. The ludic phantasm seem belong to the pre-Oedipal phase, in which "the little girl's preference for dolls," as Freud observed, "is probably evidence of the exclusiveness of her attachment to her mother, with complete neglect of her father–object."[12]

But, beyond the attachment to the mother—to the identification with her and the successive transition from being in the passive position of the cared-for baby to being in the active position of one who cares for another—playing with dolls also represents an original phantasm of the female unconscious that is worth investigating here. It is a phantasm of origins that can be expressed as the unconscious image (imago) of a female body that contains its own generative product. This is located beyond an individual's own story and phenomenal experience. In speaking of the "architecture of hysteria," Freud wrote:

> The goal would seem to be getting at the primal scene. In some cases, one reaches it directly; in others only indirectly, through fantasies. In fact, fantasies are psychic facades erected to bar access to these memories. . . . These are a combination of lived experiences and things that were heard, facts from the past (the events related to parents and ancestors) and things seen with one's own eyes.[13]

Wondering about the existence of the same fantasies in all individuals, Freud stated: "I consider these primary fantasies . . . to be a phylogenetic patrimony." We have repeatedly suspected that the psychology of neurosis has conserved, more than any other source has conserved, ancient testimony of human evolution.[14]

Recourse to the category of phylogenesis allowed Freud to justify a prestructure that is inaccessible to the individual, independent of his or her phenomenal experience. In that perspective, the parricide of primitive hordes is configured as a scene "constructed" to attribute necessity and universality to Oedipal prohibitions and to attribute an objective dimension to their psychic reality. To this end, Freud elaborated a story that precedes Oedipal organization—an antecedent that is more logical than historical. But in reality, a myth that precedes the Oedipus myth, understood as a model of human sexuality, already exists in our culture; we do not need to construct one deliberately for the sake of theoretical synthesis.

The myth of a maternal body that engenders on its own—the myth of a full body like the one represented in the story by Marianna's pregnancy, and in the symptom by Paola's pain—preceded and was replaced by the myth of the conjugal couple. The myth of independent generation is a much more archaic and undifferentiated phantasm than the Oedipal one. It is the expression of a body that is not yet gendered, of an undivided whole that holds within itself its own reproductive potential. In our culture, the idea of a primeval maternity is characteristic of "prehistory" in the most radical sense of the term—as that which is located prior to chronology, prior to any spatial boundaries, prior to the possibility of narration itself. In the sections that follow, I examine Paola's fantasy against this mythological backdrop.

ENGENDERING IN ANCIENT MYTHS

Chaos: The Original Womb

In fact, the concept of primeval, independent maternity can be found in the most ancient cosmological myth, the Enuma elish. A transcription of this myth formed the preface to the code issued by the Babylonian King Hammurabi, about 1758 B.C. "When nobody had yet made the word for a sky, above/And nobody had never thought that the earth below might have a name . . . Tiamat, the original female divinity, reigned." Tiamat represents the confusion of the swamp where polluted vapors and sweet and salt water merge and mingle; she engenders every sort of monstrous and mutinous creature in her own bosom.[15]

The reign of the goddess mother, of presexual reproduction, is equated with primitive chaos. A disordered world corresponds to her "parthenogenesis"—a world lacking time, ethics, or aesthetics, where the ordering power of the word has not yet been heard. Unnamed things sink and merge in an unregulated promiscuity, which the voice of the narrator has already condemned as the engenderer of monstrous and rebellious beings. But what are they rebelling against in a universe that lacks laws? Against a retroactive norm, without which narration would not be possible. Thus, it is through the grid of the cosmos that chaos becomes thinkable, in the light of its own interdiction.

The reign of Tiamat, the locus of blame, inexorably calls upon the male forces controlled by the wise An and by Enlil to "put things in order." But to defeat Tiamat, more than the power of reason is needed; this must be allied with violence—with Marduk, god of tempestuous winds. Besides having the aerial elements, the winds, on his side, Marduk also has technology: fire, the bow, the chariot, the net, and the sword. After a furious hand-to-hand combat, Tiamat, captured in the net (held at the corners by the four winds), is pierced through the heart by an arrow. Her skull is shattered, and her body, without a head, is divided like an oyster into two halves. One half, thrown up into the air, forms the sky, where Marduk establishes himself; the other forms the earth, which is furrowed with canals by the ordering net, divided into bounded spaces of property, presided over by walled cities, and governed by written laws.

This myth of the establishment of organization can be read in a myriad of ways. In the present context, it is interesting to observe how sexual difference is constituted in the conflict, through extreme asymmetry. All that is devalued lies on the female side, and all that is valued lies on on the male side, at least if we stick to categories that prevail historically. In reality, Tiamat's indistinct figure represents a joint world that lacks domination and violence—a world that is aphasic, because the copresence of things makes the word superfluous. It is an impossible world, but perhaps not an unthinkable one.[16] Freud would have defined it as pre-Oedipal, analogous to the mother–child relationship that precedes the entrance of the father into the primary dyad. The father's entrance renders maternal autonomy demonic, legitimizes the violent submission of the female, and sanctions her condemnation. What remains of maternal creativity is relegated to a realm outside of time and space; it is an intolerable antecedent that is finally regulated by paternal power.[17]

Another great Babylonian myth—that of Atra-hasis, which describes the gods' creation of humanity—represents the transition from an exclusively female engendering to sexual reproduction. The part played by each of each of the two sexes is definitively established:

Then the gods called and questioned the goddess, the midwife of the gods, the skillful Mami: "You are the maternal bosom, the creator of humanity:

you create Lullu [man] so that he can bear the yoke, so that man can wear the pannier of god." Nintu [Mami] opened her mouth and spoke to the great gods: "I cannot do such a thing by myself, but with Enki the work can be accomplished. He is the one who makes everything pure: he will provide me with the clay and then I will act."

Then the gods slaughtered the intelligent god Pee. Mami mixed his flesh and blood with the clay and spoke thus to the great gods: "I have completed the work you commanded."

This work involves the definitive disempowering of the goddess mother, dethroning her from the central role in origins. The constitutive asymmetry is fixed, in fact, with the creation of the very first man, which is why the father constitutes the generative principle and the mother the material vessel. The male contribution lies not so much in divine intelligence as in the bodily matter (the clay). The female contribution is reduced to the mixing and working of elements, like the potter's wheel, which transforms clay into the vase as it spins. Even the engendering power that the goddess Mami shares with Tiamat is canceled out and replaced by her servile act of manipulation. In the process of reproduction, it is the male's role to animate inert matter and the female's to contain it, to bring it to term, and to hand it over to the customer. The female body figures here as a mere receptacle; there is no hint of the annihilation of reproductive potential that has been carried out. In fact, condemnation has been replaced by repression, with its ability to conceal the prohibited and the prohibition simultaneously.

In Greece, too,[18] an Orphic myth places a goddess, Night, at the origins of the world. Fertilized by the wind, Night with her great black wings lays a great silver egg in the womb of darkness. The first offspring (Protogonos), Eros, god of love, is born of the silver egg, bringing to light all that has been hidden in the egg—the whole world. The concave space above, the sky, couples with the lower space, earth, thanks to Eros; this process engenders Okeanos and Thetis, the first couple in the world, who are both brother and sister and husband and wife. An Orphic poem goes: "The first was Okeanos, of fine course, who began the coupling: he took his sister Thetis, born of the same mother, as a wife." The mother of both, the Night, has known no marriage. Before sexual reproduction there exists a parthenogenetic generation, produced by the female womb. But a curtain of obscurity—symbol of the unthinkable, of the impossible—falls on this antecedent. The Night generates an egg within herself, and thus represents a hollow space.

In ancient language, writes Kerényi, there was a word for hollow space, the word "chaos," which meant only "wide open." "Chaos" did not originally signify "confusion" or "mixture" at all; the word only later took on the meaning that is common today, when the principle of the four elements was introduced.[19] What we see at work here are the retroactive devaluation that has transformed vital female potential into negative figures, and the symbolic forms of prohibition that language has conserved and transmitted through the historical time of culture.

Since the generative capacity inherent in the original hollow space is retroactively condemned as a primary form of evil (i.e., chaos), everything positive comes to be centered in the male element, whose appearance coincides with the birth of the cosmos. Thus, the female position comes to be configured as submission and regulation, which are violently and necessarily imposed. Freud identified this in his acknowledgment of the unconscious, but he translated it into terms of "passivity," in the attempt to neutralize what remains unfathomable in sexual difference.[20]

But it is not enough that the universe that emerged from the maternal womb is morally condemned and sexually subjugated; it is also obliterated and replaced by yet another creation. In the very ancient Orphic theogony (which recently came to light with the discovery of the Derveni papyrus[21]), the prodigious works carried out by Zeus on the advice of the mother of all gods, black Night, are related to the initiates. At the very moment he takes power, Zeus swallows the secret that the midwife of gods, the immortal Night from whom all oracles derive, has transmitted to him. Then he also swallows Protogonos, the life principle that has engendered Gaia and Uranus, from whose union Kronos has been born. With the wisdom and amorous power of Night in his possession, Zeus destroys the world that has preceded him and creates another in its place, in an act of oral incorporation: first golden Aphrodite, and then Harmonia and Persuasion together. He also conceives first Earth and the Sky that stretches up above, then the great force of Ocean, and finally another huge earth (the moon) that the gods call Selene.

As the poem tells it, now Zeus is the head and the center of the universe; he is both the first and the last because he holds the life principle and the destiny of death. The female power to engender seems to vanish along with its primordial creations, in an act of destruction and reparation that is exclusively male and that incorporates the power and knowledge of the goddess mother but adds to it Metis—cunning and ingenious intelligence. What we know is therefore a world recreated upon the ruins of a universe that has disappeared. But, surprisingly, the figure of primal maternity reappears in the concluding lines of the hymn: "Later, after he had conceived all of that, Zeus desired to unite in love with his mother." The time that governs the linear genealogy of humankind seems to retreat, to move back toward what was destroyed and concealed—to retrace its footsteps in the nostalgia for an undivided creation, a "before" that is located outside of genealogy and represents the impossible fulfillment of history.

The analogy to the return to the mother, which according to psychoanalysis constitutes the ultimate boundary of every desire, is evident. More surprising, however, is the convergence with the ideas and the imaginary of the great twentieth-century visionary Simone Weil. She could not have known this myth, and yet it seemed to animate her own conceptualization when she suggested that we enact a work of "de-creation" to uncover the hidden nothingness: "This world is the closed door. It is a barrier, and at the same time, it is a passage."[22] "In our impatience we are guilty of idolatry because we are unable to tolerate the void."[23] And yet for Weil, the deconstruction of the false images of the world and consequent confrontation with a gaping, open nothingness constitutes the assumption of the possibility of authenticity, of reality. It is as if she suggested that once the artificial icons of Metis are removed, the nocturnal work of the goddess mother—the incomplete design of a possible female universe—may re-emerge.

Another version of the origins of the universe, that of the Greek poet Hesiod, is as follows: Gaia or Gea, the Earth that emerges from the wide-open emptiness of original chaos, first gives birth without coupling to her fellow creature Uranus, the starry Sky. Then Uranus embraces Gaia entirely and becomes the eternal seat of the gods. "But all those who were born of Gaia and Uranus and were the most hideous of children, were hated by their father from the very beginning, and as soon as one of them was born he hid them all in Gaia's bosom, never allowing them to come to light; and Uranus was pleased with his wicked work, but prodigious Gaia ached within, bursting."[24]

It is interesting to observe how the rivalry Uranus experiences over the prodigious fertility of his mother and wife, Gaia, is expressed in his forbidding her to give birth. Without an outlet, the great maternal body is filled to the point that her own engendered creations have spasms and she herself contorts in a ceaseless labor. The analogy to little Paola's fantasy is clear: In Sandokan's saying "No" and opposing Marianna's request to give birth, one can read the distant echo of an age-old enactment of the relationship between the sexes, and of their basic dispute over the power to engender.

Engendering Alone

In the myths of origins, the world is self-engendered by a primal maternal womb, but every subsequent instance of reproduction comes about exclusively through the agency of a male principle. The eradication of female generative power is so great that from this point on, maternity is configured merely as an instrumental modality of taking in and increasing.[25] But, transgressing against the harshest interdictions, female fantasy continues to represent that lost power; the nostalgia for an unthinkable creative self-sufficiency causes female desire to regress toward the time of our origins. The expression of this secret phantasm, which our culture considers a self-condemning gesture of extreme rebellion, is left to a marginal myth.

In Olympic mythology, Hera is the legitimate wife of Zeus; as such, she is the protector of nuptial rites. The three epithets associated with her indicate both her threefold being and the periodicity that, like the moon, governs her life: Pais, the young girl; Teleia, the wife or accomplished one; and Chera, the solitary one. The second name indicates that she is the great goddess of marriage, who seeks not so much motherhood as unity and monogamy in her husband.[26] However, it is in the combined names of Pais and Chera as a solitary young girl that Hera asks Flora for a potion that will allow her to engender by herself. Zeus has dispossessed her of her position as his wife by bringing Athena to life, after swallowing Metis and all the wiles of the world along with her.

Flora possesses the flower needed for the job—Olene, which can engender new life and blood. Grazed by petals of Olene, Hera can give birth to Ares, the god of war, without having to yield to any sexual relationship whatsoever, but also without losing conjugal legitimacy. In the same way, thanks to the powers of damp lettuce,[27] she gives birth to Typhon and then to two females, Hebe and Eileithyia. Hebe, which means "adolescence," is a replica of her mother in the guise of Pais as a girl. Eileithyia, on the other hand, is the goddess invoked in the suffering of childbirth. But the series of parthenogenetic children is inaugurated by Hephaestus, whom Hera engenders "without union of love."

Hera's female issue is harmonious, in that it represents a duplication of herself in the guises of virgin and mother. The male issue, on the other hand, is horrible. The giant Ares, as Homer portrays him, is terrifying and grotesque at the same time. Typhon, the serpent with tentacles, the master of winds, is an awful scourge upon mortals. Hephaestus, born prematurely after perhaps having been removed from Hera's thigh, has deformed legs and turned-in feet—"visible marks," according to M. Detienne,[28] "of his power over fire and his mastery of metallurgy."

Hera makes every attempt to free herself of Hephaestus, the ugly son whom she has engendered in solitude (it is said that he is the fruit of the goddess's premarital phase) and who grows in hate. First she tries to abort him, and then she throws him into the sea. According to another version of the story, Zeus himself expels him from Olympus, casting him down upon the earth. For his part, Hephaestus tries to chain his mother to a throne he himself has forged, and only through the interevention of Dionysus (another product of transgression) is he captured after being tricked with wine. One tradition holds that Hephaestus is "the son of Wind," just as Eros is born of black-winged Night.

In comparison with sexual reproduction and the complementarity of the sexes, mythology views the desire to engender alone, to be father and mother simultaneously, as a transgressive desire for both sexes. Zeus and Hera are both emblematic figures in this sense. But while Zeus engenders Athena, a splendid virgin warrior and daughter worthy of her father, Hera's male line is marked by the stigmata of monstrosity. It is noteworthy that Athena is associated with Hephaestus and for that reason is called Hephaestia; however, the difference between the two parthenogenetic children is evident, and clearly shows how much more dangerous female desire was felt to be and how much more rigorously its prohibition came to be inscribed in the imagination itself. This was so much the case that exclusively male generation was thought to be impossible, whereas there seemed to be threatening examples in nature of female reproductive autonomy, as we will see.

Engendering with the Father

It is significant that Paola's fantasy leaves the baby out of the scene, even though it represents the motive of the dispute. But in the imagination, the status of such a "child of the night" is rather controversial. In some cases, this figure appears as the miracle child, the god of myth, or the little prince of fairy tales; in others, it assumes animal characteristics. Between these two extremes, it assumes intermediate form (e.g., a puppet, doll, gnome, elf, or anthropomorphic animal), with the characteristics of an animated cartoon. This polymorphic figure of the unconscious imagination is located in an intermediate dimension between the "me" and the "not me," between the indistinct body of the mother and the separated body of the child. As such it is difficult to define, because it is fluid, ever-changing, subject to all the variations and combinations of omnipotent infantile thought.

In its most archaic form, it can be described, however improperly, as a parthenogenetic baby, engendered within an undivided body of mother and child. In some respects, the fact that it appears *a priori* in relation to any kind of experience denotes it as an original fantasy (analogous to the primal scene), transmitted by philogenetic endowment. But as such, it is merely the possibility of representation that is activated when it becomes involved in an affective dynamic. Although it may be difficult to think of a relational process within an undivided whole, an initial separation must be produced first—a first tearing apart, during which the two poles, mother and daughter, can be alternatively experienced as "me" within a shared imaginary space.[29] Insofar as the little girl perceives her mother and herself, an early exchange of identity takes placd;[30] in this, the little girl *is* the mother who contains her, as well as the contained baby. This is the same exchange that we find with quite different effect in the game of the spool, when Heinz, Freud's nephew, identified as much with the abandoning mother as with the abandoned son.[31]

The little girl's identification with her mother, based upon the perception of bodily similarity and of their belonging to the same sex, corresponds to a primary, basic representation—to the evocation of phantasmic figures that can only be glimpsed indirectly, in their effects of alienation and silence. On the pre-Oedipal level, the child of fantasy is configured as a narcissistic duplication of the self, like a shadow produced by the ego at the moment that it separates from the maternal whole. In the face of this silhouette of absence—the "shadow child" who will never be engendered— all other figures, dreams, fantasies, or toys appear as substitute formations. Participating in the mother's feeling, the little girl experiences a precognition of engendering, an anticipation of maternity that evokes a potential child object.

Produced by the specularity of the mother and daughter, the child of the night is inscribed in the feminine triad in which the little girl occupies the intermediate position, thus participating in both the others—those of the mother and child. For the first time, we find here (in an indefinite form) the triad that Freud considered paradigmatic of the feminine, and the motherNchild interchangeabilty that Jung attributed to women.

Because it is doubly narcissistic, the first fantasy of the engendered child is always monosexual; it would be more accurate to say "presexual," because it comes before the recognition of heterosexuality. It is a fantasy destined to be submerged along with the memories of that distant phase of life, of the history of the self that precedes the word and therefore remains a prediscursive reality. A figure of primal repression that can only be seen in its effects, it remains a "thing" that can only be symbolized in the impersonal and insistent form of the symptom.[32] "A female body contains a baby." The declarative form in which this appears removes it from desire, from asking, from social contracts and laws; it simply "is," just as the little girl "is" with her doll. Its disappearance is required by the termination of the omnipotent narcissistic economy, by the detachment of its hallucinatory satisfaction.

As we will see, the void left by the images of an impossible female generation is filled by the figures of male desire—by a generative omnipotence that finds its expression in myths and, indirectly, in scientific knowledge. The universalizing power of male culture not only leaves female desire unrepresented, but also floods the void with its productions, which are all-encompassing.

When the little girl who has entered into family relationships, into the three-dimensional space of the word, confronts her maternal position, she does so from a condition of lack that is inscribed in the dimension of "being" before "having." The same girl who has shared her mother's fantasy of accomplished engendering, who has shared the full body, finds herself in the position of asking her own father for the lost baby—of asking another for something she herself once possessed. Between these two phases comes the transformation of "not being" into "not having." Female desire is suspended and turned into a question, a request that is fated to go unsatisfied because it is incorrectly formulated. It is no coincidence that Lacan, in his scheme of gender identification, has placed the mother figure under the sign of the impossible.[33] Thus, female desire moves from a condition of being unrepresentable during the pre-Oedipal phase to a condition of being inadequately represented during the Oedipal conflict, with the result that it gets lost and never recognizes itself.

Following the little girl's evolution, we see that the image of the child reappears at about three years of age, within the context of the Oedipal conflict. This time it appears in connection to the father, through libidinal desires of an incestuous nature. The little girl fantasizes that, like her mother, she has a child with the father. In this phase, the sex of the fantasized child appears changeable and uncertain, because the attribution of positions that is only reached at the end of the Oedipal conflict has not yet been realized. In this case too, the fantasy of incestuous engendering that the little girl tries her best to keep secret can be seen amplified on the backdrop of myth.

Whereas the myths of autochthony generation represent fantasies of pre-Oedipal female filiation, other stories (e.g., the cycle of Dionysus) illustrate phantasms of maternity that are more relational in nature, but that allude to the convergence of incestuous desires. Although the children engendered alone appear to be specular or monstrous, those engendered by the father cannot be placed or defined and are destined to fall from the splendor of the divine to an animal state. The degradation to which they are subjected expresses social condemnation, but in another sense, it appears to be an attempt of female fantasy to distance its own productions from the regulation of human contracts and laws.

In the Orphic myths, Dionysus, the "god of women," represents the emblem of the miraculous baby expressed by the anarchy of unconscious desire. His mother is Persephone, the daughter of Hera and Zeus. Hera shuts the young girl in a cave, where she is impregnated by Zeus, who appears in the form of a serpent as she is busy weaving for her parents an enormous mantle showing the whole universe.[34] The scene seems to correspond to the moment in which the little girl detaches from her mother and, after the "catastrophe" of abandonment, reconstructs the world in the face of the void separating them. It is precisely during this phase that the fantasy of "having a child" by her own father emerges. "With little girls the wish to have a child by their father is equally constant," Freud observed, "and this in spite of their being completely incapable of forming any clear idea of the means for fulfilling these wishes. . . . Something like a premonition of what are later to be the final and normal sexual aims governs the child's libidinal trends."[35]

The myth of Dionysus, born of the relationship between Persephone and the serpent (representing the paternal phallus as a partial object), seems to represent a typically feminine incest fantasy and the underlying intuition of a preliminary coital rapport. The incest is concealed and hidden by the absence of Zeus from the scene, who is replaced by the serpent, a recurrent symbol of temptation. The child who is born has two little horns on his forehead. In an ancient ceremony of the mysteries of the Great Mother, Rhea, the child, visibly excited, is placed on a throne while a kneeling woman holds a mirror before him. The rite effectively expresses the ambiguous placement of these precocious fantasies of maternity, which fall between narcissistic object love (the duplication of self) and the generation of the other. In Orphic myth, the story continues, describing how the Titans surprise Dionysus while he is playing with his toys and attack him upon the order of Hera, who is jealous of Persephone's maternity.

Among the toys of Dionysus—which include dolls, a golden apple, a diamond, and a top—the mirror reappears, and in it the divine child loses himself in the admiration of his own image. And it is while he contemplates himself on the distorting surface of the mirror that the Titans take him.[36] "They [the Titans] arrived like the dead from hell, where Zeus had put them, took the playing child by surprise, rent him, cut him into seven pieces and threw him into a cauldron that stood on a tripod. When the flesh was cooked, they began to roast him on seven skewers."[37]

When we compare the infantile fantasy to the myth, it is interesting to observe how the child engendered by the father is marked by libidinal narcissism in life and death. Produced by autoerotic fantasy, this child is destined to vanish with the emergence of genital sexuality and the breaking up of the Oedipal triangle. Nevertheless, insofar as the child is inscribed in a blood relationship, he falls under the power of the jealousy that a mother experiences in relation to her rival daughter. This is what causes the little girl's attempt to keep her reproductive fantasies to herself. On the other hand, Dionysus is already characterized by prohibition, as the stigmata of the little goat that mark him for sacrifice indicate: He is destined to die as a child because his incestuous birth violates an unwritten law that sacrifice undertakes to restore. In any case, there is no way for such a child—conceived at the crossroads of the two desires of infantile Eros, the one narcissistic, the other incestuous—to grow up, because both desires are condemned by societal morals and are destined to vanish with the amnesia that comes with the conclusion of childhood.

Another myth has it that Dionysus is the child of Semele, the daughter of Cadmus. Like Persephone, Semele, which means "chthony," belongs to the underworld, as if to suggest that these fantasies of premarital maternity must remain secret. There are many versions of the encounter between Zeus and Semele that engenders Dionysus. In this case too, the jealous Hera, dressed as the girl's midwife, seems to have plotted the child's death. Zeus appears to Semele in the guise of a mere mortal. It is the phony midwife who prompts Semele, during her pregnancy, to formulate a desire: that Zeus should reveal his true nature. Zeus then comes to her armed with a bolt of lightning and strikes the unfortunate girl as she tries to escape. He pulls the little Dionysus, still an embryo, from her burned body; he then sews Dionysus into his thigh, where he brings the gestation to term. As soon as Dionysus is born, Zeus gives him to the divine wet nurses, who raise him in a cave. In the various representations of his life, Dionysus appears only in relation to women. Silenus appears on the scene in later stories in the role of an educator, but he is "an old, effeminate figure, with a big belly and a feminine bosom, who is often wrapped in a long robe, all of which also characterize the bearded Dionysus as well."[38]

It is interesting to observe that Semele's guilt lies in making known what should have remained hidden—that within the figure of the partner, female desire invests the forbidden figure of the father. Her inopportune curiosity reveals that in the unconscious, all motherhood is characterized by an incestuous mortgage. The sacrifice of Semele by Zeus is also revealing of the profoundly conflictual nature of sexual relationships: The rivalry that is unleashed between the two over Dionysus's gestation is yet another manifestation of male envy in the face of the female power to give life.

In a certain sense, the cycle of Dionysus shows the conflict that arises around the child, in that all desire conspires with its Oedipal referents; that is, in a certain sense, there are always two parents on a conscious level, but on the unconscious level two other couples (grandparents) are added. Therefore, elements of love are interwoven with the rivalry and envy of the Oedipal conflict, which is never entirely resolved and arouses an ambivalent attitude toward the newborn, whom the myth presents as sublime as a god and base as an animal. The turbulence of conception reverberates in the precariousness of birth, in which the principal problem seems to be that of protecting the child from the devastation of adult passions—of removing the child from the death that threatens this new life. The rite serves precisely this phantasm of "killing a baby"[39] that pollutes human parenthood, which is disturbed in affective terms. In the final analysis, it is up to female characters, like the mother goddesses, to take in and raise the little one until the child can survive independently. The striking immaturity of the human young at birth is not only of a biological nature; it also suggests a prematurity in respect to the human capacity for nurturing, torn as it is by irremediable conflicts.

The newborn must be protected from the aggressive drives that pollute amorous drives. The infant's nurturance must be cleansed of the phantasms of death that take form around every birth, as attested by baptismal rites, in which society itself assumes a parental role. In the economy of the myth, it is up to the women to bring to term the psychological gestation that accompanies the physiological one, and that in a certain sense both precedes and follows it.

In venerating Dionysus, the women of ancient Greece writhed in the fury of love and wrath. Draped in long robes, their heads tilted backward, they ran this way and that to the sound of flutes, cymbals, and tambourines, invoking the god until they fell down in extreme exhaustion. The violence of the rite was evidently supposed to metabolize the excess of feminine passions, and purify them of the promiscuity of their phantasms. The myths of the Maenads and the Bacchantes represent these phantasms in various forms.[40] Beyond the narrative variants (the three daughters of the King of Orchomenus in Boeotia; the three daughters of King Proetus of Tiryns; and Semele's three sisters), a constant structure remains, which is worth pointing out.

First of all, there are always three protagonists of the myth—the number that, as we know, characterizes the female component in the unconscious. Second, their guilt lies in escaping from the rites held in Dionysus's honor, in abandoning themselves to *unbridled* mania. The crime that follows as a consequence—the slaughter of one or more of their children—involves a terrible series of punishments: bestiality, madness, death. One of the daughters of the King of Orchomenus rends the limbs of her own child, and she and her sisters are transformed into nocturnal birds. The daughters of Proetus, turned into nymphomaniacs, metamorphose instead into cows; they kill their children and run through the forests, dragging along all the women they meet along the way in their fury. Of Semele's three sisters, Autonoe is forced to gather up the bones of her son, who has been rent apart by her dogs; Agaue, transformed along with her sisters into a dog, takes her son Pentheus as prey;[41] Ino immerses the little Melicerte in a pot of boiling water and then throws herself into the abysses of the sea along with him. We will see later how the figure of the "bestial woman" was picked up by Aristotle to deny maternity an ethical status.

In any case, the absense of uterine fury in the rite spurs young princesses to commit filicide and leads them to the consequent bestial state. It is interesting to note how the Dionysian divinities appear exclusively in the guises of daughters, sisters, and mothers, never as wives. The little offspring in their solitude, in turn, have an uncertain social status—which pertain to something between a human child and an animal, that destines them (as it does Dionysus) to be sacrificed.

A provisional existence and an uncertain identity are characteristic of all mythic figures of the Dionysian saga. This indefiniteness arises from the sexual attributes of Dionysus himself: "he who has two mothers," "three times born," "phallic," "provided with testicles," and "the erect one," but also "the pseudo-male," "the feminine boy," "the androgynous," "the hybrid," "the tree god," "the goat god," "the god of wine," "the initiate," and "the *Iakchos*" (the name and the cry that invoked the divine child in the course of the Eleusinian mysteries).[42]

Connected to the logic of the feminine unconscious, Dionysus represents a fantasy of a child engendered by the father; therefore, he is an incestuous child who precedes the ordering of desires and of social positions that characterizes the law of laws—the one forbidding sexual relations between blood relations. His image was constantly evoked in rites, but this was done to subject his anarchy to the ordering of shared sociality. This type of social regulation of desire is what Paola, like all little girls, elaborates in solitude—in the interior theatre that has replaced the shared scenarios of myth. Her playing of "games in the head" turns out to be less futile than it first appears. Indeed, it turns out to be socially necessary for the separation between sexuality and motherhood to take place—a separation that protects the child (like Dionysus in the grotto of the divine wet nurses) from the disturbances of the passions.

MYTHS REFLECTED AND CONCEALED
IN ANCIENT SCIENCE

Theories and Fears of Spontaneous Generation:
Devaluing the Female's Reproductive Role

Through the stories of goddesses who engender children on their own and of a god who remains a child eternally, we are able to give form to the infantile fantasy of parthenogenesis and to locate it in the time frame of the Oedipal conflict. But we are also able to glimpse the system of prohibitions that such fantasies come up against, with all the violence inherent in the imaginary. If it is possible to illuminate the unconscious with the figures of myth, this is because the two realms are subject to different systems of interdictions. In myth, fantasies are set into motion, although the script always predetermines their condemnation; in the individual unconscious, self-censoring prevents the actual representation (i.e., it is repressed). The repression itself is invisible, because other representations are projected, and different discourses with normative force are inscribed on the *tabula rasa* that it produces.

On a closer look, repression is created not so much by a process of erasure as by a system of superimpressions that have a concealing effect, so that the first inscription can only be determined by deconstructing the second. "Human thought," writes Matte Blanco, "is like a game that conforms to two different rules at the same time, except that one has a legitimate course while the other only becomes visible in terms of violating the first."[43] Nevertheless, like all offenses, repression always leaves traces.

So the unconscious desire that is expressed in myth, even with all its distortions, allows us to see through omissions and contradictions in the individual unconscious. As a result, we can perceive the hyperbole that these omissions and contradictions provoke in the order of the most powerful of discourses—scientific discourse.

Therefore, it is not enough to correct the lacunae in the individual unconscious with the re-evocations of myth, because this leaves the opposition between "nocturnal thought" and "diurnal thought" unaltered and creates obscurity and inertia. Instead, one must also recover the latent imagination in the symbolic products that have taken its place to uncover the essential elements of truth.

Now that I have identified an image of the wild child, removed from the time frames and modes of social reproduction, and an image of equally undomesticated feminine desire, I will try to use a fragment from the history of science to reconstruct the epistemological conflict that comes about when scientific objectivity enters into collusion with the (male) scientist's desire. What happens at that point is that the intentional project, which is purposely impersonal, subtends another, which is sustained by an unconscious desire that expresses the scientist's imaginary, his narcissistic identity, and his gendered subjectivity. A tension is thus set up between two orders of discourse—one that pertains to things, and another that is close to the self and has evident distorting effects. In particular, when scientific theory attempts to define man and woman, the weight of narcissistic interests becomes evident and the influence of the conflict between the sexes becomes acute. For instance, Aristotle described a chick embryo precisely, but he also maintained against all evidence that women have fewer teeth and fewer cranial sutures than men.

Piaget recognized the coexistence of these two attitudes—objectivity and unconscious desire—in all scientific discourse:

> Objectivity consists of being aware of the innumerable intrusions of the self in daily thought and of the innumerable illusions that derive from it—the illusions of the senses, of language, of point of view, of values, etc.— . . . Realism, on the other hand, consists of ignoring the existence of the self and, therefore, of looking at the world from our own personal perspective as if this were something that were immediately objective and absolute. Realism is thus an anthropocentric illusion; in the final analysis, it assumes all those illusions which the history of science is full of.[44]

Many of these illusions are determined by the male desire to represent man's mastery over nature, and, indirectly, his own domination over woman. Since the result of that conflict has shaped the very foundations of our scientific patrimony and of our representation of the world, it is impossible for a woman to separate herself completely from it—to declare herself as a woman, completely beyond its effects. However, using the very intellectual tools that were forged in the climate of that cultural enterprise, a woman can dedicate herself to a philology of what is implicit, a decodification of metaphorical constructs, an interpretation of the "psychopathology" of the conceptualization.

The contrast between the sexes in the realm of reproduction seemed particularly disturbing to Aristotle's thinking and introduced elements of the imaginary into his rational project of organizing the world within an exhaustive and conclusive scientific system—an undertaking that was to take on fundamental significance in our culture.

By the middle of the fourth century B.C., the knowledge accumulated by the great schools of medicine, along with zoological experience drawn from the daily practice of "experts" (breeders, hunters, fishermen, butchers), allowed Aristotle to acquire a new field of knowledge for his encyclopedia of sciences: biology.

This field brought together tested scientific material and widely held opinions based in the tradition of socially shared discourse. But the patrimony of knowledge that resides in "what they say" is often problematic, confused, ambiguous, and contradictory. The task of both science and practical philosophy "is not so much to produce a new and opposing knowledge, which would therefore be 'paradoxical'; it is to purify this layer of truth from its dross, to free it from all the unacceptable and contradictory elements that have filtered into the opinions, to 'conserve' it, to preserve its basic and dominant characteristics, thus rendering its implicit contents explicit and coherent."[46] The result is not so much a simple systemization of what exists as it is the creation of a global vision of the world that implies a definitive anthropology and a normative ethics.

In his scientific treatment of animal reproduction, Aristotle concealed the mythic imaginary, now reduced to metaphorical repertory, and controlled the emotionally disturbing nature of his antinomies by defining sexual difference as based upon reproductive functions. This definition of difference implied such asymmetry that it legitimized female subordination and the accompanying social discipline. But it also had a much more subtle effect—that of assigning woman a mutilated and passive representation of self in the objectified and neutralized terms of natural phenomena. Men and women in their historical concreteness were never the objects of this treatment. Rather, the object became their generative production, and around it was organized a system of priority that has been transmitted unchanged for centuries and that has taken on actual procreative function in the new reproductive technologies, as we will see in Chapter 4.

When Freud considered sexual difference and wrote, "The second, or biological, meaning of 'masculine' and 'feminine' is the one whose applicability can be determined most easily. Here 'masculine' and 'feminine' are characterized by the presence of spermatazoa or ova respectively and by the functions proceeding from them,"[47] he was merely giving voice to Aristotelian theory, which had become a tradition. In this case Aristotle's theory was superimposed upon preceding beliefs while concealing them. A text from the Hippocratic school,[48] *De Morbis Mulierum*, spoke explicitly of the "sperm of the male and of the woman"; even more threateningly, however, it maintained the existence of female generative self-sufficiency, in that the female was thought to possess both the formative capacity of the sperm (the carrier of both sexual characteristics) and the material constituted by her menstrual blood. From a biological point of view, therefore, conditions for parthenogenetic reproduction were thought to exist in the female that would make the male contribution to reproduction superfluous.

Aristotle was quite aware of this danger when he asked: "Since the female possesses the same soul, and the female residue constitutes the matter, why does the female need the male? Why can't she generate by herself?"[49] In a certain sense, the Aristotelian theory of the reproduction of animals can be considered an attempt to answer this question. This theory, while it demonstrated the necessity of sexual reproduction, simultaneously sanctioned a view of the radical inferiority and marginality of the female contribution, creating an ideology that would remain dominant well beyond the social and cultural framework in which it was originally created. Generally speaking, Aristotle assimilated the traditional concept of possible autoinsemination in the female, but weakened it by treating it as a special case in the sphere of the reproduction of particular animal species, and by covering up Hippocratic theories with the censoring of silence.[50] As Aristotle saw it, the animals that reproduce by spontaneous generation are gastropods, some insects, and certain species of fish. He also believed that among birds there are some females, called "*ventose*" (perhaps referring to the myth of Night fertilized by the wind), that are capable of producing an egg on their own.[51]

Paola Manuli writes:

> The parthenogenetic idea . . . has certainly functioned like a polemical ideal in the formation of our scientific knowledge of the feminine, and we can glimpse the traces of it in the Aristotelian texts on reproduction. It is said that mares can be fertilized by the wind, that the hyena is a hermaphrodite, that all fish are female, that the cephalopods and the crustaceans enjoy agamic generation. Parthenogenesis probably corresponds to the myth of a Golden Age, in another realm of discourse, in which the earth produced its own fruits spontaneously, without being sown and plowed, and in which the analogy of earth–woman was configured differently in respect to that of phallic power in reproduction.[52]

The suspicion of a form of generation that is independent of copulation had to extend to all animal reproduction, including human reproduction.

The fear that men might be excluded from an exclusively female genealogy, ousted by a gynecocracy that would hold all reproductive power, explains Aristotle's tenacious insistence on the asymmetry between male and female in the formation of life. He wrote:

> As has been said, the principles of reproduction can be recognized in the female and the male: the male as the carrier of the principle of change and generation, the female as the carrier of the substance. . . . The male is defined as an animal who reproduces within another, the female as one who generates within herself; therefore in the universe, one usually considers the earth as feminine and motherly in nature, while once considers the sky, sun and all similar things as generators and fathers.[53]

The influence of myth on the formation of scientific theory is evident here, where the plurality of its representations was used to support a variety of different positions. In this case, in evoking the sky–earth polarity, Aristotle introduced the high–low opposition that, as M. Detienne demonstrates,[54] implied a definite value judgment, much as the hot–cold opposition would acquire a decisive role in his biology. Often, verbal expressions that seem to be referential unintentionally call up mythical images that are thick with anthropological meaning. This is the case with the Aristotelian definitions of female and male, based on the terms "within herself" and "within another," respectively. These implicitly hearken back to the generative supremacy of the mother goddesses, the only ones capable of generating in and for themselves.

In a certain sense, we can consider the myths of origins as versions of the "primal scene of humanity," where possible and impossible are synthesized. The ways in which scientific theories were elaborated over the centuries in an attempt to demonstrate and emphasize the male contribution to reproduction appear then to be defensive constructs against the mythic imaginary, which was progressively deprived of value and meaning but continued to operate, even if outside of its original context. The conflict between the sexes, evident in the violence of Marduk against Tiamat or in the envy that opposes Zeus and Hera, continued and still continues to organize the explicative models of human generation. Even if in biological works "the principles of reproduction" were recognized as belonging to both sexes, the articulation of this discourse created a radical asymmetry. Aristotelian theory was superimposed upon pre-Socratic metaphors of the female body, which was represented as a field, a furrow, an oven, a stone, and a tablet,[55] and deprived it of autonomous significance.

From the beginning, Aristotle set up his research on generation as an inquiry into the cause of generative change—that is, of the transition from nonbeing to being. How could this be possible? His answer suggested a preliminary organization of the world based on the hot–cold polarity. As

Aristotle saw it, heat, in that it functions to cook foodstuffs, functions too as an agent in the transition of human civilization from a state of nature to one of culture. As such, it always represents value. In the realm of human physiology, heat, whose "furnace" is in the heart, is what distinguishes and places the three most important elements of the body in a hierarchy, produced by the internal elaboration of foods. At the center of the classification is ordinary blood, of average heat. At the bottom of the hierarchy are the menses—thick, heavy, and cold blood, insufficiently cooked. Placed above all other things is sperm, blood that is perfectly worked by male heat so as to detoxify it of all earthly residue; it becomes *"pneuma"* ("spirit"), an evanescent mixture of air and water, the nearly immaterial principle of life and form.

Given these suppositions, Aristotle's answer to the inquiry on the cause of life already contained within itself all the implications that would ensue. In his scheme, it is the *pneuma* that, acting upon the menstrual blood held in the female body, inspires life. Here the opposition is between activity and passivity, between the male carrier of change and the passive female element, as all mere material is passive. But there is also another opposition—that between the male principle of formation and the female element of immobile reception. In the transmission of hereditary characteristics, male impulses provoke the growth of single parts and determine the modality of their structure.

"There is no difference," Aristotle pointed out, "between saying sperm and saying the impulse that makes each part grow, nor between the impulse that causes growth and the constitutive impulse at the beginning; the concept of impulse remains the same."[56] In this way the male takes on both the conception and the gestation, understood as the formation of the embryo, leaving to the female—the "mother–earth," in Aristotle's metaphor—only the containment and nutrition. Of the four causes that regulate generation, Aristotle attributed three to the father, whom he considered the carrier of the formal cause, which is final and efficient; he progressively disempowered the mother, leaving her only the material cause. Thus, as he saw it, the female enters into the process of generation as a nonengendering sex.

This scientific paradigm, which was only finally replaced in the 1800s, decreed woman's sexual impotence; it attributed to her a cold, immature, powerless body, the body of a child. Using the model of animal reproduction, science translated mythic images of divine generation, with their charged emotional content, into the cold and impersonal laws of nature. In the secular discourse, however, the conflict between the sexes, which had been so dramatically represented in the transition from myths of parthenogenesis to those of sexual conception, was hidden. The metaphor of earth and seed that organized Aristotelian theory was decisive in this

sense: The female was seen as responsible only for the task of containing
and providing nutriment, a task that does not have any impact on the
modality of the formation of the unborn child. The opposition of the two
sexes in the process of generation could not be more asymmetrical: on the
male side (agent and transformer), form and activity; on the female side
(patient and container), material and passivity. The female role in generation was thus reduced to a substratum of the other form. The woman was
seen as the container of a product to be given over to man and to the city,
which alone were thought to hold the norm and value of the citizen.[57]

In its apparent objectivity, the first scientific construct had a determining effect in delineating sexual difference. But this was not all: Since its
system of polarity shaped our thought and our relationship to the world, it
became invisible. And thus it came about that the woman was obviously
deprived of her own active contribution to human generation, and that her
presumed physiological inferiority was translated into an indisputable ontological inferiority.

Although it is now recognized that the mother and father contribute
in equal measure to conception, and that pregnancy is not only containment and nutrition (because sensory and emotional communication passes
between the pregnant woman and the fetus), the Aristotelian paradigm
remains dominant at the level of immediate self-awareness. As Barthes has
said, men and women still think of themselves within Aristotelian categories, which are now common-sense categories and find continual confirmation in society and culture. In the impersonality of political institutions,
this constitutive asymmetry between the two genders has been translated
into codes of coexistence. In this sense, the imposition of the paternal
surname on the newborn baby represents the social stamp that symbolically
sanctions the priority established by Aristotle in his theory of generation.

Thus female generation, expelled from the dominant mythology and
from scientific constitution, was finally rendered unthinkable. The
woman's formative role, which is quite obvious, was obliterated by injunctions as powerful as they were invisible. Therefore, it should be no surprise
that we must recover these elements, make them thinkable once again, in
the unconscious and the interpretation of its products: dreams, symptoms,
games, and fantasies. My examination of Paola's fantasy is intended as a first
step in this direction.

When Sandokan says "no," opposing Marianna's solitary realization of
maternity, he re-echoes ancient interdictions, prohibitions that were never
made explicit but are even harder to elude for that very reason. But we
should ask ourselves why Marianna must address an entreaty to a man in
order to give birth. Why, in the Aristotelian scheme of things, doesn't her
own substance—her own material—possess any deliberative faculty in and
of itself? Why is it completely subject to male domination? The answer is

that between these two poles there exists a dynamic of attraction that Aristotle described in his *Physics:* "Matter is the subject of the desire, just as the female desires the male."[58] Since the dynamic of drives is always activated by lack, this is the woman's role, given the inherent lack in her being. It is the woman who yearns for conception.

As Freud confirmed, only the child (male) can satisfy this privation and clear the anxiety of woman's indeterminacy. As the formal and final cause, however, it is the man (his sperm) who carries out the entire reproductive process, including its conclusion in labor, which the woman cannot fulfill without his command. It is as if we can still hear the lament of the goddess Mami resounding across the centuries—"I cannot do such a thing by myself, but with Enki the work can be accomplished"—rather than hearing the pain of the prodigious Gaia, bursting with all her children.

In their stories of childbirth, women commonly recall that they could not have gone on to the pushing phase until they saw the figure of the (male) doctor beside them. Female figures are able to sustain the labor, but the tacit assent of male authority is needed to bring the child into the world. Similarly, in the case histories of pregnant women who have had to resort to induced labor at term, we can see the unconscious adaptation to the partner's denial of paternity. Paola's fantasy makes explicit the contradiction between female desire for sexual generation, which we might call narcissistic, and the system of interdictions and injunctions that regulates human sexuality. In this sense, the labor scene represents the locus of multiple conflicts that hinge upon the obvious asymmetry and latent opposition between the sexes.

THE SON OF STONE

The interdiction that is brought to bear on the difficult maternity that Paola fantasizes—and, even more, her inability to prefigure the child-to-be—allows us to identify, through myth, the two modes of being a mother, both equally characterized by impossibility. Whereas the first, the expression of the female's omnipotent desire to engender by herself, is situated in the narcissistic pre-Oedipal economy, the second is inscribed in the Oedipal conflict, affected by its intense dynamics of love and hate. Both are fated to succumb under the pressure of repression, which separates early childhood from the succeeding period of latency. However, their effects continue to interfere (albeit indirectly) in the way we conceptualize maternity, sexuality, and the difference between the genders, as Greek tragedy vividly reveals.

"In the tragedies," writes Guilia Sissa, "the affective incompatibility between children and passionate love opposes mothers against their lovers.

And incest, where marriage and descent become confused, effectively represents the figure of the most extreme anti-family woman, who rather than being rigorously aligned in her roles with different people and different times, mixes and inverts them."[59] The encumbrance of transgression that weighs upon female desire helps us to understand why such a desire always retains a suggestion of the excessive and unacceptable, even when it would seem to be in harmony with the ego ideal and with social expectation, as in the case of conjugal maternity.

Traditionally, female desire is by definition the desire for maternity. This is inscribed in the very body of the woman, as Plato wrote in a well-known passage from *Timaeus*:

> For women, that which is called matrix or uterus is an animal within them that desires to make babies; and when it remains bereft of fruit long after the proper season, it becomes irritable and tolerates this condition poorly; then it wanders all over her body, obstructs her airways, impedes respiration, casts her into extreme anxiety and provokes all kinds of illnesses; and that lasts until the appetite and desire of the two sexes lead them to a union wherein the women can receive their fruit, as from a tree.[60]

Two metaphors recur in this passage, that of the animal and that of the tree. The first is related to dissatisfaction; the second is related to satisfaction. One refers to a process within the body and the other to an outside occurrence, according to whether the phantasmic child is evoked by desire, which is endogenous, or satisfied by fantasy, which is exogenous. Between the bodily desire to "make" a baby and the satisfaction that consists of "receiving" an already formed fruit, what disappears, in Aristotelian terms, is the woman's generative contribution and formative activity. In any case, the longing to engender that is a parasite on the female body appears to be independent of sexuality, torn away both from erotic involvement with the other sex and from the search for pleasure. The maternal subject is alone with its demon, which only the child/fruit can placate. (It has been noted, in connection with this, that the uterine fumigations prescribed as a remedy for sterility by Hippocratic gynecology included sacrificial offerings to the gods.[61]) The desire for maternity is animated by the woman's self; it is autonomous as a demon and ungovernable as an animal in captivity. The substitution of the image of the fruit tree conceals a suspicion of parthenogenesis, because the Greeks perceived plants as hermaphroditic and as generating without insemination from the outside. For the Greeks, in any case, the desire for maternity—in an intermediate position between animal and vegetable, between beastly and divine—represented something that could not be located, something disturbing. As such, it was a source of doubt and difficulty that Aristotelian thought had trouble dealing with.

We have seen how Aristotle borrowed from the archives of myth the image of the earth for a metaphor of maternity. It turned out to be particularly suitable, in fact, to represent the presumed inertia of female material, and the female's passive receptivity in respect to male seed, the autonomous master of all the potential of life and form. Aristotle was hard put to attribute to the woman any sort of appetitive activity. On the other hand, the longing did not easily suit a male principle so distant from the concreteness of the generative process. To avoid any possible complementarity of the generative roles, to avoid the possible danger that the male principle might be compromised by material, Aristotle rendered it more and more evanescent—to the point of making it comparable to spirit or to the constructive art of the artisan or scientist, which never becomes part of the material that it shapes. In his constant attempt to seal off the male principle in a superior separateness of its own, Aristotle finally placed it out of the reach of the turbulence of desire. As he saw it, since desire expresses lack, it can only inhabit the female body, which is incomplete and insufficient by definition. Man, for his part, has nothing to yearn for, because "the only passion of the wise man is being,"[63] and "if he does not experience desires it is because these are always realized (or extinguished) in the static egocentrism of auto-gratification."[64]

"The matter is subject to desire as we have seen, and it is like the female which desires the male, and the ugly which desires the beautiful but it is not by itself that the ugly or the female does this, since these are only attributes" (see note 58). Defined the teratology of the species, so to speak, women were excluded from ethics and aesthetics in a single theoretical step. In this case, the metaphor of the earth (which passively surrenders to plowing and sowing, processes regulated by the seasonal cycle) was abandoned and implicitly replaced by a libidinal, magma-like substructure as ugly as primordial chaos in its lack of boundaries, and, like chaos, in need of the order imposed by male power. The Platonic image of the uterine beast once again imposed itself implicitly, as Aristotle's definition of menstruation reveals: "It is a question," he wrote, "of a flow of blood similar to that of a slaughtered animal."[65] The reference to sacrifice hearkens back to the demonic, to the excess inherent in sacrifice. In the Aristotelian system, menarche, in fact, indicates that the girl has entered the age when the desire for amorous pleasure peaks and surpasses comfortable limits. Since abandonment to erotic pleasure pushes her to ever greater lust (because it becomes a habit), she must be strictly watched until the age of twenty-one, when she reaches the age of procreation. At this point female sexuality can and must be regulated by motherhood, because "Women who are intemperate in amorous relationships become more settled and moderate after they have given birth a number of times."[66]

In Aristotle's scheme, then, the erotic desire of a sterile adolescence is

transformed, in due time, into the desire for maternity, disciplined by a
sequence of pregnancies and childbirths that precipitates the female body
into a precocious and pacified old age. Once again, an adept game of more
or less explicit metaphoric constructs has guaranteed the asymmetry of the
positions: for males, domination; for females, submission. In the course of
its advancement, scientific ordering has apparently exorcised the phantasms of female desire, which are transgressive (whether in their narcissistic
omnipotence or their incestuous promiscuity).

But on further examination, we can see these phantasms reappearing
in the heterogeneity of the generative products—in their departure from
the resemblance between father and child hypothesized by of Aristotelian
genetics. If all faculties were precisely transmitted and the male form
could predominate and dominate over the female material, the pure and
simple duplication of the individual would be the result. This remains an
abstract paradigm, however, because the resistance of the material or the
weakness of the impulse is such that every offspring digresses from
perfection, thus constituting varying levels of "monstrosity"[67] or, more
precisely, "anomaly." "Whoever does not resemble his own parents,"
Aristotle stated, "in effect constitutes an anomaly [teras] because nature
in these cases has in some way strayed from the gender. The first instance
of such an anomaly is to be born female and not male, but this is necessary
in nature because the gender of animals in which female and male are
separate must be preserved."[68]

Femininity itself is thus translated into an anomaly or monstrosity,
which is both exceptional and necessary. Another deviation from the
teleological axis is represented by the male who resembles his mother,
which is to say her father, or neither parent. Others, finally, do not resemble
a man, but share the likeness of a monster. In all of these cases, the child
represents a diminution in respect to the perfection of the paternal model.
The disregarded female desire seems to intervene in the divergence between
the expected form and the actual baby that is born, as the duplication of
the mother in the daughter reveals, or the resemblance of some males to
the maternal grandfather, or, finally, the disturbing arrival of a monster. In
those cases where the informational power of the sperm seems to fail, the
female residue demonstrates unexpected causal capabilities, revealing a
dangerous compromise between material and form.

Everything that Aristotle tried to exorcise—the generative autonomy
of the female body, a formal causality of its own that is both final and
efficient—seems at last to be transgressively concretized in the formation
of a "mole" or teras. Even worse than a female child, the mole is a derisive
product of the female body that seems, in its complete negativity, to deprive
the material cause of any possible value. It is a shapeless and inert thing
that takes form in the belly of a woman during a pseudopregnancy in which

a clot of menstrual material grows together. The fantasy of parthenogenetic generation seems to find realization in the mole, which represents its harshest punishment: A child of stone, never developed and often never born, seems to be the final condemnation of a failed body that is not open to desire, that has not yielded to the imposition of the male form. Aristotle wrote:

> The so-called mole is rarely produced in women, but is produced in some when they are pregnant. . . . A woman who has had relations with her husband and believes she is pregnant will first see the volume of her belly increase and everything else will occur normally according to expectation, but after the time to deliver arrives, she neither gives birth nor does the size of her belly diminish, but three or four years pass until . . . she gives birth to a fleshy mass that we call a mole. Some women, on the other hand, age and die from the effects of this. The moles who come out turn so hard that it is difficult to break them even with an iron implement.[69]

Aristotle asked himself why on earth this morbid phenomenon should happen only to human females among all other animals, and responded by identifying the abundance of menstrual blood, which makes it hard to cook. He therefore configured this "raw" femininity as a petrified lump, the expression of a shapeless and worthless body that, left to itself, can only realize a nonpregnancy, a nonbirth, the opposite of health and life.

"The parable of the mole," observes Paola Manuli, "is nothing more than a metaphor for female impotence, of the material that cannot heat itself, and at the same time, it represents the definitive sanction of the polarity between sperm and menses: one carries an extremely positive connotation—of completion, of life, of form, of heat; the other the negativity of all its opposites."[70]

To return to the fantasy of a real baby removed from sexual complementarity and social conjugality, we have now seen that its image is marred in myth by monstrosity, and in Aristotle's biology by fatality. The scale of denigration ranges from the bestiality of the sacrificial god (a combination of the sublime and the base) to the inanimate reification in the mole. In any case, there is no place for an imago that threatens to upset the supremacy of male generative power, in its incontestable singularity. The woman must see herself simultaneously as inert earth and as yearning for fruit, because in the game between passivity and desire, the male spirit accomplishes its reproductive task from a distance—just as the sun warms matter with the energy of its rays and brings about life. Yet it remains outside of that viscous process in which life is transformed into a body within another body, the maternal one.

Maternity is seen, then, as a mindless machine of production that destroys itself in the exhaustion of its own potential—in silence, because silence, as Aristotle declared (quoting a well-known line from Sophocles), "is fitting for a woman."[71]

Fears of Female Excess: Gynephobia in Greek Science and Culture

To Aristotle, the regulation of the female body seemed a task that is neither easily or ever completely accomplished. When he opposed the lust of virgins with the punitive therapy of multiple deliveries, he revealed how violently the mythic imagination erupts in the calm neutrality of scientific treatment—in the ideal model of organic reproduction. The conjugal figures, *dramatis personae* who should have remained off stage, are surprisingly superimposed upon the articulation of the generative material. In assigning the spouse the task of regulating the excess of the young girl, Aristotle opposed sexuality and maternity in a schema that would dominate female education and gynecology from the fourth century B.C. until the nineteenth century A.D. In opposition to the virginal state, conjugality carries with it the suggestion of two kinds of bleeding: deflowering and birth.

The sacrifice of Iphigenia seems to be repeated in the rites of passage of female existence. The constitution of the family is punctuated by these rites, and natural reproductive capability is transformed into social reproduction. The animal that Plato felt stirring in the female body finds its bloody sacrifice in reiterated conjugal sexuality. The violence and blood that the scientific text attempted to conceal (along with the mortal conflict that forms the furthest horizon of the sexual act) return here with all the coercive impetuosity of repression. The disappearance of the Aristotelian "cold" female gestation reveals that his conceptualization could not withstand the weight of opinion that is sufficiently emotionally charged to resist neutralization by science.

The fear of a female nature that cannot be reduced to social requirements also re-emerged in the *Nicomachean Ethics*,[72] where in a discussion of intemperate figures, Aristotle exemplified "bestial dispositions" by citing "the woman who is said to devour fetuses after having disemboweled pregnant women." He associated this woman's actions with the cannibalistic rites of savages, and distinguished her from those who fall into bestiality as a result of illness, madness, or force of habit: "for example, those who have been the victims of violence since they were children." Aristotle went on to say that women must have a "natural disposition" for bestiality that reveals itself precisely in connection with maternity. This passage shows how male phobia transforms the power to receive and form the fetus in gestation and to bring it to light in childbirth into its opposite—into the disembowelment and devouring of fetuses. Gynecocracy, as Vidal-Naquet has shown, is the nightmare of a dreadful state of nature, a threat feared by

Greek culture from its very beginnings.[73] Weren't the violence and grieving of the Trojan War caused by Helen, the most beautiful of women?

Representing the misogyny of archaic culture, Hesiod attributed all the world's ills and griefs to Pandora, "terrible scourge."[74] In this kind of oppositional scheme, it is not insignificant that Pandora, "this truly beautiful evil," turns out to have been artfully produced by the horrible Hephaestus, Hera's son. Therefore, in the final analysis, the members of the "cursed gender, the tribe of women," are actually descended from themselves—as a result of the most abominable of female transgressions, autogeneration. Since Zeus takes language from women, their power (granted by Aphrodite) consists solely of beauty. In the face of the seduction caused by beauty, Hesiod expressed a fear bordering upon phobia.

Plato more shrewdly projected this phobia upon women themselves in an opposite form, so that their segregation would appear to be the inevitable consequence of their uncontrollable savagery. He wrote: "There's nothing that would be harder for this race of women to bear [than taking food and drink in the open], for it is habituated in a retired, indoor way of life; it will use every means to resist being dragged by force into the light and will prove much superior to the legislator."[75] A further expression of gynehobia can be seen in the common somatic metaphor that "women's habitation" seems to be located in the viscera, like the lustful soul—separated by a diaphragm from the noble parts of the body, the heart and mind. Women's wild behavior and visceral nature, revealed in their uncontrolled dedication to eating and sex, constitute a leitmotif of Greek misogyny.[76] The fear of the female sex, the closest of the figures of otherness, found its most passionate singer in Simonides. The violence of his bestiary expresses the sadistic components of the masculine imagination with unparalled clarity:

One he made from a long-bristled sow. In her house everything lies in disorder. . . . And she herself unwashed, in clothes unlaundered, sits by the dung heap and grows fat.

Another he made from a wicked vixen, a woman who knows everything. No bad thing and no better kind of thing is lost on her; for she often calls a good thing bad and a bad thing good. Her attitude is never the same.

Another he made from a bitch, vicious, own daughter of her mother, who wants to hear everything and know everything. She peers everywhere and strays everywhere, always yapping, even if she sees no human being. A man cannot stop her by threatening, nor by losing his temper, and knocking out her teeth with a stone, nor with honeyed words, not even if she is sitting with friends, but ceaselessly she keeps up a barking you can do nothing with.

Another he made from an ash-gray ass that has suffered many blows; when compelled and scolded she puts up with everything, much against her will, and does her work to satisfaction. But meanwhile she munches in the back room all night and all day, and she munches by the hearth; and likewise when she comes to the act of love, she accepts any partner.

Another he made from a ferret, a miserable, wretched creature; nothing

about her is beautiful or desirable, pleasing or lovable. She is mad for the bed
of love, but she makes any man who was with her sick. She does great damage
to neighbors by her thieving, and often eats up sacrifices left unburned.[77]

Simonides's catalogue includes additional typologies such as the horse
and the monkey, characterized respectively by unbridled greed for food and
sex and by an innate incapacity to set limits. Or the temperament of women
seems to depend upon the substances that they are composed of: earth or
water, equally ill-omened. Only the woman-bee—the asexual guardian of
the house who is completely used up in the period of nurturing and
reproduction, and who is isolated from the contagion of other women—
seems to constitute a positive presence. But she only exists so that

> Each man will take care to praise his own wife and find fault with the other's;
> we do not realize that the fate of all of us is alike. Yes, this is the greatest
> plague that Zeus has made, and he has bound us to them with a fetter that
> cannot be broken. Because of this some have gone to Hades fighting for a
> woman. . . .

Such gynephobia seems to function so that the homosexual bonds that
are necessary for the Polis (the city–state), for war, and for the transmission
of values can be formed. This can be seen in the extent to which women
and their horrific qualities constitute a fundamental element of the tragic
passions in the drama of Euripides. One thinks of the invective tone of the
misogynist Hippolytus, shut in his defensive virginity: "Oh Zeus, what a
cunning evil/you have brought into the light of the sun for men:/women!
If you wanted to propagate the human race, couldn't you have done
it/without recourse to them?"[78] Or the grotesque figures of the comedy of
Aristophanes come to mind—for example, Lysistrata's use of sex to gain
power and the Ecclesiazusae's use of power for sexual satisfaction. In any
case, in their limitless sexual availability, women represent a threat that is
transformed, in a man's eyes, into excessive desire and nymphomania. This
is why Aristotle placed them outside the space of the Polis, along with the
profiteer and the tyrant.[79] This exile sets them outside the perimeters of the
rationality of Logos and places them in opposition to the law, which is
"thought devoid of desire."

REGULATING FEMALE DESIRE: RITES FOR GIRLS
AND WOMEN IN ANCIENT GREECE
What Does Woman Want?

In Aristotle's science, ethics and politics converged to expunge the female
body from the linked representation of man and world upon which Western

civilization is based. For Plato the place of women constituted a problem that was open to ambiguous and contradictory solutions, as the different roles envisioned for women in the *Republic* and the *Laws* demonstrate. In the first work, which is decidedly utopian, woman's emancipation is a consequence of the end of the family, and of the equality that is produced in the deconstruction of its system of exchanges. But with the restoration of the family in the *Laws*, woman once again comes to be subordinated, first to her father's authority and later to her husband's. And whereas the revolutionary Plato attributed the difference between the sexes to education, he ultimately decreed it to be founded on a natural inferiority. Accordingly, presenting an epiphany on possible reincarnations in *Timaeus*, he wrote: "The more cowardly and unfair men were reborn as women in the second generation."[80]

But if the existence of the other sex constituted an obstacle that Plato had to confront in his philosophical system[81] and his political project, Aristotle enclosed women definitively within the circle of their "natural difference," with much less ambiguity and contradiction. In the Aristotelian system of social exchanges, women are relegated to the private space of the house (*Oikos*), which seems to duplicate in the city the "inside of the self" that characterizes the generative capacity of the female body. In Aristotle's shrewd topology—which is misogyny, with its components of fear, hate, and sadism—the female body no longer pollutes the neutrality of science, the serenity of ethics, the equilibrium of politics. For he felt that the turbulence of female desire, deprived of representation, could be adequately ascribed to pathology and entrusted to the realm of medicine.

In fact, the field of medicine was thus prepared to take on female desire and relegate it to one of the most resistant categories it ever devised: "hysteria," a pathology that has come to be characteristic of the female sex. In the history of science, the hysteric, with her numerous symptoms and their multiple meanings, has come to represent a recurrent epistemological obstacle that, in its irreducibility opposes all comprehensive theories, all conclusive systems. The hysterical symptoms, expressed as enigmas, have revealed the insufficiency of pre-existing medical categories, the inadequacy of medical methods, and the impotence of treatments, and have thus prompted new research.[82] And it could not have been otherwise, because female excess can neither be contained within the house nor regulated within the body, since the place in which it resides is elsewhere.

Once again, a myth served to represent "the other scene" long before Freud inscribed it in the intimate dimension of the unconscious. It is told in the Theban plays that Tiresias, who is well known to us for his knowledge of Oedipus's dark past, was once called upon to settle a disagreement between Zeus and Hera, who "were disputing with each other as to whether the male or female kind got more pleasure of love. . . . His decision ran thus:

ten, the man enjoyeth but one part/Nine parts the woman fills, with joyful heart." Enraged, Hera blinded him as punishment. In return, Zeus made him a seer and granted him seven generations of life.[83]

In the economy of pleasure, we see that the sexual asymmetry that favors man in terms of power is reversed in the woman's favor. "The re-allotment of pleasure on the part of one who knows," comments Lacan, "indicates that along with man's simple *phallic* enjoyment, there is *another female enjoyment*, which is greater, more complex, more important: nine tenths of the pleasure in love. The fractions serve here to quantify enjoyment. . . . Nine months of pregnancy so that a new being may be born. . . . Does female pleasure revolve around childbirth?"[84]

The part that we cannot see with impunity is female desire in its connection to maternal power. Only the magical and divining function of numbers can elude the interdiction and reveal the secret of sexual difference. This is a secret that only Tiresias, who is both male and female, holds—and that Hera, on the other hand, placing herself on the side of maintaining the distinction, defends tenaciously. It is meaningful that the same goddess represents both the omnipotence of maternal desire and its interdiction. By punishing Tiresias with blindness, she perpetuates the sentence of silence, to which she is first victim and then accomplice. Maternal desire survives now in the interior reservoir of the female imagination—removed from the contractual nature of conjugal exchange, erratic in comparison to the time frames and modes of male desire, condemned to perpetual exile and misunderstanding. What the hysteric feels, even if she is unaware of it, is withheld tension, pleasure seeking a representation it can grasp hold of. The blotting out of narcissistic or Oedipal fantasies of engendering leaves powerful libidinal energies floating—an affective legacy that will "lie fallow" during latency, to be summoned in the course of adolescence and put to use in the construction of the self, in the personal libidinal economy that translates female desire into an unspeakable life story.

The woman's "greater part" in the reproductive undertaking, which myth exorcises (except to recover it in "greater pleasure") and which science denies, seems to have found its provisions in fantasy. However, this is a delicate and unproductive arrangement if it does not attach itself to appropriate objects and to conscious processes, or if it remains floating between the psychic and the corporeal realms, where it is open to all the conversions of neurosis. Girls can use the latency period, from six to ten years of age, to elaborate childhood phantasms of maternity in a nonconflictual manner and to inscribe them in the archives of memory and in images of self-representation. But this process appears to be forbidden, and maternal passion finally lacks images, as Paola's problems and her flight into somaticization demonstrate.

On the other hand, the existence in classical Greece of a complex and elaborate series of rites to lead a young girl through nubility attests to a greater awareness of the struggle required for infantile passions to be directed and prepared for their ultimate goal: the reproduction of citizens. In *Lysistrata*, Aristophanes described the stages of the initiation process: "As a child of seven years I carried the sacred box; Then I was a Miller-maid, grinding at Athene's shrine; Next I wore the saffron robe and played Brauronia's Bear; And I walked as a basket-bearer, wearing chains of figs, as a sweet maiden fair."[85]

The First Rite: Abandoning the Mysterious Child

It is interesting to note, in the correspondence between rites and psychic processes, that the first stage of the female initiation process fell on a girl's seventh birthday—exactly when both the elaboration of the unconscious phantasms of autogeneration and the regulation of their anarchy begin, as in Paola's case. The rite brings to light the hold exerted by society on the energies and images that each young girl possesses and has received in the family, the first organization. The imago of the child, which we have seen in connection with the narcissistic and omnipotent economy of childhood, must be abandoned to leave room for the figure of the son who springs from the father. The little animal–god of the infantile imagination must disappear so that his place can be taken by the son, future citizen of the Polis. In Athens, the sacred sphere was the place of this transmutation, and the first rite of passage was its expression. A description of this process is in order here, because its gestures are more eloquent than words.

The Arrephoria, the first level of sacred service dedicated to Athena, was carried out each year by two little girls chosen by an *archon* (a high official of the state) from among four girls belonging to the most illustrious Athenian families. The two arrephoroi, dressed in white robes and bejeweled with gold coins, lived during the initiation period in a segregated area away from the Acropolis and were fed special food, probably bread shaped like a phallus. During that time they had to help the priestess of Athena, who began the weaving of a *peplos* (shawl or scarf) that would be consecrated to the goddess during the celebration held in her honor. Another service required of the two girls took place in the late spring, between May and June. During the night, crossing an underground passageway, they had to transport a basket with mysterious contents from the Acropolis all the way down to the sacred precinct of "Aphrodite in the gardens." Having deposited their burden, they loaded up with other secret objects that had to be taken back up to the Acropolis. "The secrecy that this endeavor suggests, the difficulty and danger of the nocturnal and subterranean transit, the prohibition against discovering the nature of the transported objects are all significant elements of a true test."[86]

The significance of this ritual is suggested by a mythical precedent—the saga of the first Athenian king, Kercrops. Having arisen from the earth, half man and half serpent, Kercrops represents the transition from chthonic generation to conjugality. "He had discovered," it was said, "the double origin of man: procreated not only by the mother but also by the father; he had instituted marriage between one man and one woman, an institution that had to come under the protection of the goddess Athena."[87] The secret relationship between Kercrops and the goddess was only remembered in dark, mysterious ceremonies. In the myth, Athena turns out to be the mother of his three daughters, who become inhabitants of the Acropolis, the first women to take up weaving. Athena gives them the task of guarding, but never opening, a basket with mysterious contents in which Erichthonius is hidden—a child who emerges from the earth, born perhaps of the seed spilled when Hephaestus makes a futile attempt to rape the goddess. Two of the three sisters disregard Athena's injunction, open the basket, and see the infant Erichthonius wrapped in a serpent; the sight results in their deaths.

The myth and the rite similarly symbolize the beginning of the transition from childhood to adolescence, which includes the woman's entrance into the social sphere (represented by weaving) and her access to the mysteries of sexual reproduction. In this sense, food in a phallic form alludes expressly to the necessity of accepting oneself as lacking and of giving oneself up to the other in the complementarity of reproductive function. But we can only understand the abandonment of the mysterious child, of little Erichthonius, if we keep in mind the pre-existence of self-engendering phantasms that must be sacrificed to socialized reproduction. The difficulty of this act of denial is effectively represented by the arduous nocturnal course of the children's procession, while the preconjugal nature of little Erichthonius is indicated both by his birth from earth and by the dispersed insemination of Hephaestus, the deformed offspring of Hera's parthenogenesis. Moreover, the serpent that is wrapped around the divine newborn seems to allude to the half-serpent Kercrops, thus suggesting an incestuous bond. The death of the two sisters who want to see what is in the basket seals within the unconscious the dangerous infantile fantasies of maternity; like all rites, it also inaugurates a second life, a rebirth after the end of childhood.

Without any social affirmation, Paola attempts to elaborate these very same tests in the realms and ways available to her: fantasy and symptom. Both contain a secret, because "Marianna has not gone out since she has been expecting, because she is ashamed to have such a big belly." This shame, a reaction to an implicit judgment, isolates the imaginary realm from communication and from social relationships (even the servants don't know anything). On the other hand, it leads to "not wanting to see" what is represented on another stage. The pain of childbirth expresses the sacrifice demanded by the abandonment of the secret baby, while the tormenting uncertainty over whether to hold it in or expel it represents the unspeakable nature of maternity: Is it the voiding of a fullness or the filling up of a void?

At this point, the "beautiful baby boy" who is only born because Sandokan, the custodian of male power, gives his permission, appears to be another form of little Erichthonius—an impossible baby to be abandoned in Aphrodite's nocturnal gardens so that the woman, relieved of her burden, can return to the Acropolis, the emblematic locus of social dominion. Paola's fantasized childbirth entrusts the "child of the night" to the unconscious and prepares her for maternity—the real, socially recognized maternity that will occur within the time frame and according to the modes determined by society and culture. Cleansed of the promiscuity of infantile fantasies, of their corporeal materiality, she is ready to accept the "child of the day," a man's child who will be born "in the name of the father." Neither Paola's fantasy nor her "illness" has any sequel, and the latency period lays a curtain of forgetfulness over this event.

Years later, Paola's mother tells me that the girl, now in puberty, is assailed by the fear of being sterile or of giving birth to monstrous children. This is the consequence of repression, which (as is always the case) has not completed its task, and which therefore allows the twisted phantasms of the forbidden imaginary to filter through.

Paola's text, in its extreme particularity, takes on an emblematic value because it brings to light an event that all women share. As in Anna's case, the child's language permits us privileged access into the representations of the unconscious. But we must recover them in myth, rite, and in the weaving of scientific discourse if their complexity is to be revealed and if they are to take on meaning. In the timeless dimension of the unconscious, desire and law confront each other in a conflict that has already taken place but is nevertheless reactivated in each life story.

The Endless Domestication: Further Initiatory and Religious Rites

As we have seen, the first stage of the female initiation process in Athens, the Arrephoria, constituted the threshold a young girl had to cross to enter the shared space of the Polis and to move toward assuming her position as a mother of citizens. But female initiation required further rites of passage, and in some sense it was never completed, since the religious calendar included special annual rites that confirmed her function.

The second initiatory level—the rite of Alteris, the grinder of grain—

appears to be poorly documented. It is only known that Athena was believed to preside over this ritual service, which consisted of preparing flat loaves of bread from grains cultivated in sacred earth for the sacrifice. Ten-year-old girls, at the boundary between childhood and puberty, were selected for this rite (as for the Arrephoria) from the daughters of aristocratic families. The ritual apparently alluded to another vital function that a young woman had to perform after her marriage: domestic food management. The reproductive task that the city assigned to women was, in fact, carried out on two levels: receiving and elaborating the conjugal seed in pregnancy and childbirth, and seeing to the survival of kin through the manipulation of the earth's seeds.

Thus, the maternal and alimentary functions were the two cornerstones that the rite proposed to etch in the female imaginary, thus inscribing the law of the city as it applied to the roles befitting women—subjects who lacked political and legal rights, and who were constantly subjected to the tutelage of male authorities (fathers first, husbands later). But women must have presented a fierce resistance to their social domestication, because the third initiatory stage, set at the threshold of adolescence, was focused on elaborating the remnants of untamed savagery.

The rite of the Arkteia, or of "playing Brauronia's Bear," took place outside the city of Athens at Brauron (a locality in eastern Attica)—a wild place dear to Artemis, goddess of the hunt, of birth, of childhood, and of nubile youth. The goddess Artemis, in her double role as protectress and avenger, was thought to preside over all female biological events: menarche, coitus, childbirth. Girls dedicated their first childhood toys (balls, dolls, twine) to her, and later robes stained with their first menstrual blood. Finally, they invoked her in the struggle of labor. In cases of happy childbirth, they dedicated a whole piece of woven cloth to the goddess; in other cases, they dedicated a piece of fabric only half-finished, incomplete like their generative task. At Brauron, the young girls put on and then took off yellow robes during a secret ceremony. It is said that, instructed by a priestess dressed as a she-bear, they played the parts of she-bears and mimicked these animals, running and leaping nude upon overturned vessels.[88] Identifying themselves with animals, the girls atoned for the original sin of their sex: the offense committed by a girl who, having been scratched by a bear, forced her brothers to kill the beast inside the temple of Artemis, thus contaminating a sacred place. An epidemic ensued as a consequence, and only ended after the father agreed to kill his daughter by order of Apollo. Playing she-bears permitted the Athenian girls one final wild act—a regression that was also a transgression—before they entered into the ranks of wives and mothers.

The rite is of interest to us mainly because it brings to light an obscure female substratum (connected to blood, birth, and death) that the city never succeeded in completely normalizing, and that could only be circumscribed in space and precisely defined in time so that it did not spread like an infection. Infantile sexuality, with its sterile nature, its omnipotent economy, and its solitary regime, came to be constantly supervised, represented, and connected to prohibition, guilt, and punishment.

Finally, the last stage of the female initiation process, the Kanephoros, took place during the Panathenaea festival and required girls approaching marriage to carry the instruments of sacrifice enclosed in a basket. The holiday took place on the supposed birthday of Athena, so that the female initiatory cycle began and ended in the name of the city.

But an Athenian woman's whole life was punctuated by an annual rite, the Thesmophoria, which confirmed her position as wife and mother. This took place in the autumn, in the month of sowing, and was dedicated to Demeter. In Greek myth, Demeter is the goddess of grain and agriculture who oversees the life cycle and human labor, whether this is devoted to taking fruit from the earth or from the female womb. The followers of Demeter Thesmophoros, who were limited to legitimate wives, practiced a "female government," or "city of women" for three days, safe from the eyes of men, thus simulating the political structures that excluded them. As S. Campese and S. Gastaldi have observed,[89] the ritual's content was modeled on the myth of Demeter and Kore (Persephone)—the separation of the mother and daughter for a portion of each year, thanks to Hades, and their subsequent reunion.

The first day, which re-evoked Kore's descent to the underworld and her mother's desperation, involved attitudes of mourning and supplication. The second day was characterized by a purifying fast and a strange ritual that consisted of recovering the putrefied remains of young pigs from sacred subterranean passages, which were reached through cracks in the earth; these remains were then placed on the altar, mixed with seeds, and later returned to the soil. This gesture—meant to ensure the fertility of the soil and of female wombs—established an association between the generative capacity of the earth and that of the women, which was emphasized on the third day and last day, dedicated to "Demeter of the good stock."

During this whole period, the wives dedicated themselves to chastity, resting on pallets made from "chaste trees" (a plant thought to block sexual desire and promote the menstrual flow). The dampening of desire in favor of fertility in the Thesmophoria was meant to confirm the position of the legitimate wife, who was as distant from the virgin as she was from the Hetaera. However, the allusion to slaughter and bloody sacrifice introduced a disturbing note that is difficult to decipher. It may have involved exorcising the nocturnal product from female fantasy—the impossible child sprung from the cracks of the chthonic goddess, whose incumbent threat of transgression disturbed the order of the city and the sleep of men.

But the necrotized remains of the little pigs also hearken back to an unusual myth of cannibalism. In the myth, Tantalus invites the gods to a banquet at which an infant is the main dish, in order to provoke them. All refuse the terrible food, except for Demeter, the mother goddess, who takes "a little, little piece." This is sufficient nevertheless to associate the nurturing mother with the devouring mother, life with death.

A dark side of maternity exists that must be hidden, placed outside of the order of the day and the gaze, and constantly exorcised. But since maternal power, generative force, resides in this too, it is necessary to come to terms with it—to create forms of mediation that permit the coexistence of male power and female strength. In this sense, we can interpret the myth of Demeter and Kore as an attempt to dissolve the mingling of life and death, which makes the figure of the mother in the cycle of the seasons so disturbing. When Zeus intervenes to mediate the quarrel between Demeter and the infernal god, Hades, who has abducted her daughter, he decides that Kore will spend a third of the time with her husband in the bowels of the earth and two-thirds with her mother in the light of the day. The antinomy is thus dissolved in the succession of opposites inherent in the natural cycle; this provides a metaphor of a possible conciliation of opposites.

In classical Greece, the abduction of Kore or Persephone symbolized matrimony. In fact, the wedding ceremony was the decisive moment in the passage from infantile sexuality (which was likened to untamed nature) to adult sexuality (which was likened to the agricultural cycle of wheat). To symbolize the transition from "raw" to "cooked," the day of the wedding the bride brought a pan to toast barley, while a pestle (used in the grinding of grain) was hung at the door of the nuptial chamber. The decisive act in the ceremony occurred when the father entrusted his daughter to her husband with these words: "I give you this girl for a work of plowing that she may produce legitimate children." The daughter herself declared: "I have escaped the worst, I have found the best." The social economy replaced the instinctual one; the symbolic replaced the imaginary (in Lacan's terminology); the planning of legitimate filiation replaced the spontaneity of amorous desire.

Although the Athenian nuptial and initiation rites undertook a comprehensive regulation of the female gender and an ordering of female phantasms, in their lives women maintained a stubborn desire that did not yield to manipulation. Their gusto for opposition and for desecration was effectively expressed in the rite of the Adonia—a profane ceremony of anti-initiation, a paradoxical rite of nonmaternity, and a provocative omen of sterility. According to Aristophanes's description in *Lysistrata*,[90] in August under the constellation of the Dog, when heat waves seemed to provoke female licentiousness, all classes of Athenian women gathered to dance on the roofs. In the process they destroyed crops they had planted in rooftop "gardens of Adonis" eight days prior, during a period that was utterly anomalous in respect to the agricultural season for sowing. They planted a mixture of wheat and aromatic essences; the heat and abundant watering quickly resulted in precipitous and ephemeral germination. Once intoxicated with the god, the women yanked out these plants and destroyed them with salty water, moving in accompaniment to the sound of cymbals, tambourines, songs, cries, and invocations of Adonis. The rite was apparently a parody of the fertility ceremonies and can be read as a denial of conjugal generation, which, as we have seen, was associated with the production of wheat. The desperate jubilation of a carnival was evident in this topsy-turvy world, which stood in opposition to politics, agriculture, conjugality, and maternity.

But who is Adonis, the divinity whose worship led to these most serious of transgressions? He is a divinity of Oriental origin who never really becomes a part of the Olympic tradition. He is born of an incestuous relationship between Myrrha, the daughter of Cinyras, king of Cyprus, and her father. Myrrha deceives her father by lying with him precisely during the Themosphorria (a period, as we have seen, of sexual abstinence for women). To protect her from her father's murderous fury, the gods transform the girl into myrrh (the aromatic plant that bears her name), from whose ripped skin Adonis is born. Sought after by Aphrodite and Persephone (Kore), the young god lives, as Zeus wished, part of the year alone and the rest with the two goddesses in turn. But this well-loved god is not long-lived. In fact, a wild boar kills him after he tries in vain to hide under a lettuce plant, which is said to provoke female autogeneration. Adonis is a figure of incompletion, a phantom of the unrealized female imagination. His birth falls under the sign of transgression and violent death, which seals his interdiction.

Whereas the Thesmophoria celebrated the triumph of the social imagination, the Adonia represented its defeat. Indeed, it affirmed the priority of sexual pleasure (the aromatic essences) over generative fertility (the wheat), of the relationships between women over the marriage bond, of Dionysian abandon over denial, of waste over conservation and care, of night over day, and of the open spaces of the roofs over the closed rooms of the houses. The derisive overturning of the values imposed by male society undoubtedly constituted a liberating moment, but its dissolute, exceptional, licentious nature only served to validate the normality of the established power. Like the events occurring during Carnival time (the period before Lent in modern Catholic countries), the apparent transgressions of the Adonia served to maintain the status quo—in this case, the male pact that based the political system on the exclusion and seclusion of women.

While the "gardens of Adonis" symbolized all that was ephemeral and fleeting in desire, the organization of the city methodically pursued its task of social reproduction, of control over female generation, and of the inscription of the citizens in a male genealogy. Plato wrote in *Phaedra*:

> And now tell me if an intelligent farmer, if he has the seeds he prefers, and he wishes them to bear him fruit, will hasten at the height of summer to sow them in Adonis' gardens, for the pleasure of seeing them luxuriate in eight days? Or would he do these things merely on account of the celebration, and for pleasure if he did them at all? On the contrary, for those seeds he really cares about, the farmer will follow the rules of agriculture, will sow them at the right moment, and surely he will rejoice when, after the eight months have passed, all those he sowed have grown to maturity.[91]

A time of impotence as opposed to a time of power, a time of desperate revenge for autonomy, the Adonia represented "the other side" of the city—that which never happened and which was nevertheless preserved uncorrupted in the dimension of the unconscious, in the archives of the imagination.

Just as sexual morality, which regulates the presence of women in the political order, does not depend upon laws and edicts but conceals its prohibitions and impositions in the ambiguity of rite and myth, so too are female transgression and overwhelming subordination revealed in this realm. A striking and unusual myth concerns a strange, monstrous, solitary figure who emerges from the earth: Baubo, whose name means "belly."[92] Whereas the laws of men separate mother from daughter, the generating body from the generated offspring, physicality from thought, childhood from maturity, sexuality from fertility, and pleasure from pain, Baubo reunites the opposites within herself. Like a successful caricature, she is both immediate and syncretic; like a children's game, she is both obscene and innocent.

Baubo is such an infamous and marginal divinity that her presence seems to debase the noble cycle of Demeter. It is told, in reference to an ancient rite, that a desperate Demeter is wandering the world in search of her abducted daughter when she stops, exhausted, in a modest house after Baubo invites her in and offers her a drink made of barley (the grain consecrated to Demeter). Demeter refuses because she does not want to break her penitential fast. At this point Baubo does an unforeseen thing to console her, a thing that has no equal in Greek mythology: She raises her robe up to her head and shows her naked belly. At that sight, Demeter bursts into peals of laughter, suddenly breaking her mourning and silence.

What does Demeter see? We now know the answer, thanks to archeological finds that have come to light in Asia Minor: amphorae and wine jars that are made in the form of bellies, but that also seem to have faces. The coiled lids seem to be hair, the breasts eyes, the navel the nose, the pubic fold a laughing mouth. In some of these a laughing newborn sticks out from the base, which represents the vagina. The newborn is Iacchus, venerated in the Eleusinian mysteries, whose initiates could not reveal what they had seen. Nevertheless, the feminized amphorae, which are among the scarce ancient artifacts depicting scenes of childbirth, represent infringe-ments upon a powerful prohibition, with clearly pleasurable consequences. The infernal goddess Baubo—both belly and head, female figure and halved member, mother and son—is an extraordinary product of the psychic process that Freud called "condensation."[93] This is a modality of thought that characterizes oneiric formations and witty expressions, and that con-stitutes a stratagem for saying what should be repressed; it permits prohib-ited figures to pass through the barrier that separates the unconscious from the conscious, and to elude the watchfulness of the internal censor.

Baubo appears to be an enigma, and, I think, must remain as such—a coagulation of the visible and the invisible, of body and mind, of container and contained, of pain and joy, of solitude and the capacity to give, of life and death. She is a perennial reminder of the impossibility of reducing maternity to thought, of reducing female generative capacity to social reproduction.

After this long digression in the area of mythology, it is now time to reconstruct the main thread of the discourse. In Chapter 1, the case of Anna permitted us to glimpse the mental anguish that foretells, in the uncon-scious of little girls, their actual future motherhood. We have thus been unable to discover that, in infancy, the feminine identity is linked to the fantasy of generating by oneself the "child of the night," narcissistic fruit of the unconscious omnipotence. Suddenly, however, this imago disappears, leaving in its place an emptiness that leads women to ask the opposite sex for the child they want, behaving, in the encounter, as if they possessed nothing of their own. Paradoxically, the woman arrives at the joining that will make her a mother without being aware of her contribution: incapable of recognizing to the end that the child is at least half fruit of her genetic patrimony, of her physical capacity, of her creative imagination.

Subsequently, the case of Paola shows us that such renunciation is the effect of a conflict with the masculine sex, with the claim of men that they exclusively possess the power to bring other human beings into the world. The conflict, which remains hidden in the institutional culture, reveals itself, however, as we have seen, in the mythopoetic production, and, in particular, in the ancient rites and myths of fertility. These remind us that a defeat that happened at the beginning of history produced the subordi-nation of the mother to the father. This arbitrary act was then rationalized by science, which concealed its elements of violence under the neutral justification of natural necessity. The effects of masculine domination have been particularly serious in that, for centuries, women have carried out the

desires of others, recognizing, in the complementary inferiority, the legitimate position of their sex.

But now things are changing. Women are trying, with intuition,
curiosity, and courage, to recover their own part in the generative process,
to redefine the maternal authority, starting from themselves, from their own
specific imagination. The task is producing new relations between women,
in particular between grandmother, mother, and daughter, as the extraordinary birth diary written by Francesca Grazzini tells us, in Chapter 3.

CHAPTER 3

Exploring Maternity

THE NEED FOR A NEW DISCOURSE

Among the tasks we must urgently confront for the development of humanity is that of describing the adult female experience from the point of females themselves, and especially from the point of view of the female unconscious. In this chapter, I attempt to do this in regard to the experience of maternity. My exploration is a wide-ranging one, covering biological, evolutionary, and historical as well as psychoanalytic perspectives. However, as in the first two chapters, I begin with one female's story—in this case, the experiences of a new mother, Francesca Grazzini.

"That's it: When I think of my desire to be a mother, I think of the adjective 'rhetorical.' In respect to motherhood, I begin to get rhetorical, and I still don't completely understand why. I have to look at myself from a rhetorical vantage point. I had two children. Before them, I thought of myself somehow like the song 'I'm Not Worthy of You.' I mean, I wasn't worthy of my mother's body; I wasn't equal to my own female body. As a child, I felt like a strange fruit of nature, and my defect was that I wasn't like my mother. Her figure was associated, for me, with the idea of beauty and procreative power. My mother knew how to produce bodies. Mine, and then right afterward my brother's and sister's, one after another. I was the first-born, a little monster, a botched attempt at a son who came out wrong. It must have been true

115

if my mother tried again right afterward, first managing to have a little
boy, and then a real girl, and putting me aside to hold them in her arms.
I was always hungry. Hungry for her. My stance toward life was this
terrible hunger. I wanted to be full. Of food. Of children."

Beginning her "birth story"[1] with the term "rhetorical," Francesca
Grazzini clearly expresses the inadequacy of our words and our thinking
to elaborate upon the experience of maternity. They are inadeqate not
only because they don't seem capable of capturing the wealth, the
mutability, and the contradictions of life as it comes into being, but also
because a heavy curtain of pre-existing discourse screens out new expression. Pre-established semantic and lexical constructs keep any possible
definition of its meaning and value shut within impersonal objectivity.
In a certain sense, there are no words for maternity, or at least no
ready-made ones. But if the available discourse finally appears to be
rhetorical, it means that a new awareness is taking shape—an urgency
that produces a schism between what is said and what is felt to be loaded
with possibility. And it is precisely through the adherence to personal
history and the struggle to make meaningful and communicable those
experiences that women believe to be essential to themselves that the
widespread practice of women's consciousness raising has come into
being. They are becoming conscious of their own being and their capacity
to become mothers—not only of bodies, but of social meanings as well.[2]
This practice has revealed the need to construct new horizons of value
and meaning as points of reference, to find a discourse that fosters social
bonding among women without any pretense of supremacy.

FROM MOTHER TO DAUGHTER:
THE SENSE OF DEFICIENCY IN MATERNITY

As always, exploring maternity means first considering the figure of one's
own mother—as Francesca does—and opening up a comparison or a
conflict that hinges on some failing, some lack of vital nutriment. Freud
heard such recriminations in his first cases of hysteria, from patients who
claimed they did not receive sufficient breast milk; he interpreted these
complaints as protests at their having been born female, having been denied
penises. This may well be the way that a woman recognizes her privation
and her desire in a male society. But this does not explain the connection
between her protest and maternity—the conflict between her sense of
deprivation and inadequacy, and her sense that she should be able to carry
out the generative undertaking precisely because she is female. We see
nevertheless, again in Francesca's words, how this conflict remains operant

even when the woman is about to become a mother herself, when all sense of inadequacy should have vanished:

> "Having said that, when I found out I was pregnant, I was walking down a street downtown in a summer dress; I was 'full of grace,' in a state of ecstasy. And it didn't seem possible. I mean, *could* I really? Was there really such a possibility in my flesh and blood? Could my body have managed such a magical task? . . . I was caught there, hovering between being worthy and being unworthy, between the existence and the nonexistence of the shadow of a baby. This meant the life and the death of my woman's body, which was finally reconciled to itself."

"*Could* I really?" This question echoes the one addressed by Marianna to Sandokan in Paola's fantasy (see Chapter 2). The answer—"No, yes; no, you can't, you mustn't, but you can and must"—always sounds ambiguous and contradictory. But who formulates this answer? Who holds the prohibition against reproducing or the permission to reproduce? The unconscious says the mother, but also the person who takes the mother's place as the love object—first the father and then the partner.

We know that the little girl fantasizes giving a baby to her mother, to fill the shadow that has crept between them and that grows menacingly as their separation continues. The gift is meant to console the mother in her mourning; as such, it is meant as reparation. But it is also a means of satisfying the daughter, to the extent that it is eccentric to the subject and always a desire for the other, in a dual sense: the identification with absence and the offer of love. It is as if the little girl were saying to the mother, "Love me, because I have what you want."

The sexual identity that is transmitted by the mother's gaze and confirmed by the imitating perception would seem to authorize her to actively enact that generative act that she once experienced passively.[3] Her hollow body[4] allows her to fantasize herself as a container when she has actually only been contained within the other,[5] except for the consuming of food, which makes the mouth the antecedent of sexual receptivity. Her body provides her with proof, in other ways, of productive power: Saliva, urine, and solid feces come out of her orifices intermittently. So it seems possible to "to make" of that inner mortal clay a puppet, a doll, an offspring to offer the mother who is suffering abandonment, and thus to repair the guilt that every separation carries with it.

But this gift is not seen as part of her own maternal merit, as her implicit request for equivalence with her mother demonstrates. In fact, the mother welcomes the feces that the little girl offers as proof that she has achieved control over her body—as the child's manifest capacity for cleanliness and obedience—but she misunderstands the little girl's pretense of offspring and of the procreative competence that it implies as a symbol of a baby. The daughter thus feels that her gift is misunderstood, yet at the same time she is constrained to play the part of the "good girl," with all the passivity that this carries with it. From this moment on, all she can do is conform to the role that society assigns her, or else rebel against it. However, every rebellious act will be seen in the context of "being a tomboy"—in other words, as a masculine protest, a manifest penis envy. How can she express the fact that she wants to be a different girl? That she wants to be able to recognize her power to produce, to reproduce, to create, before her body is fertile, independent of its physiological capacity? She cannot express this because her own mother is deprived of her power and of her procreative phantasms, believing as she does that she was impregnated by the father, saturated by his (the other's) generative power and competence.

The phallic mother of early childhood is merely a deception of infantile omnipotence—an extreme attempt to deny what she lacks and the consequent "conjugality" of generative sexuality. The first castration figure is always maternal, because the child knows she is deprived herself. Against all evidence, however, the unconscious desire brings back the figure of the omnipotent mother, whom the daughter reproaches for not wanting what she is capable of, but also for not being capable of what she wants. Her fury is not altogether unmotivated if we consider that the mother, as a woman, has lost the awareness of her own part in reproduction; she has blotted out her own generative phantasms and no longer recognizes the procreative force of her own female desire. What every mother in every generation of women is accused of is the historical defeat in the sexual conflict. While the little boy will receive from his father the phallic emblem, and thus procreative power, the little girl is prepared to receive from outside even that which that she already possesses for the reproductive process.

THE SHADOW OF THE OBJECT: THE PHANTASMIC CHILD VERSUS THE REAL CHILD

When the course of the first fantasized maternity is completed, the void (which always presumes a fullness) is transformed into a lack (which always presumes a taking away). But little trace remains of this first feminization. Only myth allows us to glimpse what remains invisible within us. I think what is at work here is the original privation that connects the little girl to her mother and that produces the "hunger" for her that every possible gift will leave unsatisfied. An unending question binds and divides the two women, in that one asks the other for something the other does not possess.

The writer Marguerite Yourcenar captured this gaping void in writing of herself: "I wasn't born for restlessness, but for pain, for the infinite pain of loss."

And it is also because of this nonfulfillment that the little girl turns later to the father to obtain from him the baby she cannot give to her mother. But in this turn to the father, "having it," which is presumed by the prior attempt to give (a baby to the mother), is transformed into "not having it," which is implicit in asking (the father for a baby). It is, once again, a request fated to remain unanswered, prevented by Oedipal prohibitions like the one that has come before it. But in this case, the father's denial is not absolute: It is resolved by the prompting to wait for the child that her husband will give her, in another time and another place.

Already in her first heterosexual relationship, the woman comes up against the misunderstanding that, as Lacan points out, will characterize her relationship with the opposite sex.[6] The girl wishes for her father to confirm her own generative potentiality, to share her dream of maternity, to see her own inner child recognized by him. However, the father only glimpses a lack in her and responds to a request that arises from the realm of the imagination with an answer that arises from the realm of reality. Nevertheless, this precocious infantile desire never completely disappears. It often reappears in the dreams of pregnant women and is made apparent in the joy with which a young mother offers her newborn to her own father, as if to fulfill an old pledge.

The Oedipal law, however, sets the child of man, the social child—reward of a sublimated desire that has denied its own hallucinated object, and of the defused urgency of satisfaction—against the "child of the night," the manifestation of the pleasure principle. The paternal prohibition is confirmed by social and cultural injunctions and their system of promises. As such, it makes the little girl herself its agent, for she is eager to gain social validation for her feminization, as Anna's dream of her own hollowness (see Chapter 1) demonstrates.

Now everything has been prepared for the "second period" of human sexuality during puberty, when the curtain of latency is raised, and erotic and generative desires can be expressed in the practice of mature sexuality. But at this point the asymmetry between the two sexes, between the male who gives life and the female who contains it, is already defined: The girl has lost her weapons and her emblems long ago, in the crossfire of the Oedipal conflict. Her mother has not elected her into the ranks of mothers, has not transmitted the emblems of female power to her; this has allowed the phantasm of the child generated by infantile fantasy, to vanish into thin air, like a premature fetus that lacks identity and name.

The dolls and puppets that have formerly satisfied the little girl's procreative feeling and represented her generative product become frozen in an affective sense and progressively estranged; finally, they become the supports of an idealized ego built upon social expectations and upon stereotypes of mass consciousness. The transition from the warmth of the transitional object to the cold Barbie doll mercilessly characterizes the little girl's detachment from her interior imaginary realm, her surrender to the gaze of the other. The "child of the night" thus remains sequestered in the unconscious, along with the associated desires for autogeneration; Only in dream, in symptom, and (in the best of cases) in artistic creation will it be possible to glimpse the products of its remote existence.

Therefore, the woman approaches actual maternity without any pre-cognition, any prefiguration of expectation, as Francesca's account clearly attests:

> "When I finally arrived at the hospital one night with strong labor pains, and the nurse told me to unpack the outfit for the little girl who was about to be born, I did it reluctantly. As I handed the little outfit to the nurse, it looked to me like a ghostly sheet, which would never be filled with substance."

The woman who approaches the moment of becoming a mother thinks of herself and the coming child in a manner that is inadequate to her body and is the result of the lacking maternal mandate. The empty little outfit, in its immateriality, represents the "child of the night"—that figure of the infantile imagination that has been relegated to the unconscious, where it continues its oneiric life sheltered, like all the contents of the unconscious, from any further elaboration. This figure now stands in opposition to the real child like a rival: The substantiality of the "child of the day" is destined to frustrate the shadows of its nocturnal alter ego. An invisible psychic conflict plays itself out in the labor scene[7]—a conflict that can only be glimpsed in the woman's momentary withdrawals from the generative task, in the little acts of self-distancing that are almost always interpreted as laziness or fear. But the woman herself has no awareness of her reluctance, because the shadow that has given form to her expectation has not entered into her intentional and conscious thought.

Beginning in childhood, the form that female castration takes, in its specific connection to the empty body, is the disappearance of the phan-tasmic child. Freud distinguished between the conscious loss of an ideal object, as in mourning, and the unconscious loss of a phantasmic object, as in melancholy: "In mourning it is the world which has become poor and empty; in melancholia it is the ego itself"[8] To the extent that the woman's ego is identified with the imaginary child (nor can it be otherwise, given the enormous narcissistic investment), it will remain indelibly marked by the separation from the child. "The shadow of the object," Freud observed, "fell upon the ego, and the latter could henceforth, be judged by a special agency, as though it were an object."[9]

The lacking recognition of the phantasmic baby, the demand that it remain beyond the threshold of the mind, has made gestation a blind process. Again Francesca's description makes this clear: "To 'feel' the inhabitant of my womb more than I did—I couldn't do it. There was nothing more than my intestines, my stomach, my kidneys." Only her mother, in fact, knew how to manufacture bodies; only she possessed the creative power. But she could not transmit this to her daughter, who was now waiting to receive from the outside, from the hands of the nurse or doctor, what she actually possessed within herself. Francesca notes that she tried several means of grasping this elusive knowledge and power, but failed:

> "I tried meditation and training, which I never considered only techniques for labor, for a path into myself. I would have liked to see myself within, to develop not five internal senses, but one acute, essential that could synthesize like an intense love pang, that could apprehend *what* was happening. I couldn't do it. I couldn't grasp . . . what? I couldn't grasp that *what*."

A gaping chasm seems to separate the pregnant woman from her child—so near her that it is confused with her own body, so far as to appear unnamable to her. Only the violent impact of labor can break the glass walls that seem to divide them. Francesca's account of her own labor depicts this graphically:

> "The pain doesn't let up. I am afraid. I'm overtaken by panic. I'm burying the 'thing' inside this endless pain. The thing dies. I die. What confusion; it was supposed to be a birth, and it's a death. They say that my belly is contracting. I can't feel anything, I can't react. I push with all my strength against my self. I explode. The pain is horrible, they've cut me. It's not a horrible pain; why does it feel like it is? The baby (a girl) is already out. So fast. It's simple. It's terrible. I don't want to have any more children. Don't put her on my stomach. Yes, put her on my stomach now, please. She's on my stomach; she's covered with blood and a white coating, She slides up, toward my breasts. What does she want, to eat? After all that struggle? She's a monster. She's going to sap all my energy. She's beautiful, and I'm happy."

Francesca Grazzini is able to communicate clearly the turmoil of the disassociated, and sometimes contradictory, sensations that characterize the experience of labor and that make it so anxiety-producing, as well as the cathartic resolution that ends it. Mother and daughter are now two women, and from the very first moment in which they face and recognize each other, they reproduce, in inverse form, the same plea of incorporation and the same reaction of moving away that has bound and divided the preceding generation. Whereas Francesca has said of her own relationship with her mother, "I was always hungry. Hungry for her. My stance toward life was this terrible hunger." Now, looking at her daughter, she thinks: "She's a monster. She's going to sap all my energy." What the little girl asks for, as the mother once did, is to be recognized for her own identity, to emerge from the mortal condition of "thing" to be filled with the vital flow that milk represents. However, the identity that will be assigned her is the one that awaits all little girls: She will be considered a sterile individual, of the female sex.

The woman attributes the status of daughter to her newborn girl but not that of mother, because no female genealogy based on maternal right exists. The energy that the little girl, this devouring little girl, demands will be neutralized in such a way that she will never have any sexual representation that she can recognize as her own. I do not know whether it is possible for a mother to transmit something that she herself has never received: generative power, the awareness of self that includes a prefiguration of the child within, who alone can bring the woman to fecundity, bearing as she does her gifts of capacities and powers. Rather, what the woman perceives is an empty sense of self, like an ancient jar that, even with its protuberences, *mastoi*, breasts, represents the female body.[10]

HUMAN VERSUS ANIMAL
MATERNAL COMPETENCE

If we observe women in their actual experience of maternity (gestation, delivery, breast feeding, early maternal care), we can only be stunned by their radical lack of skill. Everything must be learned. First of all, in the majority of cases, the moment of fertilization passes unnoticed. Only a few women attest to having had a vague awareness that something extraordinary, something beyond the range of normal physiological processes, was happening inside them. Such women describe the experiences as an occurrence beyond their will, a sudden burst of impersonal vitality, a violence that came from "elsewhere" (as in the experience of something sacred).

Although the psyche registers all physiological occurrences on the unconscious level, fertilization is not registered, except in a few rare cases such as those noted above. This experience remains relegated to the unknown, allowing the gestation process to proceed without any corresponding thought. In other mammals, fertilization is immediately recognized, and the female becomes unavailable for mating. For humans, the first signal consists of the cessation of menstruation; however, since this is an ambiguous sign, the phenomenon is not reliable. At this point a woman relies on the doctor or on a home pregnancy test, so that, paradoxically, she asks a modern soothsayer what is happening within herself. In the absence of vital signs, a chemical sign comes to the rescue: A color, a geometric shape, tells the woman of an occurrence that can alter or overturn the course of her life. The Angel Gabriel, announcing the Virgin Mary's impending motherhood, has been replaced by the index of a positive or negative chemical reaction, a commercial product of the pharmaceutical industry. In both cases, however—both in the Christian tradition and in everyday reality—the awareness of the woman's state seems to arrive from the outside and to invest a thought that is apparently unconnected to the body. Thus, in many ways, psychic gestation and physical gestation proceed separately.

Now and again, we hear of sensational cases of women (for the most part, very young women) who give birth claiming that they didn't even know they were pregnant. In their experience, no gestation precedes the birth. Usually these are girls who are still dependent on their parents, and for whom a pregnancy represents an undesirable and dangerous occurrence, a trauma they cannot face. A repression is then set off, particularly concerning external changes (because the internal ones remain unnoticed by many women, even though they know what is happening). It takes only a somewhat greater repression for the vital process of gestation to proceed completely unacknowledged, isolated by the hiatus that separates the mind from the body.

But even more interesting to me than these unconscious gestations is the psychic work that each woman undertakes to reconnect thought to a vital dynamic that takes its course inside of her, through her body, but without requiring her consensus and deliberate participation. From the very first moment, the empty silhouette of the imaginary child of early childhood—which is later blotted out by the amnesia that accompanies its ending—is reactivated. The figures created in childhood and adolescent reverie, only to be abandoned like old dolls in a corner of memory, are now projected upon the adult woman's mind. These now must become integrated in a single image and must be internalized, so that they are identified with the fetus's movements, its formless "fluttering." But the woman must also fill the emptiness of her expectation, prefigure the guest who will arrive in the house, and prepare her own partner to welcome him. It is often the case that the future father has many more plans of a specific, reality-based nature than the mother, who is more involved in this imaginary elaboration of expectation.

Many of the disturbances of pregnancy that have no physiological basis can be traced to the gap between the psychic and the corporeal—the conflict created by two processes that occur within the same organism, but that follow different time frames and forms of logic. To judge by the dreams of gestating women, it seems that the imagination reacts in a delayed fashion to physiology and is incapable of adapting to physiological timing. Dreams that the layette is not prepared in time (so that the child cannot be wrapped in the appropriate clothes and remains cold and naked), or that there aren't enough little outfits or they're the wrong ones, are common.

Indeed, the layette is an element that has powerful imaginative and emotional content. In some ways, it informs the maternal imaginary and prefigures of the newborn. It is amusing to see the differences among the various layettes in mothers' suitcases at a maternity ward or clinic, in anticipation of the "happy event." Some mothers have prepared the tiniest garments; others have brought outfits for a year-old child, in which a newborn would be swallowed up. Little silk shirts and woolen sweaters are mixed together for the same season. Brilliant colors and bold patterns clash with all-white or pastel-colored clothes. The ghostly sheet that Francesca mentions has as many shapes and sizes as there are mothers and the images that accompany their waiting.

The animal's competence in giving birth presents a sharp contrast to the human's incompetence. When a cat is near labor, for example, she prepares the bed that will accommodate the litter; she knows exactly what she is doing and does not err in either direction, shortage or excess. Even if she has had no previous experience or is completely isolated from her own kind, she reacts competently and efficiently, directed by a precognition of the newborn kittens that leaves no margin for the indecision of fantasy.

But the human female's lack of preparation for the generative task is never as apparent as during labor. The most sophisticated preparation courses do not succeed in preventing moments of complete bewilderment and annihilating anxiety. Sometimes it seems that the laboring woman does not know what is happening to her or what she should do. For this reason, the figure of the obstetrician is psychologically irreplaceable: Unlike the doctor, the obstetrician identifies with the woman to the point that, notwithstanding her competence, he can identify also with the woman who is totally unexperienced. Nevertheless, in the body-to-body struggle of labor, in the violence of the pushing stage, the newborn imposes his or her bodily identity: The infant's weight, pressure, and movements announce his or her impending "arrival in the real world."

Between these two bodies that were initially joined in a morphological and functional enmeshment that has no analogy, an intentional proximity is now established. But in comparison to an animal's precision and efficiency, a new human mother's gestures often end up being timorous and clumsy. The newborn must be recognized as a son or daughter, despite a basic otherness; he or she must become someone "other" than the phantasm that has animated gestation, his or her nocturnal double. The "recognition" scene, the cathartic moment in classical tragedy, repeats this fundamental event in each individual's life because the audience derives pleasure from thus being reassured.

The first mother–child interactions, which are so undervalued by everyone from hospital assistants to the new mother herself actually structure the relationship of the new couple. The physiological mechanisms of gestation are replaced by intentional maternal behaviors. The expression of intentionality is shaped by the imitation of the woman's own mother, as well as by the internalized image. It is therefore affected by unresolved conflicts and by distant emotional tensions, which can only be resolved in communicative interaction with the baby.

The importance of labor in allowing the mother to recognize her child in the baby as he or she is is indirectly confirmed by the greater degree of difficulty that women who undergo Caesarian births face. From my own continuing observations,[11] it appears that these women experience a greater degree of hesitation in synchronizing themselves with the needs of their infants and in establishing an intimate connection to them. This difficulty has numerous causes: the passivity imposed by any surgical intervention; the absence created by anesthesia; and the postpartum suffering, which appears to be useless. Lacking a concrete signal of interruption, the unconscious pregnancy sustains its imaginary existence with its phantasm of a baby. A fantasy of the gestation, the remote echo of an unfinished task, wanders through the body of the woman who has undergone a Caesarian. However, it takes only several days of maternal care before the real child takes his or her place in the arms and thoughts of the mother. The physical exchange that occurs between the two bodies, as in the process of breast feeding, establishes emotional contact with much greater fluidity than any outside intervention could. Nonetheless, the "nonbirthed" baby (which is perceived as a charm, like the childhood presents of Christmas) tends to be particularly receptive to the idealized projections of the mother—the narcissistic love that no actual birth can impinge upon.

For some time, I have had the opportunity to observe the initial nursing attempts of first-time mothers in a maternity ward. Almost none spontaneously assume the posture that favors the flow of milk, or find the position that the sucking infant should be in. All this must be taught, but it is a particular kind of teaching, full of sporadic questions, silent waiting, and wary yet trusting glances. It does not take long, however, for the ancient competence to be reactivated—one that has been forgotten but that is still available to be reappropriated, as in the remembrance of forms that Plato described in the "Meno." Considering that nursing requires synchrony, the initial dissonance between these two beings who have lived in unison up until a few hours earlier is astonishing. Yet their existential distance is rapidly filled by a gift of feeling, a communicative emotion that has the gratuitous and pleasing grace of artistic creation. Nevertheless, the attitudes of young mothers remain extremely varied, for they never conform to a single behavior.

A vaguely impersonal homogeneity of instinctual behavior prevails between female mammals and their young—a harmonious program that seems to carry on the process of gestation outside the body and to be continuous with it. For the human female, on the other hand, the dissociation between the imaginary baby and the real baby, between fantasy and life, has the result that the child that is born never coincides completely with the expectation. The appearance of the baby at birth means the evanescence of his or her nocturnal double, with the inevitable effects of melancholia.

The frequent occurrence of postpartum depression in new mothers, even when it is minor, appears to be a paradoxical event: After all, the baby's birth constitutes the end of a long wait, the defeat of anxieties related to possible sterility and inadequacy, and participation in maternal power. But instead, the sensation of triumph appears to be veiled by a feeling of loss that can only be understood as the consequence of the ancient filial imago's disappearance. The experience of having lost a familiar mental presence is less intense when the newborn is fragile, handicapped, or sick, as if its incompleteness could prolong the oneiric work, the persistence of its surreal figures. A feeling of continuity and contiguity with the imaginary baby in the mother's unconscious corresponds to the feeling of disappointment caused by the reality principle and social demands. The unconscious favoring of the disadvantaged child is well represented by fairy tales, where often (e.g., as in the story of Thumbelina) the child who is not as well endowed physically is also the one who is more highly prized and loved, the only one who knows the path that leads to the maternal home.

When postpartum depression turns into a genuine syndrome, this can be attributed to the newborn's inability to fill with his or her presence the void left by the imaginary double, so that the melancholia takes on the violence of overwhelming mourning. A mother's recognition of her off-spring as her own son or daughter seems to be made difficult or impossible by the lack of an identifying mark that permits her to say, "This is it!" In spite of the long period of cohabitation, the two bodies remain divided by an estrangement without figures; in extreme cases, only death can overcome this estrangement, obliterating the emptiness with nothingness. For this reason, the combined act of infanticide and suicide, which in a very few instances is the result of the most acute form of this depressive syndrome, is experienced by the mother as a supreme gesture of love—as the inevitable conclusion of the procreative course that cannot be realized.

For this reason, she withdraws into herself in the desperate attempt to connect the real baby to its shadow.

Without making generalizations about these extremely rare cases, we must nevertheless admit that there is some conflictual and unresolved element of maternity that goes beyond the biography of each individual woman, as well as beyond the history of women—something that evokes the realm of human evolution. I believe that the key to this enigma must be searched for in the unconscious of little girls, in the cultural imagination, and in the transformations of the human species, rather than in the behavior of women. In the next section, I turn to an evolutionary perspective in order to explore this enigma further.

THE LOSS OF ESTRUS: POSSIBLE CAUSES, POTENTIAL CONSEQUENCES

If we categorize human maternity among other natural behaviors, we lose a sense of its social and cultural functions, and reduce the historical and anthropological variety of its instances to a single paradigm. This has the effect of transforming an empty general formula into a binding moral and legal norm, in that what is natural is set forth as universal and necessary. But if we consider it as one of our many socially induced behaviors, we misunderstand its rootedness in the body, in the imagination, in the impersonality and atemporality of the unconscious. Rather, maternity is located in a pivotal position between what we presume to be natural and the historical placement of its agents—between the preverbal substratum and discursive formations.

In the psychological realm as well, maternity occupies an intermediate position between what is inside and outside—between elements of autarchy and narcissism that support the the autonomy of the ego and the relational function of the self. Despite every fantasy of self-sufficiency, every dream of "self-generation," fertilization is always the outcome of a relationship between two parties, even when it is limited to the meeting of gametes (as in artificial insemination). For this reason, after examining maternity as an autonomous psychological construct, we must reconnect it to the sexuality to which it is so closely interwoven, as Anna's case has shown. But the coordination between maternity and sexuality is not guaranteed for us as it is for animals, because an event took place in prehistory to dissociate them. We are still feeling the destabilizing effects.

In order to pinpoint it, we must adopt the viewpoint of Darwinian evolution, which forces us to recognize ourselves as part of the animal kingdom—as humbling as this may be to us, in our narcissism[12]—and subject to the same processes that control the evolution of other species.

Basic among these is instinct, which spurs individuals to ensure the survival of their genetic message through the impulse to increase the number of births, and thus the probability that their offspring will survive.

Sexual selection occurs as a result of two processes: the choice of the female by the male, and the battle among males for power over females. This competition is determined by the scarcity of ova in comparison to the abundance of sperm, as well as by the relatively modest investment that the male makes each time he mates; for this reason, it is advantageous for him to copulate with as many females as he can. On the other hand, the females do not increase their reproductive success by copulating with many males, but rather by mating with the right males. Within the two sexes, the competition is much stronger among males than among females and is the principal cause of violence within the group.

For most of the year nonhuman animals refrain from sexual behavior, so that copulatory activity is of a sporadic rather than a continuous nature. Only human beings copulate regularly during periods in which conception is impossible. The "intemperance" that characterizes humans has been culturally perceived as an infraction of the natural order. In his *Natural History*, Pliny wrote: "Only man has a sense of remorse after his first coupling, which is evidently a sign that life has an origin that one must repent of. If for the other animals there are fixed seasons each year for reproduction, in man this can happen at any hour of the day or night; if other animals are satiated when they mate, man is hardly satiated at all."[13]

But whereas adult human males, to the extent that they are always fecund and potent, behave like the males of other species, human females actually appear to be unique in their sexual profile. For this reason, most evolutionary hypotheses are based upon the modifications that came about in female sexuality, particularly the loss of estrus.[14] There are various components of estrus: the hormonal changes that determine the fertile phase; the morphological changes, such as the swelling and reddening of the genital area (which provide visual cues for males); the production of pheromones (which produce an olfactory stimulus); and, finally, behavioral changes.

The conduct of nonhuman mammals during the course of estrus is characterized by attractiveness, procreativeness, and receptiveness. Attractiveness consists of the sexual stimulation the female provokes in the male; the procreativeness is the activity the female undertakes to initiate and favor mating; finally, receptiveness consists of positioning herself so that copulation causes fertilization. All these functions are favored by a high level of estrogens, whereas the procreativeness also seems to be brought about by a high level of androgens. Estrus lasts for a relatively short period of time, which usually, but not always, coincides with a brief fertile period.

If fertilization occurs, estrus is interrupted for a time until after the birth of the young, or at most as long as the animal is lactating.

According to anthropologist Donald Symonds, since the widespread occurrence of estrus leaves no doubt that it was part of the original condition of mammals, it is likely that at a certain point our female ancestors were suddenly deprived of this condition.[15] For this reason, unlike the females of other species, human females do not "publicize" their fertile periods. The single observable event that signals their reproductive cycle is menstruation. The preovulatory increase of estrogens, however, is not accompanied by more intense desire or by an increased attraction to males. Unlike that of all other mammals, the sexual conduct of human beings has become independent of hormonal control, in that the female is always receptive.

It was upon this observation that Pliny "scientifically" based the Aristotelian belief in female "excess" and thus continued:

> Messalina, wife of the Emperor Claudius, thinking that this would have been the trophy of a regal triumph, chose a girl who was most famous of all the prostitutes for a competition and defeated her, making love twenty-five times in twenty-four hours. In the human species, males have devised ways to enjoy the pleasure of love, all of them the fruit of violence to nature; women, instead, have invented abortion. In this area, we are more guilty than the beasts.[16]

It is interesting to observe that for men this degeneracy is located in the realm of sexuality, while for women it is located in the category of maternity. In the name of civilization, ancient women were accused of lasciviouness and modern women are accused of frigidity, but in both cases they have been found guilty of an "intemperate" sexuality, whether excessive or lacking.

Symonds notes that barren sexual relationships that occur outside the estrous cycle have been observedions among diverse animal species, but these generally appear in conditions of captivity. It is not impossible that such phenomena are among the artifacts of captivity, as is the stereotypical ambulatory behavior (pacing back and forth) displayed by predatory mammals after a certain period of captivity. Symonds's observation (which is validated by experimental studies) seems to me of great interest because it indirectly connects the loss of estrus with the domestication of women—that is, with their segregation within the house and with the conjugal control of their sexuality. The range of conjectures advanced to explain this unforeseen event is quite broad, and the underlying ideological assumptions are decisive, as the discrepancy between the reformulations proposed by androcentric and feminist theorists suggest.

Some explanations have emphasized the socially unifying role that sexuality may have played; that is, the females' availability for coitus would have increased the group's cohesion. This hypothesis is refuted by the existence of highly developed social organizations among primates who only mate during brief reproductive periods. Others emphasize that the females' sexual availability may have been aimed not so much at socialization in general, but at sustaining the bond of the pair, which would have been cemented by the reciprocal gratification of the partners. The slow development of human young would have required the permanent association of parents, which, it is thought, the evolution of the "sexual bond" would have promoted.

Among the most "popular" hypotheses, the best-known is that of Desmond Morris,[17] according to whom the primordial human group was the nuclear family. In his view, the male hunter had to be induced to carry the catch back home rather than eating it all by himself (as his primate ancestors would have done), "because home is where he would have found the little woman who was constantly receptive to his sexual attentions."[18] As has been repeatedly observed, in this case the model of the modern nuclear family has been mistakenly applied to the primitive form of social organization. Yet another scenario has recently been proposed by C. Owen Lovejoy,[19] who after analyzing the fossil remains of "Lucy" (an early hominid female discovered in Africa in the 1970s) has linked bipedalism to the loss of estrus, dating both events back four million years. Since an erect position would have rendered the morphological signals of estrus invisible and the olfactory stimuli imperceptible, they would have had to be replaced by other "systems of stimuli" (e.g., hair, skin, and anatomical forms), which were equally arousing and, more importantly, could be continually activated. Thus a "natural" stimulating function has been attributed to those features of the female body that are culturally valued for other reasons.

A rather different explanation has been proposed by the sociobiologist Sara Hrdy,[20] who has countered the theories of the couple's bind, maintaining that the female's sexual availability would mainly have increased the likelihood of her own reproductive success, the possibility of transmitting her own genes. In Hrdy's view, after a male had sexual relations with a female, he would be induced quite often to save the young that he would have otherwise overlooked when the territory was claimed. Her position stands in opposition to the androcentric explanations described up to this point, but suffers from the same individualistic vision of evolution.

A scenario that is quite different, in that it emphasizes the group rather than the individual or the reproductive couple and attributes an active role to females, has been proposed by the anthropologists Nancy Tanner and Adrienne Zihlman.[21] They ascribe the loss of estrus to the numerous changes that would have been produced in the transition from an economy based on hunting and gathering to one based on agriculture. The work of the new economy would at first have been done by females, and only later would have been shared by males and enlarged upon by the construction of tools. In this scheme, the new mode of production would have required a cooperative modality of work and of the distribution of resources; this would have included the joint raising of offspring, which tends to promote the transmission of learned skills. The need to control the environment; to recognize the seasons, animals, and plants; and to make tools for the gathering and transport of food would have caused decisive changes in the codes of communication, favoring those symbolic exchanges that would prove to be the principal adaptive resources of the human species. In this scenario, the loss of estrus would have allowed for a flexible sexual relationship and the possibility for the female to select her own partners. It thus would have permitted her to become an active agent of evolution rather than a passive one, if not eventually to shrink from coitus.

The sexual exchange, thus disconnected from reproductive ends, constitutes a formidable tool for social communication, as the cosmological meanings attributed to copulation demonstrate. Removed from natural rhythms, regulated by the norms of the group, sexuality has become a powerful element of social unity and cultural transmission. Although the loss of the signals of estrus as erotic stimuli has permitted a great variety of sexual behaviors, it has also resulted in the prevalence of conventional signals.[22] In a certain sense, the culturalization of sexuality constitutes what is natural to the human species, because it is part of our biological inheritance, of our particular mode of adaptation.[23]

MANKIND'S WOMAN: CULTURAL CONTROL OF SEXUALITY AND FERTILITY

The inquiry into the loss of estrus in human females has led us all the way back to the line that separates human beings from the animals—exiling them forever from the economy of nature, to which they nevertheless belong, as their "mortal nature" demonstrates. The sudden slackening in humans of the hormonal mechanisms that regulate mating in other mammals constitutes a "biological movement" that is difficult to reconstruct in terms of ends, but may be easier to understand (although difficult to appraise) in terms of its effects. There is no doubt that sexuality without estrus has freed women from the laws that regulate the fertility of other species, from a single determining factor. Released from the control of the ovular cycle, female sexuality is theoretically open to all expression—flexible, responsive to a woman's own body, synchronized with the time and mode of her own desire. This seems to our eyes to constitute an unforeseen possibility. In allowing infertile coitus, the loss of estrus has opened up the possibility of the manifestation of nongenerative sexuality—of those erotic expressions aimed exclusively at pleasure, at creativity, at exchange, and at play, all of which we usually label as immature.

But these potential elements of liberty and autonomy, of a cultural elaboration of libidinal energies, have never been realized and have never become a part of our history, because the civilization of man has always connected female sexuality with the capacity to engender. The period of "hetaerism" (in which sexual relationships would have taken place on the basis of the natural law of promiscuity) assumed in Bachofen's *Matriarcato* never existed, except as a utopian vision of the past, because our history cannot be separated from the domestication of women.[24] Likewise, there is no historic documentation of a society of female law, which would actually constitute patriarchy's logical precedent. It was in this sense that Engels evoked the "great defeat" that would have preceded male acquisition of power and female's submission.[25]

Among the enduring mechanisms set up to control human sexuality in general and female sexuality in particular, the institution of marriage as the basis for the family occupies a central position. "Family" is used here in the sense defined by Lévi-Strauss as "the more or less lasting union and socially approved union of a man, a woman and their own children."[26] F. Hertier lists a wide range of family structures and then comments: "Nevertheless, even if the monogamous conjugal mode with the common residence of relatives is certainly the most common, the extreme variety of rules which contribute to the family's formation, its makeup and survival, shows that it is not—in its particular modalities—a fact of nature; on the contrary, it is a truly artificial phenomenon, a construct, and thus, a cultural phenomenon."[27] Nevertheless, matrimony has come to be considered as the "privileged locus of biological reproduction."

As far as female sexuality is concerned, marriage, in whatever form it assumes, constitutes an attempt of control aimed at reproduction. The order of conjugality makes a woman unavailable to the threatening promiscuity of exchanges and to the license of pleasures. The woman passes, then, without any possible continuity, from the natural control of estrus to social regulation—from one form of control to another. When we speak of the "control" of reproduction, we generally think of interventions intended to limit fertility, forgetting that these represent only one particular instance of such control and that the first and principal preoccupation of man has been to *maximize* the fertility of the female body. The most ancient votive statues—dedicated to the Great Mothers, divinities whose maternal attributes were greatly emphasized—reveal this. Manipulations that aided fertilization became necessary, as anthropologist Paola Tibet notes, because of the relative infertility of the human species. In comparison to those of other mammals, our chances for fertile coitus are decidedly scarce. Because each month only one ovum (or two at the most) comes to maturation and there is no synchronization between fertility and desire, nothing signals the existence of the fertile period; the menstrual cycles are often irregular and sometimes anovulatory, and in any case, only continue for a limited period in the female's lifetime. The influence that higher psychic functions exert on the other systems also provokes momentary or permanent disturbances of the reproductive process. Conception occurs through the casual correspondence between an ovulatory cycle and a sexual calendar. The most effective way to reduce this element of chance is for a woman to submit to more frequent and regular intercourse, which is to say maximal exposure to fertilization.[28] This is a condition that can be best realized in marriage—a pivotal element between the natural arrangement and the social organization of man.

By controlling the mother, a man is assured maximal biological productivity and the possession of his children; through his children, he is guaranteed the safeguarding of his patrimony and the continuation of his spirit. Franca Basaglia Ongaro writes:

> When the nomad stops to cultivate the earth and, shaping his first tools, takes possession of it, inequality and submission are already confirmed: women and earth are subjected to the designs of man. . . . Their parts are already marked: the different, troubling, and autonomous realm represented by woman is no longer fearful once it is confined within the walls of the house, invalidated by a force that appropriates it, defining its nature and its borders. The woman becomes everything which will be shut within these walls, and her history is that of a body enclosed within a property and invalidated by a guardian.[29]

However, marriage alone is not sufficient to reap the maximum profit and control of female reproductive potential; a complex and flexible apparatus of ideological pressure is also necessary to exert both physical and psychic constrictions, leaving sexuality no natural margins and molding its every phase. Injunctions aimed at directing sexuality into conjugal coitus are enforced in every society, even if they take extremely varied forms. To this end, rites of initiation, marriage, and fertility (which often include injury and mutilation) are utilized, as well as threats and physical violence against those women who outwardly rebel against legalized rape.

In Western society, an intermediate form of female upbringing prevails, based on the ideology of maternity as a woman's single goal and of obedience as a wife's greatest quality. "The conjugal duty," a structuring moral and legal obligation, is supported by an extensive system of economic pressures along with psychological injunctions—which, to a greater extent than one might believe, include threat and rape. This does not mean that marriage cannot create harmony between the spouses' sexuality and fertility; it does mean that these are subjected to a social demand so pressing as to leave the couple little room for freedom and spontaneity. For centuries a woman was denied any control of her own fertility, left her in ignorance of whatever gynecological knowledge had been gained by medicine, and forbidden to use methods of birth control. Moreover, the man was given exclusive control over the possibility of infanticide—a eugenic form of population control frequently employed in the ancient world.

Childbirth, then, represents a moment that is too important in its symbolic and social significance to be left in the hands of women.[30] The crucial function that this fact plays in social reproduction reduces the margins of childbirth's privacy and intimacy. With the transition from home births to hospital births in the last century, labor, which is divided into stages, has been subjected to a rigid ritualization of postures, positions, time frames, and responses—all of which exclude all possibility of spontaneity in the experience. Childbirth is thus equated, as much as possible, with the industrial production of merchandise.[31]

This alienation of the birth process from women has been facilitated by two fundamental aspects of patriarchal culture: the devaluation of the natural, bodily, and material elements of maternity, and the corresponding privileging of the symbolic elements of paternity and rebirth. This devaluation and privileging are represented by the ceremony of the newborn's integration into the community and the imposition of the father's name.

Aside from the direct ways of controlling fertility, there are also indirect modalities—for example, the variations of marriage age, the celebration of celibacy and virginity, and numerous prohibitions of a religious nature against intercourse. On the other hand, a practice that is specifically aimed at maximizing the female's fertility and eradicating the postpartum "dead period" is the interruption of maternal breast feeding, which speeds up the recurrence of the menstrual cycle and makes the woman fertile again. In this sense, the institutionalization of wet-nursing, limited in the eighteenth century to aristocratic families but widespread in the following century among the middle class, constituted one artificially induced form of increasing female fecundity. This was not an absolute increase, because there was always a quota of women who subordinated fecundity to nursing, but only an increase among those belonging to the socially and economically stronger classes. Since wet-nursing carried with it a higher rate of infant mortality, a vicious cycle between the number of births and newborn deaths was established, and women and children of the last two centuries fell victim to the practice.[32]

Historically, the social control of fertility has been aimed at increasing the number of births, while interventions aimed at birth control, condemned by secular and religious morality, have remained relegated to the clandestine and ambiguous practices of midwives. It was only in the middle of the nineteenth century that restrictive birth control, practiced mainly through the interruption of sexual relations, become socially widespread and culturally recognized. In fact, Freud listed it among the principal causes of neurosis.[32a] Now birth control plays such an important role in a couple's and particularly in a woman's sexuality, and represents an ethical and legal problem of such consequence, that we forget that the imposition of reproduction is one of the structural aims of marriage. Although few incidences of sexual intercourse cause fertilization to occur even in the lifetime of the most prolific woman, her sexuality has been connected to maternity. In fact, it has been believed that only her maternal function could justify her concession to desire, to physicality and its pleasures, which for her are otherwise indecent and inopportune. The idealization and the glorification of the maternal role carries, as a counterpoint, the repression of other female potentials—those connected with nonreproductive sexuality.

The certain existence of a sterile sexuality that tends to be undefined, erratic, and anarchic has been seen as a residue that is socially controllable through a series of mechanisms, among them the division of women. In this regard, I must quote the words of Demosthene (*Against Neaera*): "We have courtesans for pleasure, concubines for the daily care [of the body], and wives to have legitimate sons and to be the faithful guardians of our house."[33] This was an emblematic subdivision, which the ancient world enlarged upon through a minute series of ritual codes and behavioral prescriptions.[34]

It is evident that a woman's social position was and still is not autonomous, but dependent upon her relationship to a man. While the bride is prepared for reproductive sexuality and finds her place in the conjugal house, the others—who exercise sterile sex, subordinated to economic gain, pleasure, and play—move in the promiscuity of extradomestic realms. A man is permitted to exercise his sexuality at both levels and to pass from one to the other.[35] Women find themselves ascribed by birth to the ranks of wives or prostitutes, and only with great difficulty can they escape this iron-clad system of determination. In both cases, sexual experience remains partial, and the possibility of self-representation is precluded by social rules.

But in the logic of exchange, it is not only women who are divided into categories of hierarchical value; a second type of division runs through the various stages of life. Although it is conceivable that a young girl might experience an erotic sexuality before puberty, marriage signals the prevalence of reproductive sexuality. The girl is the object of male desire, but not the bride, for whom marital intercourse represents an order to perform the work of reproduction. In traditional societies, the female body is so weakened and damaged by the uninterrupted cycle of pregnancies and childbirths—made so "physiologically ill"—that Shorter translates the condition of "economic misery" that Mare attributed to the proletariat into woman's "biological misery."[36]

The most revealing aspect of this second division is the way that the rearing of daughters has imposed the opposition between sexuality and maternity. Up until a generation or two ago (and in some milieus even today), a mother forced her daughter to remain virginal by portraying the dangerous prospect of premarital pregnancy. In fact, such an event would have cast the girl into shame and and discredit, relegating her to the socially shameful position of "child mother." Any possible desire she might have to be a mother was felt to be dangerous and quickly repressed, only to be reactivated in a passive form later in the context of marriage, where it was principally a question of giving her husband a child. It is interesting to note, as we will see more clearly later, that a girl's first encounter with sexuality and maternity took the form of guilt and punishment, and the agent of this intimidation was the mother herself. Thus the hostile elements that opposed her in childhood were confirmed and would be reactivated during her first pregnancy, when regressive processes re-established the old rapport of affective dependence.

If society has traditionally connected female sexuality to maternity, it has done so in a selective fashion as far as women are concerned (only for wives), and also in a limiting fashion as far as the stages of life are concerned (not for little or young girls). The woman has had to deny any desire for maternity that appeared premature in respect to the conjugal state—to identify with a body sealed in virginal integrity, only later to confront the horror of rape at the moment of coitus. Her conjugal sexuality finds its one legitimate source of desire in what Francoise Dolto calls the "fertilization drive,"[37] but only provided that it is passive and conforms to the timing and modes of marital desire. Sexual complementarity is reawakened in marriage by a whole series of reciprocal services, based upon socially induced inabilities that seal the woman's subordination in her role of wife and mother.[38] The matrimonial mechanism functions, therefore, to regulate sexuality, especially female sexuality. Its injunctions are rendered invisible, however, by the presumed "natural" basis of her tasks. As F. Hertier writes:

> If there is a cultural characteristic that is truly universal, this is the ethnocentric certainty, shared by all the members of a human group, that their institutions are laws of nature and therefore almost automatic, and that, consequently, there cannot be any others. Our own civilization escapes this rule even less as it covers a great part of the world, includes millions of individuals, and spurred on by its own weight, by the force of its arms, by religion and by commerce, has succeeded in imposing its certainties on the peoples on whom its shadow fell.[39]

Reducing female sexual potential to a single goal of maternity, as our civilization has done, has meant that we have elaborated an extensive imaginary, obliterating instinctive figures and superimposing other images.

For this reason, we must work from the loss of these natural configurations to recover "an archeology of the female imagination." The figures of this archive will then appear to be "constructs," aimed at compensating for the blindness of instinct that characterizes the human animal. The constructs will be elaborated out of the tension in the conflict between the sexes, as this conflict is acted out in the actual family structure and in the internalized form that we call the Oedipus complex.

It is mankind's woman who fantasizes a child all her own, only later to obliterate this child and hide his or her shadow in the unconscious. It is mankind's woman who carries out maternity as if it were a conjugal duty, who hands her newborn over to the father's authority, who denies her daughter the generative power she herself lacks, who does not recognize the symbolic potential of her knowledge of "bringing into the world." However, at least in recent years, it is a different woman who has come to know herself again, to name herself, to redefine herself—and who, in attempting to redefine herself, has bent language in order to create new realities.

THE INCREASING DISCOMFORT OF MOTHERHOOD

For centuries women saw themselves in the figure of the mother and absorbed the idealization of this role as a dutiful homage to their own functions; they were admirably responsive to the ends of nature (as these were portrayed) and of society. But slowly, suspicion has been aroused, and the preconstituted harmony has been transformed into conflict and discomfort. The psychoanalyst Marie Langer writes:

> Once society imposed severe sexual (in the narrowest sense of the term) and social restrictions on women, but favored the development of maternal activity and function. The consequences of these restrictions were the great frequency of hysteria and of other psychoneurotic manifestations in women. Nevertheless, they seemed to have suffered from relatively few psychosomatic disturbances in her procreative functions. At present the landscape has changed. In the last century, the woman of our civilization has acquired a sexual and social freedom completely unheard of only three generations ago. The present circumstances impose rather grave restrictions upon maternity. As a consequence the typical neurotic manifestations (the great hysteria) have diminished, but psychosomatic disturbances of the reproductive functions, a symptom of the latent conflict between maternity and femininity, have increased.[40]

The change of woman's position in our society is not a sudden and unmotivated occurrence; rather, it is the outcome of historical movements of some duration. Marie Langer correctly cites the French Revolution—in particular, the declaration of equality based on the common nature of all human beings—as the beginning. Whereas nature was traditionally invoked to justify the differences between the sexes and the inferiority of the female gender, now the same term became the basis for legal equality. For the first time, the woman was co-opted in political society for her potential contributions to the political realm. It was more a co-opting in principle than in fact, but it was nonetheless capable of bringing about real change—not immediately, as the difficulty women experienced in obtaining the right to vote shows, but when the historical conditions made it possible.

In the meantime, formative social and cultural processes were taking place in the elaboration of the image of women. The collapse of the *ancien regime* brought the end of the medieval image of human beings as part of the religious vision of the world, belonging to a particular lineage, bound to the earth, and subjected to a tightly knit network of social controls and to the daily regulation of time and of life. In the modern conception of humanity, which replaced the medieval image, people are (at least in their self-representation) free of subordination to the divine, independent of the community to which they belong, and autonomous in respect to political powers—sovereign individuals, masters of themselves, and of their own lives.

But the dissolution of contractual ties to others carried the stipulation of new, internalized contractual ties to the self. Along with the internalization of morals came the importance taken on by family education. This education, aimed more at intention than at behavior, was suspicious of the autonomy of thought, of the imagination's freedom, of the autarchy of pleasure. The transition of social control from without to within provoked "the paradox of democratic societies": in which the disappearance of external determination will be translated in a radical internal dependence.[41] The individual's social emancipation seems to have brought, as compensation, a psychic subjugation—a self-discipline that became the principal preoccupation of moral education. This was all the more intensive and programmed for the female psyche, which was felt to be savage and linked to an interperate body—intemperate both in its excess and in its lack.

One of the most widely read nineteenth-century texts of female upbringing, *Nymphomania or the Uterine Fury*,[42] by the French physician J. D. T. de Bienville, seems emblematic; it would eventually be translated and read all over Europe. This book can be considered together with another greatly successful book of this period, *Onanism: Dissertation on the Illness Produced by Masturbation*.[43] Both volumes were concerned with adolescent autoerotic sexuality, which was considered a pernicious practice for young persons and degenerative for their descendants—therefore, dually dangerous for the social body. One distinction was made, however: for boys the *behavior* was stigmatized, but for girls the *imagination* was blamed. In the case of boys, educators were advised to scrutinize their actions and to prevent any bodily contact through the use of orthopedic devices; in the case of girls, mothers were exhorted to scrutinize their daughters' thoughts, dreams, and feelings. For a young girl, the reading of novels, idleness, the company of peers (even that of other girls), and keeping a diary were all considered dangerous, as were looking at herself in a mirror, adorning herself, eating spicy foods, drinking alcoholic beverages, and (worst of all) fantasizing. Every infraction carried with it the danger of falling prey to nymphomania, which was considered to be both an acute and incurable illness and the expression of woman's profound nature. Only marriage held the remedy for the unnatural excess of her sex, and only the sequence of pregnancies and childbirths would definitively subordinate desire to procreation. The suspicion that arose between mothers and daughters as a result of the former's educational responsibility became the daughters' suspicion of themselves, the refusal to accept their own images and to recognize their own desires.

This traditional social repression allowed more and more room for self-censure, and for that psychic repression in which Freud located the cause of female illness *par excellence*—that is, hysteria. It is interesting to see how at the beginnings of psychoanalysis, in the preliminary *Studies on Hysteria* (1893–1895), Freud and Breuer glimpsed the cause of psychosomatic disturbances in the imaginations of their patients. However, they saw the imagination as an empty dimension, a hypnotic "twilight" state, where the forbidden would block out all representation of desire and of emotion. "The girl," Breuer observed, "senses in Eros the terrible power which governs and decides her destiny and she is frightened by it. All the greater, then, is her inclination *to look away* and to repress from her consciousness the thing that frightens her."[44]

Given this changed awareness, marriage no longer appeared as the remedy *par excellence* for the "female illness," so that Breuer could state without hesitation: "I do not think I am exaggerating when I assert that *the great majority of severe neuroses in women have their origin in the marriage bed.*"[45] It is upon this profoundly innovative position in respect to tradition that psychoanalysis has based its program to redefine human sexuality and to denounce the repressive mechanisms that function (often invisibly) precisely because they are self-induced. Psychoanalysis has not proceeded alone in this undertaking, but has taken part in the vast movement of cultural criticism from Nietzsche onward that regards tradition and the presumed naturalness of its formative assumptions with suspicion. The clearly liberating work of psychoanalysis is aimed almost exclusively at human sexuality, however; it leaves the question of maternity unconsidered. Or, from another point of view, it reattributes maternity to the cosmic and impersonal dimension of classical nature, which can only be represented through myth.

In psychoanalytic anthropology, woman possesses a sexuality that is different from but coextensive with male sexuality. Sexual evolution ends, in both cases, with the acquisition of the procreative function, an equally unique corporeality. There is no psychoanalytic theory whatsoever on menstruation, pregnancy, childbirth, nursing, the puerperium, or any of the particular questions of female generation. Women psychoanalysts have set forth the most convincing criticisms of Freud's[46] speculative schema,[47] but have not yet formulated a new explicative framework of femininity. For all the profound changes that have come about in the social condition of women since the beginning of the twentieth century, no corresponding cultural representation has been found as far as maternity is concerned. If as a lover woman shares in the elements of modernity, as a mother she finds herself relegated to seventeenth-century iconography and its stereotypes and to the system of codes that Francesca Grazzini stigmatizes with the term "rhetorical." This term includes a broad variety of cultural artifacts, which are unified by the idealization of the maternal duty and by its reduction to a single dimension, which is defined as "natural." For this reason, formulating a new discourse about maternity presumes that, without giving up the cultural instruments that have allowed for this criticism, we can liberate ourselves of cultural encrustations. It presumes that the coordinates that organize maternity, the images that sustain it, the words that conceal it, can all be disassembled. In the emptiness thus obtained, new images and unforeseen configurations of meaning, different ways of relating to ourselves and to others, may emerge. Above all, we must manage to resist the urge to fill the void with new, definitive inscriptions and limit ourselves to practicing "a long-lasting research."

UNPLANNED PREGNANCY: A FAILED ACT, A SUCCESSFUL DISCOURSE

The decision to consider maternity "from the point of view of the female unconscious" has broadened the coordinates of the discourse well beyond the organic economy and individual biography. The difficulties evoked by Francesca Grazzini's "birth story" are revealed to be long shadows, determinations that come from somewhere; we can only make vague conjectures about these, but they permit us to shatter the false image of a self-sufficient ego. In human evolution, the instincts that organize animal reproduction have disappeared, along with the control of estrus. The imago of the child, informing generative drives, has withdrawn into the margins of our psychic geography and sends us pale and indistinct signals from there. In myth, we have also seen how infantile representations of autonomous or incestuous reproduction have been marked by condemnation and punishment, and have thus been rendered unthinkable. As a barrier gainst these unthinkable fantasies, culture, in its attempt to reconnect sexuality and maternity, has created a catalogue of images, of languages and practices, from which it is difficult to extricate ourselves—especially since they have been progressively internalized to the point that they now seem "endogenous." Only recently has sexuality moved far enough from maternity to appear as separate. In fact, through the so-called processes of modernization, historical events have brought about the material conditions that may finally permit the formal equality of "the rights of man" to be transformed into actual female emancipation.

With World War I, a huge number of women left the family environment for the first time to work in roles that traditionally belonged to men. This activity beyond the domestic sphere brought women a modicum of economic independence, self-determination, and mobility; above all, it overturned the age-old identification of "woman" with "mother." Higher levels of education, the acquisition of political rights, a new contract of family reciprocity—all these forced woman to redefine her own images. Essential to this process was what Renate Siebert defines as "the progressive pluralization of the worlds of life," meaning the new possibilities now open to women so that they could aspire to different realizations of self and to different potential autobiographies, rather than to the single script that was traditionally expected.[48] In this context, contraception became a widespread practice and the planning of births a social reality.

But it has only been since the 1970s (with the appearance of dependable and widely available contraception) that female sexuality has actually been made independent of maternity, and that the dissociation between the two, which occurred in the distant reaches of time with the loss of estrus, has become autonomy. But whereas sexuality can be completely cut off from procreation, procreation still remains mainly connected to the heterosexual relationship. This connection is no longer necessary, because since the 1980s the widely publicized successes of artificial insemination and other forms of reproduction that do not depend on coitus ("artificial reproduction") have made the independence of sexuality and maternity at least theoretically possible for all. Even though relatively few women have made use of this almost guaranteed birth control, our way of understanding procreative function has been radically changed. If for millennia maternity was a destiny, now it has become a choice. The desire for maternity that invested the woman's fecundity—inducing her to accept all pregnancies, both planned and accidental—has now been transformed into an intentional goal, in a plan that knows no exceptions. What occurs now is that aside from one or two occasions, every other event of fecundity is felt to be an error.

Paradoxically, the potential fecundity of the female body, the perpetual renewal of its resources, provides more chances of "accidents" than of successes. Within the current code of sexuality, which only allows fertilization as the rarest exception, an unplanned pregnancy represents a "lapsus," or even better, a "failed act." These terms, taken from Freud's *The Psychopathology of Everyday Life*,[49] allow us to conceptualize the gap that exists in every unwanted pregnancy between the prospect of not remaining pregnant and the failure to take the necessary action. Usually there are understandable oversights (e.g., forgetting to take birth control pills, miscalculating fertile days, inserting a diaphragm incorrectly), but these are not accidental ones, as we would have thought before.

In fact, the elements that upset and deflect conscious intentionality go back to an unresolved psychic conflict between the exercise of nonreproductive sexuality and an unconscious desire for fecundity, which has been pushed away by consciousness but not completely stripped of its capacity to express itself. Sometimes the involuntary transgression of a birth control plan constitutes the single possibility for the desire for maternity to be realized, and a woman may acknowledge in such a case that the unwanted pregnancy accomplishes what she would not otherwise have been able to recognize. The same woman who easily resorts to the category of the accidental pregnancy, as far as the failed act is concerned, is nevertheless ready to admit to a psychological motivation when her analysis comes to consider the unconscious desire for motherhood that is revealed by the pregnancy. In other cases, it humiliates the woman to feel that she has been outwitted by an uncontrollable event with such high stakes, that she is so little her own mistress of her life. Therefore, an inscription of the event in her own story is elaborated, rightly or wrongly, and is justified in the rational realm of autobiography. The meaningless and the insignificant later acquire sense and communicative value; they become "a narration of self," a human event.

For adolescents, unplanned pregnancies are usually a means of overcoming their fear of sterility, of proving their own reproductive capacities to themselves. For other women, they may be a way of obtaining rights to male partners, of occupying the place historically filled by the wives. In still other cases, such pregnancies may represent the undreamed-of possibility of breaking the circle of solitude, or else of denying the approach of menopause and with it the end of reproductive potential. We also must not forget that the man's conscious or unexpressed desire and his connection to procreation (which is not always linear) play a part in the complementarity of fertility. In all these cases, fecundity is surreptitiously reunited with sexuality; indeed, they were never completely separate, as the phantasm of fertilization that frequently appears in the female unconscious during the sexual act, and that makes the act so distant from pornography, reveals.

But if we also consider mental life, in all its complexity, as a weaving of conscious and unconscious motivations, we must admit that the individual's boundaries are too narrow to justify the eruption of a vital project that transcends its limits. We are thus directed to another, transindividual dimension, which one often finds difficult to attach to one's self-representation. But Freud's theories once again provide support: In his later years,[50] he inquired into a human being's place in the life cycle, and therefore in death. Following the biological model of the epoch, he introduced the idea of a radical difference between the "soma," which is subject to natural death, and the germinal cells, which are instead potentially immortal:

> The individual does actually carry on a twofold existence: one to serve his own purposes and the other as a link in a chain, which he serves against his will, or at least involuntarily. The individual himselfs regards sexuality as one of his own ends; whereas from another point of view he is an appendage to his germ-plasm, at whose disposal he puts his energies in return for a bonus of pleasure. He is the mortal vehicle of a (possibly) immortal substance.[51]

In this perspective, fertilization is located at the intersection of two vital processes: one impersonal, aimed at the continuation of the species; the other individual, aimed at the realization of self. On different temporal scales, both oppose death. It is in the extreme vulnerability of recognizing oneself as mortal that the figure of the child arises, and all of the unanswered infantile narcissism converges in it.

"Parental love," observed Freud, "which is so moving and at bottom so childish, is nothing but the parents' narcissism born again, which, transformed into object-love, unmistakably reveals its former nature."[52] We know, however, that the link between love of oneself and love of the child by the imaginary baby—that intermediary figure between the ego and the other, which evolution represses in the unconscious. But from there it attempts to reappear in the scene of life by using those stratagems that we call "by-products of the unconscious." These by-products appear in dreams, in games, in symptoms, in daydreams, and in this case in the failed acts that show themselves to be "successful discourses," as Lacan calls them.[53]

Unwanted pregnancies, as eruptions of the unconscious, lie outside of women's possibilities to predict and control, which can eventually take over at a later time in the recourse to voluntary abortion. In such a case, abortion constitutes the outcome of the failed elaboration of a "psychic womb" in which the pregnancy can find the necessary mental acceptance. In a certain sense, the synchronization between the impersonal time of the unconscious and the historical time of the subject has failed. On the other hand, no one can point out a human group that has completely reclaimed the unconscious, tamed its indomitable and indestructible resources. Relegated to an

extremely primitive psychological level, isolated by the barrier of repression, the unconscious is always ready to assert its demands, to seize satisfaction in some way. "To this is due the instability of the proud superstructure
of the mind,"[54] observed Freud.

Nevertheless, psychoanalysis is based on the conviction that it is
always better for us as human beings to know than not to know, and that
our awareness of our limits—of the natural and cultural determinations to
which we are subject and that are bound in an inextricable weave—may
constitute our freedom. It is therefore a residual freedom that is only
rediscovered when the limits of our capacity to reconstruct the past and
control the future have been tested.

CHAPTER 4

Metaphors of Motherhood

... Psychoanalysis was born as a therapy. However, this is not
the reason why I mean to recommend it to you, but for its
contents of truth, for all it teaches us about what is in the heart
of man above and beyond all other things—his own essence—and
for the connections it makes between the most divergent
human activities.

—SIGMUND FREUD

EXAMINING OLD IMAGES
IN THE SEARCH FOR NEW ONES

Analyzed through the psychoanalytic grid, motherhood, at a crossroads
between the "internal world" and the "external world,"[1] appears to be subject
to innumerable erasures and superimpositions; these may make us feel that it
lies beyond our reach, estranged from our cultural codes. Actually they merely
hide the historical conflict that has produced them beneath their apparent
neutrality. However, it would be ingenuous of us to think that we might ever
make motherhood a completely transparent process through our own reap-
propriation. A bridge between the biological and social realms, it will remain
partially concealed by the shadows that emanate from both. In a certain sense,
the psychoanalytic commandment "Remember the forgotten" will never lose
its relevance in regard to motherhood.

Nevertheless, new forms of female self-representation may be constructed upon the areas of darkness, and new ways of understanding pro-

creation may be proposed. In fact, motherhood is a central theme in the elaboration of our identity, and a laboratory of images and signs capable of producing a cultural dialogue.[2] To this end, it is necessary to begin with the self—not with one's own body, as has often been stated, because the body is a presemiotic reality that does not create meaning directly; but only with the representations that come out of it, with the materiality of its fantasies, with the life projects that it contains. It is in the imagination rather than in the anatomy that our sexual identity is constructed. This does not come about immediately, as a product of the reflection of the body in our thought, but through an anxious definition of the self in relation to others, as Anna's case shows (see Chapter 1). To this end, a knowledge of self that is rooted in the gendered unconscious represents a valuable possibility of thought that is "faithful to itself and connected to the other."[3]

Although necessary, self-awareness is still not sufficient, because the construction of a female subjectivity cannot be limited to taking on an infinite series of individual stories. These must converge in shared representations, in socialized figures that can mediate between individual lives and shared experiences. In the face of the suppression and reification of our imaginations brought about by the mass media, there is a temptation to flee from communication and to shut ourselves within our own private lives. But the intrusion of society occurs even if we are unaware of it, and silence has never protected us from being expropriated. It is better for us as women to formulate a language about ourselves, to give voice to the feminine, even if we must cross back again over sedimentary collective representations; in any case, these constitute a centuries-old history we certainly cannot ignore, in an illusion that we have no foundations whatsoever.

"The process of becoming a woman," writes Patrizia Violi, "the construction of our identity as women, identity which is both individual (internal) and social (collective), depends precisely upon the way in which we elaborate the images we get from being women in a certain culture at a particular time."[4] The deconstruction of what exists and construction of the new are not distinct programs anyway, but proceed in unison. Since cultural forms are always the outcome of a conflict (in our case, a sexual one), they contain the rejected reasoning of the losing side.

Among the most powerful images that culture has elaborated both to represent and to govern women, is, without a doubt, that of motherhood. In some ways, this image is atemporal; in others, it is manifested in historically determined metaphors. Motherhood, understood as bringing a child into the world, is a universal experience, if it is true that each of us finds our first home in a woman's body. Freud wrote:

> The dwelling-house was a substitute for the mother's womb, the first lodging, for which in all likelihood man still longs, and in which he was safe and felt

at ease. . . . There is a joking saying that "love is home-sickness"; and whenever a man dreams of a place or a country and says to himself, while he is still dreaming: "this place is familiar to me, I've been here before," we may interpret the place as being the mother's genitals or her body. . . . (Occurrences of '*déja vu*' in dreams have a special meaning.) These places are invariably the genitals of the dreamer's mother; there is indeed no other place about which one can assert with such conviction that one has been there before.[5]

Precisely because of its elemental and universal nature, maternity has always been utilized as a metaphor of the "other," but has remained of little significance in and of itself.

"The discourse relating to the mother," wrote Artemidorus in the *Book of Dreams*, "because it is so varied, has diverse aspects and must be analyzed in detail, has escaped the attention of many dream critics."[6] When he tried to identify its symbolic meanings, he discovered that (on the basis of the sexual rapport that the dreamer dreams of having with his own mother) this can mean different things from one time to the next: profession, homeland, inheritance, nature, death, earth. In the atemporality of the unconscious, all these figures coexist because "in the unconscious nothing can be brought to an end, nothing is past or forgotten."[7] "Like every archetype," wrote Jung, "that of the mother possesses a nearly infinite number of aspects."[8] But in the history of culture, the metaphors follow and take on a particular historical importance. Each represents a way of relating to the self and to the world that is chronologically delimited. In this chapter, I examine some such metaphors that seem particularly significant: the mother as earth; childbirth as productive labor; gestation as intellectual labor; maternity as creativity, and vice versa; and the care of children as morality. Not all of these metaphors have equal power, equal duration, equal relevance. But all contain unexplored elements—possibilities and considerations that might represent the maternal process outside the narrow confines of biology in general, and of gynecology in particular.

THE MOTHER AS EARTH; CHILDBIRTH AS WORK

The metaphor of "mother–earth" is the strongest of the explicit connections, because it contains within it the two extremes of the procreative process: birth and death. I have already analyzed in Chapter 1, in connection with the triadic figure that represents woman in the individual unconscious and in myth, how the earth may be mother to us in the double sense of producing vital foodstuffs and acting as the pall that covers our bodies in their ultimate dwelling place.[9] These two aspects of the metaphors affect each other in turn, and both make the relationship of humankind to nature conceivable—not only the relationship that has become eternal in the unconscious, but also the one that was historically determined, that characterized premodern culture. "Women and nature," writes Carolyn Merchant, "are united by a millenarian association, an affiliation that has persisted throughout the entire course of culture, of language and of history."[10] The earth as mother was a central concept for organismic cosmology, which was then supplanted in the 1600s by the mechanistic model of the scientific revolution. With the beginnings of modern Europe, the relationship of humanity with nature became different at the same time that its relationship with maternity did.

In the course of the modern break with the ancient order of the world, the figure of the witch and of the midwife took on a symbolic value. The witch became the symbol of the disorder of nature, which required the control and dominion of man. The midwife, on the other hand, symbolized the incompetence of woman to manage human reproduction, which had to be taken away from her and given over to the representative of an acknowledged profession, the doctor. Without wanting to indulge in any nostalgia for the past, we must admit that in this transition the values that were the foundation of the female care of labor were rejected, along with ignorance and error. "It is necessary to underline," writes the historian Claudia Pancino, "the process of exclusion intrinsic to innovation, but also to to refute the myth of that exclusion and of those women who were excluded that has been created in recent years; the truths of their history can, in any case, teach us something."[11]

When midwives lost their centuries-old monopoly over the assistance of birth, an unwritten inheritance came to an end. This inheritance—of knowledge, of movement, of dexterity, of natural pharmacology—had served as a vehicle for an uncultivated imagination and had provided a familiar lexicon. As such, it had been able to produce empathy, participation, and social interaction among women. As far as reproduction was concerned, the doctors preferred to reactivate the old Aristotelian theories, above all through the biological works of the great naturalist William Harvey.[12] As we have seen in Chapter 2, these theories placed particular emphasis on male predominance. The female figures who had for centuries transmitted forms of knowledge and management of women's bodies were now subjected to social prohibition and cultural discredit. "The witch," notes Merchant, "and her counterpart, the midwife, came to find themselves at the symbolic center of a battle over the control of substance (material) and nature, control that was essential to new social relationships in the sphere of production and of reproduction."[13]

The triumph of the mechanistic model of nature, more suitable to an attitude of domination and of the exploitation of its resources, resulted in the progressive obsolescence of the mother–earth metaphor. Thus, a great and solemn conceptualization of maternity and of the cosmic dimension of its time frame was lost. The rhythms that punctuate the life of the female body are ruled by an astral temporality connecting them, through invisible consonances, with the cycle of seasons, the phases of the moon, the movements of the tides, and the alternation of day and night. But such consonance became insignificant when man began to think of himself in opposition to nature, as standing outside its vitality. The synchrony between microcosm and macrocosm that Renaissance naturalists had perceived failed when man began to represent himself as a self-sufficient and complete machine. In the social life of capitalist economies, the dominance of biological rhythms was broken; they were subordinated to the chronological measure of time and and to civic rhythms. Once they were disconnected, mother and earth simultaneously lost the possibility of being conceived of as symbolic forms powerfully endowed with value and meaning.

Nevertheless, the consequences of the waning of the great metaphor were not merely negative, because the mother–earth analogy inscribed motherhood wholly in a natural dimension—which, as we have seen, concealed the elements of social conditioning and individual responsibility. In the face of a fecundity regulated exclusively by the rigid laws of the cosmos, a woman could do nothing but subject herself to its domination. Although in traditional culture motherhood was validated in the sublimated form of divine will, it was also considered an ineluctable imposition that should induce an attitude of obedient acceptance. The image of the Madonna receiving the Angel Gabriel's announcement with a bowed head effectively expressed the nobility and the limitations of motherhood seen exclusively in the context of the sacred, where natural time and supernatural time were thought to converge in the intensity of the occurrence.

The mother–earth metaphor was an impersonal way of understanding the occurrence of maternity in the lives of women, who were progressively relegated to the margins of the social imagination and of the personal unconscious. The decline of the metaphor allowed the individual experience, conscious intention, and the concretions of the corporeal to emerge. The pain of childbirth ceased being viewed as an inescapable punishment, but took on the fortuity of a morbid event, and was offered as such to the understanding and care of the doctor.

However, the social management of maternity by a class of professionals, and then by hospital institutionalization, once again imposed a passive position on woman—an impotent and mute stance of waiting in the face of the reproductive event, of which she herself was the agent. The development of knowledge and of technical devices (among them the notorious forceps) accompanied the establishment of a specialist lexicon that excluded women from the communicative events taking place at the scene of childbirth. They were thus left without information about their own bodies, unable to engage in dialogue with the doctor, and even incapable of communicating with one another. This aphasia still continues in a certain sense, creating quite a few difficulties in the doctor–patient interaction, which is marked by a radial asymmetry of the respective positions—all the knowledge and power being concentrated on one side, and all the ignorance and dependence on the other.[14]

Outside of medical terminology, the few terms used to express the making of children go back to the metaphorical realm of work. In this sense, the word "labor," which means both the struggle of childbirth and the suffering of work, assumes a particular significance. "I would formulate the hypothesis," writes Costantino, in the beginning of an interesting linguistic analysis, "that childbirth (and the generative process) might be taboo not because of their relationship to sex but because they are work, since it is work in our society that gives one the right to profit and power."[15] The comparison between procreative process and productive work is a claim often advanced by the women's movement, in the hope of making known what both the struggle and the management of child- birth involve for a woman along with her social function, which is normally concealed by the presumed naturalness and spontaneity of the events.[16] It is often maintained that women's participation in productive work is limited by their biological function. But isn't the production of human beings a kind of work? And isn't it as important as the production of a means of subsistence? Both demand an expenditure of energy decid- edly greater than that which an organism normally expends to live. Although the physiological process of gestation is common to all mam- mals, only for human beings can we speak of "work," because human reproduction at present is relatively free of instinctual imposition and is brought about by intentional decision.

It seems that one can extend to human reproduction Karl Marx's definition of "work"[17]—a process that passes between human beings and nature, in which people put in motion their natural physical forces (their arms, legs, heads, and hands) to appropriate natural materials that will be useful. But, in acting upon external nature, modifying it, people also modify their own nature. Paola Tibet carries this hypothesis to its conclusion by observing how the domestication of human reproduction (through the manifold forms of control we have examined) transforms a natural process into a work of a social nature. Through this work, humanity directly modifies its own species.[18] But in the system of private property, work, which is alienated, undergoes expropriation and loss of the object. Alienation and deprivation can also be extended to generative female work in that the offspring becomes the socially acknowledged "child of the father," inscribed exclusively in his succession of descent, as the imposition of the paternal surname indicates. But the differences are such that they prevent a recognition of the similarity between the production of bodies and the production of goods.

The work of gestation does not take place outside of the body, like other forms of work; moreover, except for breast feeding, the expenditure of energy is carried out within the organism. Furthermore, human labor utilizes tools that integrate or substitute for the limbs of the worker, whereas this has not yet occurred in the process of gestation, except in a few cases of premature birth. Nor, on the other hand, can we attribute the same intentionality of human labor to gestation. A worker decides the scope of the work and chooses the most suitable means to carry it out. In the course of the work, an act of intentional vigilance is always in process. In biological reproduction, on the other hand, the moment of fertilization can be chosen; once it is under way, however, the process continues without any pause, according to its own intrinsic plan, independent of and sometimes even against the will of the pregnant woman. Only at the moment of childbirth is it possible once again to assume a form of voluntary control over the generative event, and even then it is only partial. Furthermore, the child remains an object of love and of self-validation for the mother, in that it is socially removed from the father. And then, generation is never "re-production," in the sense that every newborn is different from all others—an original who cannot be copied.

In a certain sense, maternity resembles intellectual more than physical labor. In fact, thought also has an autonomy of its own in relation to the thinker. We cannot interrupt an association of ideas on command, guide thought to our liking, or decide not to think. In addition, intellectual activity is carried out within the body and has no need of external instruments to proceed. Finally, the intellectual product always maintains a relationship to the person who produced it; it appears to be an emanation of that person's subjectivity or essence.

The analogy between the production of bodies and the production of ideas is provocative, and culture has always made use of it to conceptualize intellectual activity. We need only think of the extensive use of the term "to conceive" and of its strong metaphorical value. However, in generation, the conception occurs in a close relationship between bodies, an interpenetration of the two; the mental activity of conceiving an idea, a plan, a project, or even a joke takes place within a single body—traditionally that of the male, the only one permitted to think. The opposition between the conception of ideas and the conception of bodies brings us back to the scenes of myth discussed earlier, and to sexual conflict that myths represent and that continually distorts cultural products.

CONCEIVING BODIES, CONCEIVING IDEAS:
GESTATION AS INTELLECTUAL LABOR

In the attempt to give symbolic form to gestation, we have once again come upon the effects of the concealment produced by a culture based on the denial of female generate power. Paradoxically, human thought has considered itself through the metaphor of the procreative process, and at the same time has denied any contaminating connection with the female body, forcing conception into a position of headless maternity.

The dialogue Plato dedicated to love is emblematic in this sense. In the conversation he recorded in the *Symposium*, love—between men, of course—was discussed. The discussion pivoted upon the nature of love, and whether this might be characterized by perfection, completion, and unity, as Agathon maintained, stating that Love is the most beautiful, the best, the bravest, and the most knowledgeable of the gods; or whether it should be characterized by division, as Pausanius argued, claiming that Love is double like Aphrodite herself, who is both "heavenly" and the "vulgar prostitute." Beside him, Aristophanes reconstructed an imaginary anthropology; he linked the desire for unity and for love to the halved state of the original spheres.

When it was Socrates's turn, the discourse suddenly diverged because Socrates raised it from the mundane level of the prior discussion. He maintained that an encomium must tell the truth; however, because nobody present had done so, he was willing to tell the truth about Love, although in his own manner and not in contest with the preceding discussion. In the solemn name of truth, Socrates made an unheard-of gesture: He invited a woman to join the wise men. Moreover, this woman was a foreigner, Diotima. When Diotima joined them, Socrates then assumed an unprecedented position for him, that of disciple. What bearing could the word of a woman have in the most powerful of male discourses, the philosophical one? She could introduce the body—not the body in the abstract, the animation of geometric order, like that represented by Aristophanes's semicircles, but the real body that desires, copulates, and procreates.

I want to pause for a moment to emphasize the importance of this textual moment, which is a foundational representation in Occidental rationality. But we can only understand how unusual it was by recalling the dual interdiction that it violated. As we have seen in Chapter 2, women in ancient Athens were rigorously excluded from banquets because as Plato noted (almost with regret), should they have been forced to eat alongside men, they would have found some way to escape.[19] Furthermore, birth was believed to be incompatible with beauty, as the two prohibitions—those against birth and death—enforced at Delos, the sacred island of Apollo, reveal. A boat carried laboring women and the dying to the shores of a nearby island, Mykonos, for both these states were thought to be symptoms of the transience of time and of human mortality; these were viewed as incompatible with the god of eternal youth and uncontaminated beauty.[19a]

However, through Diotima's words, the body, the sexual body, could be thought of in the realm of beauty and of eternity through the intermediation of love. Diotima stated:

> We are all of us prolific, Socrates, in body and in soul, and when we reach a certain age, our nature urges us to procreation. Nor can we be quickened by ugliness, but only by the beautiful. Conception, we know, takes place when man and woman come together, but there's a divinity in human propagation, an immortal something in the midst of man's mortality which is incompatible with any kind of discord.[20]

Diotima's truth, which Plato simultaneously made explicit and concealed, pertains to the pregnancy that exists prior to every event of fertilization—the implicit divine nature of the union of the sexes before procreation occurs; the immortality that resides in being human and in the longing for beauty.[21] "In Diotima's discourse, *eros* is transposed—from the desire for beauty of bodies to the beauty of souls and ultimately moves towards the beauty of actions and laws."[22] Plato let the foreign woman articulate this, but he inserted her words in a system of coordinates so powerful that their innovative significance was all but neutralized. The element that Diotima introduced into the order of discourse was explosive, because it broke the material–form opposition upon which the subordination of the feminine and the hierarchy of the world was founded. Attributing the value of eternity to pregnancy would seem to purify birth of that shadow of death that rendered it impious, and to place fertile bodies in the Apollonian genealogy.

Continuing in her representation, Diotima attributed the same love of immortality to all the animals: "Haven't you noticed," she asked Socrates, "what an extraordinary effect the breeding instinct has upon both animals and birds? . . . With men, you might put it down to the power of reason, but how can you account for Love's having such remarkable effects upon the brutes? . . . I don't know how you can hope to master the philosophy of love, if that's too much for you to understand."[23]

In Diotima's representation, love would seem to invalidate the distinctions that set man and woman, man and animal, and man and god in opposition. The antinomies are eluded by a dynamic that transcends them, by a dimension of eternity that levels them. But this potential overturning of the constituted order was not made explicit in the Platonic dialogue, because the irreducible sexual asymmetry re-established the predetermined positions. Diotima continueed, in fact:

> Those whose procreancy is of the body turn to woman as the object of their love, and raise a family in the blessed hope that by doing so they will keep

their memory green, "through time and through eternity." But those whose procreancy is of the spirit rather than of the flesh—conceive and bear the things of the spirit. . . . [These things are] Wisdom and all her sister virtues. . . . And hence [man's] procreant nature will go about in search of the loveliness on which he may beget. . . . And if besides he happens on a soul which is at once beautiful, distinguished, and agreeable, he is charmed to find so welcome an alliance.[24]

In the dialogue, however, order, which was disturbed by the eruption of the female, quickly took shape again in homosexuality. The reproduction of bodies was returned to the level of semibestiality, entrusted, as it should be, to the management of women and of inferior men—to each his or her station. The making of a child was deemed to saturate female potentiality and to transform desire into need, distancing woman from the transcendence that should rightly belong to the philosopher. The work to which Plato would give birth, in the name of love and beauty, paradoxically actually reflected the laws of the Polis, in which the woman found her exclusion definitively sanctioned. Thus, for the thousandth time, the female was silenced; her value and meaning were negated. More importantly, the woman who was silenced, in great mockery, was one who was defined as "learned in this and many other questions."

As an icon of declared female discourse, we are left with Need (Penia), the protagonist of the myth of the birth of Love, which Diotima recounted. In the myth, Need wants to partake of the banquet organized by the gods to honor the birth of Aphrodite, so she lies with Resource (Poros), son of Craft (Meditea), whom she finds drunk and asleep in the garden. From this embrace, which is realized in cunning, Love is born; he becomes a follower and servant of Aphrodite, because he is conceived on the day of her birth. It is the coincidence in the realm of time that attributes value to the child—a symbolic contiguity, since the wretched carnal parents have nothing to transmit, especially Need, who is an exaggerated representation of our poverty of figures and of language.

Therefore, to consider maternity means to start again from the part of Diotima's discourse that was misunderstood and rejected. It means rediscovering the female capacity to procreate in her body and in her spirit—the commonality with both animals and gods that constitutes the specific status of human generation.

MATERNITY AS CREATIVITY

The metaphor of creativity challenges the Platonic schism, proposing the recovery in maternity of the related generation of bodies and of ideas in maternity. The baby represents the realization of the female desire for fecundity, of her imaginary figures. Formed in the course of gestation by a secret synchrony, the infant is brought into the world by a maternal discourse that reformulates personal biography and family genealogy. The child's birth is accompanied by an auspicious desire—by a wish for happiness, by a presumption of greatness that will make him or her feel inviolable, the subject of himself or herself. All this takes place by means of a process linking both mother and child's body and mind, of which we only have an inkling; nevertheless we must presume it accounts for the existential condition, which is uniquely human—the singularity of the self and of its story, the inescapable mastery of the body, and the "right" over one's own mind. We cannot easily conceive of gestation as both a physiological and a conceptual process, or of a baby as a product both of the body and of thought, because this idea contradicts powerful symbolic injunctions, as we have seen.

The philosophical scenario endorsed by Plato in Diotima's recounting of the myth of Love's birth closed on the confirmed triumph of the opposition between material and form. This opposition not only divided woman and man, but also constituted a criterion for the ordering of thoughts, words, and things, not to mention the relationships of power in the cities of the present and future. Male discourse could only construct a universe based on these deep structures, and on their reassuring power to transform sexual differences into the superiority of one gender over the other once and for all. For the most part, women opposed this with silence, the single exception being the contribution of women mystics.

Visionary discourse, rooted in the imagination, brought to light important hidden connections between the female body and thought. Maternity, which was denied by the monastic condition, became a metaphor for the relationship of woman with the divine. Through the imagination, the female body was explored indirectly; it was rediscovered and re-presented, with surprisingly truthful results. For example, Hildegard of Bingen, a renowned mystic of the thirteenth century A.D., wrote: "The pleasure of woman is like the light of the sun that spreads, sweet, continuous, and soft, over the earth, warming and making it fertile; it if burned any brighter with its constant flame, it would burn the fruit instead of ripening them. In the same way, a woman's pleasure in love possesses a gentle, sweet and constant power, that permits her to conceive and grow a child in her belly . . ."[25] In Hildegard's vision, the mother was no longer represented as a container, but possessed a feminine power analogous to the pleasure of love that gives life and form to the embryo. Nevertheless, these elements of female awareness never succeeded in disassembling the traditional discourse and the power of its metaphors; they were definitively silenced by the prevalence of scientific rationality, and by the capacity of this rationality to provoke "a disenchantment of the world," as Weber put it.[26]

The vitality of the maternal body remained silenced until it was ultimately sequestered by the medical model—by its impersonal mechanization, separating every link between visible and invisible. But current criticism aimed at the mind–body opposition, and the acknowledged awareness of their interconnection, now permit us to recognize the mingling of elements that have been disjoined for too long. Yet a discrepancy still remains between highly advanced theoretical elaboration[27] and medical empiricism; this is particularly evident in obstetrics, which is considered a technical and marginal application of medicine. Paradoxically, an antihistorical movement, which includes the recovery of prescientific superstitions, allows us to keep its reassuring mechanization at bay.

The history of science has restored an ancient enigma, that of maternal cravings, and a long-banished topic, the craving mother. "Of all the female figures that come into play around the event of maternity," writes Claudia Pancino, "the one we have the least information about is, once again, the mother."[28] Although the pregnant woman belongs entirely to a private sphere and to the quotidian realm, the period of pregnancy has been subject to numerous traditional restrictions, such as, limiting or even prohibiting sexual relations, and to a variety of prescriptions, such as the recommendation that the husband fulfill the sudden wishes of the expectant mother. These are generally dietary wishes for such things as fruit out of season (e.g., strawberries in the winter). If these bizarre wishes fail to be satisfied, there will be serious consequences for the fetus: The infant's body (often the face) will be marked with stains (desires) of the same color as the denied fruit.

This theme often appears in fairy tales to suggest, in this reassuring and familiar context, a dimension of the unknown, a halo of magic. Its evocations express a condition of privilege, because it has always been the role of the princess to desire, or rather to submit to the adventure. To recognize a transgressive maternal desire is to concede a position of power to the pregnant woman, but at the same time to confirm that the female is subjected to outside forces as a rule of life. She is subjected to the course of stars and to the cycle of seasons, but also to the wonder of a new life that is developing mysteriously inside a body unknown in its anatomy and in its bloody physiological processes.

In the popular tradition, the generative event has been accepted as an inscrutable natural phenomenon and as an indication of the presence of the sacred. However, medical science, which in the eighteenth century came face to face with this unexplored faculty of the human organism, had first to apply some order, to separate affinity and toleration, to isolate what could be rationally explained from what had to be left to the underground of superstition and fear. The female organism's reproductive function was disconnected and isolated from its psychological dimension.[29]

At the beginning of the seventeenth century, Mercurio Scipione wrote: "It is clear that the imagination and generation are actions that depend upon the same animal faculty connected to the same supposition; and that although they are born of the same source, they are quite alike and suitable together; and are like all the other faculties that man generates, however distant their sources."[30] But imagination, of which only the disturbing effects were recognized, was one of the invisible causes that the new sciences intended to do away with; as such, it could not become part of an anatomical–physiological model of the human body, objectified in the eyes of medicine. Throughout the 1600s and 1700s, a fervid scientific discussion set the two fronts of medicine in opposition: the imaginists and the anti-imaginists.

The first group maintained that aspects of maternal imagination, such as an intense emotion or a frightening vision, could leave their stamp on the fetus. In 1745, Ludovico Muratori wrote: "It was clear that these [the cravings] arose from the strong imagination of the mother, who in her pregnancy felt some powerful craving for some fruit, or food, or to touch some part of her body, or even not to touch it, would then leave an impression, that is the figure of the desired thing, in the tender little body of the fetus; which is the reason that they are commonly called 'the cravings of women.' "[31] But in spite of its proclaimed efficiency, the female imagination came to be defined as "passive" by Voltaire, who wrote: "This passive imagination of brains that are easy to shake up sometimes pass onto the babies the evident marks of some feeling the mothers had. The examples are many."[32]

In the imaginist's clinical descriptions, the maternal power to "impress" the fetus assumed the form of witchcraft because it only brought deformity and monstrosity; such conclusions reveal the projections and the anxieties of this group of medical-theorists. Their opponents, the rationalistic doctors, could not recognize the existence of "cravings" because there was no place for desire in explicative models that took the "bodily machine" as a point of reference. This "machine" was split up into the presumed autonomy of its apparatuses, deprived of any sort of intention whatsoever, and given over completely to the normativeness of the rationalistic view. The belief in "cravings" was to remain the heritage of women, "the sex that chatters and gives birth."[33]

But the current interest in this remote scientific discussion suggests the view of a possible active relationship between the mind and body, between the mother and fetus, and between the dreamed child and his or her real double. Here, imagination, which we are in the habit of placing in opposition to reality, reveals a real capacity to conform, demonstrating a "maternal reaction" that is not only an unintentional organic process. This hypothesis was proposed as a nondemonstrable possibility in scientific

psychology at the beginning of the century. Henry Rutgers Marshall wrote
in 1905:

> It is true that, from what we know, the nervous system of the embryo is not
> directly linked to that of the mother. . . . But in spite of that, a new lesser
> consciousness is developing in the mother, which even if only slightly
> integrated into the mass of total consciousness, is still a part of it. . . . If this
> is so, one must then say that during intrauterine life, the psychic activities
> of the embryo constitute part of a complex consciousness that is both the
> mother's and the child's.[34]

Recent neurological studies of the relationships that link mother and
fetus, involving comparisons of maternal and fetal electroencephalograms
recorded during sleep, are proving that "cravings" symbolize a link between
material and form, between body and soul, between gestation and thought
that medical science has denied since cravings were first recognized and is
only now struggling to rediscover.[35] The mother and her fetus sleep and
dream together, united by a shared psychophysical condition that may
perhaps predetermine the exclusively human possibility of "thinking
thoughts"—of transforming, through protomental processes, the emergence within the self of "things" into the form of subjective "thoughts."[36]

We should not forget, however, that along with these unconscious
processes, conscious re-elaborations of the family story and imaginary
predictions concerning the future child and his or her life take place during
pregnancy, placing the child in a preformed social framework. The wait is
rich with anticipation, which will influence the personality and destiny of
the newborn. Writing about this, Jules Michelet, one of the keenest male
observers of the female spirit who ever lived, commented in the emphatic
style of the late Romantic period: "It is the desire of our mother, her attempt
to generate a divine child that allows us to become what little that we are,
and it is the best part of ourselves that she puts into us with that dream.
And if one is strong on the earth, that is because she conceived us in
heaven."[37]

After birth, at the moment of the first awareness that passes between
mother and child, she reshapes that imagining; she focuses her vision of the
already familiar figure on the real protagonist. As if by a spell, the previous
fantasies, still characterized by the omnipotence of thought, by the mega-
lomania of infantile narcissism, are remeasured to the dimensions of reality.
But their eclipse does not provoke disappointment and regret, because a
thread of felicity links past and future. Clarice Lispector captures this
transfiguration with great psychological sensitivity in the short story "Via
Crucis", relating how a simple, impoverished woman, Maria das Dores,
experiences her maternity (perhaps suggested by her name) like that of the
virgin Mary. But after the last labor pain, when the anticipated baby Jesus

comes into the world, the divine image disappears and a mortal baby, Emmanuel, remains. Lispector concludes, "It is unknown if Emmanuel had to bear his cross. Everybody bears his own."[38]

However, it happens in some cases that the fantasies persist and the actual child, at a constant disadvantage in comparison to his or her imaginary predecessor, is hounded by an unexpressed maternal judgment of inadequacy. The proliferation, sometimes violent, of orthopedic interventions (e.g., eyeglasses, devices to straighten teeth, corrective gymnastics, speech therapy, reconstructive surgery) reveals the failure of the initial recognition of the real child, and the persistence within the figure of the child of a phantasmic umbilical cord that links him or her to the omnipotent womb of the maternal dream. But the overly coddled child, as well as the inadequate child, can also be the outcome of a painful attempt at gratifying these inexhaustible maternal expectations. In the case of overcoddling, the inadequacy has been filled by the establishment in the child of a "false self" that wavers between grandiosity and depression.[39]

I think that the "child of the night" remains in every mother–child relationship, in any case, as an invisible shadow—doubly protective, a prolonging of the mother's attentions and diligence, as the image of the guardian angel in popular iconography reveals. The child's false self is nothing more than a reflection of the maternal false self that wants to find, in its product, the positive value that it could not find in the reproductive process. Dispossessed of the meaning and value of her own images, as from her own generative capacity, the mother asks the idealized child to function in such a way as to restore her own existential lack of being. The greater the mother's sense of her own meaning and value—the greater her awareness that the fabric of her own images is open to the creativity that animates the world, and that the life project inherent in her fertile body can take shape in a variety of human expressions—the less likely it is that the relationship with her child will be burdened by affective demands and social compensation.

Melanie Klein maintained that envy is directed first toward maternal creativity.[40] And yet, as a mother, the woman misunderstands this power of hers and identifies instead with the kinds of dependent and querulous figures that tradition transmits to her. In this sense, she is subject to that "mystified self-comprehension" that Habermas speaks of.[41] We must replace the completed image of motherhood—the one that has been handed down to us through the religious iconography of the Madonna and Child—with the image of the process of "bringing a child into the world" if we want the full efficiency and flexibility of the female disposition, and the full range and variety of its manifestation, to emerge.

Maternity, which does not begin with gestation or end with childbirth, is a creative act at every moment. When a mother looks at her offspring she has a metaphorical vision, because she sees in that generic infant the subject of a story that has already found its protagonist—although it has yet to be written. The maternal gaze glimpses "somebody in something," and that gaze creates the child, allows him or her to be a presence in the world. When the poet compares the moon to a silver coin, from that instant onward something new exists in the world aside from the moon and silver coins: the "moon-as-silver-coin." Similarly, from the comparison between the imaginary baby and the real baby, the unique, irreplaceable baby that is only like himself or herself emerges—a synthesis of possibility and reality that cannot be reproduced. Because no newborn coincides fully with his or her imagined predecessor, the imaginary project always remains unfinished. Its state of incompletion can be compared to what Simone Weil called "our uncreated part."[42] Accepting the part that is discarded in the process constitutes the very condition of female creativity, the motor that pushes imaginative invention toward reality. This is all the more true because the real infant, disjoined from the ideal one, presents itself as an open-ended project, like a work that contains its own ends but not the self-sufficiency of its own means.

The first question that the newborn addresses to the mother in the course of their life long dialogue is actually nothing more than the reflection of her expectation. Their dialogue only possesses an elementary genetic code[43] from which an infinite series of shared thoughts will evolve. But how does this game proceed? Without question, totally unpredictably. No machine endowed with artificial intelligence could possibly program it in advance. As in any creative experience, there are pre-established links and given determinants, but within this framework the possibilities are open, and the rules are formed as game itself unfolds. Freeing oneself of one's own images, keeping possibilities open, trying new approaches, and tolerating not knowing what one will do next are all conditions both of intellectual creativity and of bringing into a world a being who is really "other" but is not alien. In order to express its creative faculty, the maternal experience requires a space of shared silence, a suspension of time in which conceptual (imaginative) forces can coverage. Concentration, intentionality, force are only hindrances; what matter are the conditions of distraction, relaxation, and availability. In a certain sense, these are the same conditions that Freud recommended for would-be analysts and that Bion synthesized in his prescription for therapists—to suspend knowledge, memory, and desire.

It is told that a Chinese painter asked a great artist what the best way to start a painting was. "Let it happen," was the wise man's response. Similarly, the child's design takes shape on its own; it delineates itself in the space between maternal vigilance and inattention. What matters is that the child is not received as a thing, but as the outcome of the interaction between two subjects: The mother tolerates the child's changes, which are not always predictable, and these changes modify the mother. To the extent that life, at its beginnings, does not proceed along pre-established tracks, it brings a margin of ignorance and risk that is not always easy to tolerate. If the mother is not afraid, if she can have faith in what occurs, we witness the wonder that happens daily all over the world—the birth of a new individual, who is in some ways inscribed in the thoughts and bodies of those who have come before, but in other ways is unpredictable and new. Envisioned in a myriad of figures, shaped by the complete range of maternal emotions, the child moves from the imagination to reality, from the inside of the body to the world outside, from the atemporality of the unconscious to the history of events. In this way, the child embodies the outcome of human creativity; he or she is living proof that the material–form opposition is a mere artifice or fiction, and that in the concreteness of generation, the material is thinking and thought is material.

CREATIVITY AS MATERNITY

If female generation is a process that takes place at a high level of creativity, we should now ask ourselves whether our intellectual conceptualizations can be rooted in the maternal imagination and can exploit its expressive potential. In other words, can we transform the metaphor of the thinking body into its opposite, that of the corporeal thought? The process of maternity involves a broad spectrum of expressive possibility and entails definite elements of creativity, but it is by no means the only way for a woman to realize herself. However, we need not envision a polarity between motherhood and other forms of creative expression for women; on the contrary, a rigid dichotomy of "mothers" versus "not mothers" risks impoverishing both alternatives. The psychic energies that are directed toward bringing a child into the world can find other objects, as occurs when people fall in love, or different ends, as occurs in social accomplishment and cultural production. Whereas maternal behavior in other animals is preprogrammed by genes and instincts, the maternal project in humans is open to other endeavors. But it is not enough to formulate an intentional purpose, a merely intellectual program; one must actually organize the psychic economy, one's management of libidinal energies, differently. In other words, it is necessary to divert oneself from all that is pre-established in motherhood—from its object, from its means and ends—in order to direct oneself to another goal, which may be rather far off in time and space and rather uncertain in its outcomes, but to which one can bring the potential of maternal competence.

The psychoanalytic concept of "sublimation" provides us with a model for considering such an existential contortion. Sublimation is a psychic mechanism that directs the drives toward objects that are sexually neutral and socially valued. It is still a matter of working toward satisfaction, but this is delayed and indirect. Sublimation—which mainly makes use of pregenital impulses, because they are more flexible—remains conditioned by the nature of the forces that it exploits. Anal impulses, for example, can be sublimated in the accumulation of money or in the endeavor of art collecting, among other things, but what remains constant is the retention of contents that are highly valued. Sublimation, insofar that it utilizes pregenital impulses, is extremely close to perversion.[44] In the present case, however, it is a question of sublimating genitalized psychic forces—strongly directed, as we have seen, toward the realization of an object that lies outside of the narcissistic economy. In such a transfer, the emotional inclinations toward caretaking can be used (inhibition of aggression, self-denial, understanding) as they are in the traditional figures of the nun, nurse, teacher, and cook, and in all forms of motherhood. But if we privilege creative aspects, these will become the imaginative materials that are transferred to sublimated motherhood— the imaginative codes, the capacity to reconnect oneself to the bodily (physical) roots of thought.

Freud maintained that only sexual energies neutralized for preventative ends can be sublimated. We might ask ourselves, then, whether psychophysical forces characterized as feminine, such as maternal resources, can be used in the realm of social and cultural action. One way to respond to this question positively is to analyze female cultural activity throughout history, such as the work of women mystics and poets. This process has already revealed the existence of a culture of women who have expressed their sexual identity truthfully and transposed maternal potential into symbolic forms.[45] But if we do not want to view these products as exceptional events, reserved for a chosen few, we need not have to limit our research to these "historic mothers." We must reconstruct the ways in which each of them reached feminine expression and a creative attitude, independent of the outcome of her work, in her own sphere. Lou Andreas-Salomé wrote in this regard that "the sublime and the unusual do not consist in finding what never existed before, in announcing the unthinkable, but in bringing what has become most common, that is known to everybody, to the fullness of its possibility."[46]

The maternal attitude, once redefined, can be transformed into a perspective on the world, a communicative style, a quality of life, and a way of standing in relation to oneself and to others. But it is also a question of seeing whether the endowment connected with the possibility of becoming a mother, and the experience connected with being maternal, can be invested in life projects that are personally gratifying and socially useful beyond one's private realm. The social commitment of the maternal aspect is an established fact, except that female subjectivity often remains separate from processes of work, and female pleasure is negated by the fact of duty.

Recognized maternal dispositions have always been utilized in caring endeavors. The female capacities to attend, contain, preserve, nourish, protect, andheal are redirected from the child onto the environment, from the infantile body to the social body, according to modalities that are rigidly predetermined.[47] However, this type of redirection is not a matter of sublimation, but of simply transplanting these maternal capacities. Sublimation, in fact, requires that drives directed towards the object be turned back onto the self; only at a later point in time are they transposed onto external objects and directed toward autonomously predetermined ends. In every woman's psychic evolution, libidinal energies are displaced and rearranged numerous times, at the end of which they are usually fixed by her education in an opposing typology: the "motherly woman" versus the "narcissistic woman." This is an artifice that deprives both types of depth and life, with one difference: Society is concerned about bringing the narcissistic woman to motherhood, but not with the opposite. The mother/nurturer is, in fact, too useful to the community for it to allow her to abandon the role that is presented to her as both a necessity and destiny.

Before looking at these psychological considerations in terms of their social outlets, it may be useful to quickly review the evolution of female libidinal investment, to identify the injunctions girls and women receive from the outside and the unused possibilities they contain.

When the little girl withdraws the undue amorous demands she has made on her parents at the end of the Oedipal period (at the age of five or six), she turns the correspondent erotic energies back onto herself (secondary narcissism). If she does precisely what her father asks by delaying love and motherhood, she will direct part of these energies onto her partner and child—first anticipated in her imagination, later experienced in the fullness of realization. Some girls and women, however, direct the whole affective load onto themselves. "Strictly speaking," Freud observed, evidently fascinated, "it is only themselves that such women love with an intensity comparable to that of the man's love for them."[48] But he did not see that in a woman even narcissism is maternal—that one part of herself takes the place of the imaginary child. We need only notice how women care for their own bodies—how they look at themselves, brush their hair, nourish themselves, and see mother and daughter joined in themselves.

The possibility of narcissistically appropriating within oneself libidinal energies—even those meant for generation—makes the woman, as Lou Andreas-Salomé wrote, "a happy animal." Not only is the entire surface of the female body erotic; there is also an interior pleasure, an endogenous happiness that has no comparison in the male libidinal economy and that determines a particular attitude toward happiness in women.

Although every woman may be characterized by a greater or lesser possibility to express maternal feelings, the outcomes as envisioned by Freud and others are quite different. The "nurturer" projects onto the other the greater part of her own libidinal energies and remains "impoverished," so to speak, as a result, while the "narcissist," in identifying her own self with the figure of the child, establishes an affective autarchy that gives her value. Self-sufficient as a child, a domestic cat, or a great feline, observed Freud, she exercises an irresistible attraction over protective men who, having denied all of their own narcissism, are in search of a love object. And he concluded that is "the type of female most frequently met with, which is probably the purest and truest one."[49] The mother, in fact, utilizes in an active way (which is therefore considered masculine) those same impulses that the narcissist turns passively back onto her own image. In reality, there is no such absolute polarity; rather, one tendency or the other prevails in a woman's balancing out of her libidinal energies. The two registers are psychologically interchangeable, but life fixes them in stereotypical opposition.

Considering maternity as the realization of all female aspirations, Freud worried that all women cannot enter into the love of the object (male). In fact, he wrote: "A mother is only brought unlimited satisfaction by her relation to a son; this is altogether the most perfect, the most free from ambivalence of all human relationships."[50] It is not worthwhile to reopen the old debate on this point, but it is worth pointing out, once again, how incalculable psychological interferences (threat, exhortation, flattery, allusion) have been used to make all female desire crystallize in motherhood, as man wishes it to be. As we know, social expectations and family structures tend to fix and hold women in the position of mothers, regardless of their deepest intentions and of their conscious convictions.

"Even a marriage," continued Freud, "is not made secure until the wife has succeeded in making her husband her child as well and in acting as a mother to him."[51] Although these words (true as they may be) may represent an unexpected decline into the banality of popular thought, his convictions are interesting because they unintentionally reveal the coercive mechanisms that transform the maternal experience—which is only a possible, even if a central, dimension of female life—into a role that is psychologically induced. The generalization of maternal experience into the perpetual condition of motherhood cancels the creative value inherent in giving life and transforms procreation into an obscure reproduction of bodies, of ideas, of foods, and of things. When women today refuse to identify with motherhood, they are correct in wanting to reject the burden of that status; however, along with throwing off the restrictions of the past, they may be wiping out the possibilities of the future.[52] A recognition of motherhood, from the present point of view, attributes value to what cannot be considered insignificant, so that we do not risk "throwing the baby out with the bath water."

Whereas Freud wanted to demonstrate that even the narcissistic woman could become a loving mother—by locating a part of herself in the baby, thus making the infant lovable—I wonder instead through what process a mothering woman can enter into another form of self-representation and realization. I do not mean by this to describe how it might be possible for a mother to become a manager, because the integration required for such assimilation is quite obvious; rather, I mean to inquire how a woman can transplant those elements of creativity that I have traced in her generative competence to other contexts.[53]

We know that through the process of sublimation all instinctive energies can be redirected to ends different from their original ones, provided that they are withdrawn from the self beforehand. From this point of view, motherhood appears to oppose sublimation. Therefore, it would seem necessary for the mother who does not intend to become "stuck" in this role to detach at a certain point from her child—to make herself emotionally open to other projects and other points of reference. But even women who are not mothers carry within themselves a potential maternal project. Motherhood, understood as creativity, is a modality that a woman may or may not realize in a child, but that remains inscribed in her instinctive energies. It is not necessary for her to neutralize herself to enter into the sphere of social interactions. It *is* possible for her to transpose her sexual energies and her maternal creativity to that sphere, once they are recognized as forms of energy that are made up of mind and body, of the unconscious imagination and of recognized fantasy, of both the individual and social economies of exchange. Naturally, all of this carries with it a redefinition of the symbolic field and a renegotiation of social relationships. This belief has given female thought the strength to see womanhood as a source of extraordinary innovative capacity, rather than as a distressing diminishment of thought.

A book by Evelyn Fox Keller about Barbara McClintock, who was awarded the Nobel Prize in 1983 for her work in genetics, provides an opportunity to debate these issues. McClintock's discovery of the mobility of genes transformed the very concept of the genetic program from the earlier static model, by recognizing in it an internal dynamic and an environmental interaction aimed at adaptation.[54] "What allowed McClintock to be able to see further and deeper into the mysteries of genetics than her colleagues?" Keller's answer is simple, and comes up repeatedly: McClintock had the time to look, the patience "to hear what things have to say," and the intellectual openness to "let them come to [her]."[55] Without getting into the merits of a rather complex text, I only wish to point out how the creative attitude attributed to this scientist has many points in common

with the characteristics of maternal experience. The relationship that the
geneticist maintained with stalks of corn is analogous to that of a mother
with her child. And yet the role played by her being a woman is not as linear
as it might appear, because McClintock never recognized a professional
female identity in herself, in that she was attempting instead to practice a
neutral knowledge.[56]

Therefore we cannot consider the specificity of female intellect as a
consequence of social identity. Belonging to the female gender, as society
and culture have shaped it, creates a traditional mentality forged, as we have
seen, by the projections of male desires and fears. More likely, biological
sexual identity does not guarantee any sort of intellectual autonomy whatsoever, because it does not necessarily create a way of thinking that is
faithful to a specific sex. If that were so, all women would automatically
bring a sign of sexual difference into their activity, whereas we know that
most of us find it easier and more convenient to camouflage ourselves in
neutrality. Only by placing the realm of imagination between the body and
thought can we discover a locus for the interaction between our sense of
being female and our existence as social subjects. But the imaginary realm
is not the reserve of uncontaminated nature (as even a short clinical history
like Anna's reveals); rather, it is the battleground of a thousand struggles,
of which the struggle between the sexes may be most prominent. This is
why we will not find immediate liberation, spontaneity, or authenticity
there, but only the possibility, sometimes unexplored, of becoming ourselves. Just as the mother brings a child into the world and, in some sense,
invents the child by creating from the little that is there, projecting him or
her onto the figures of her desire, presenting to him or her the combinative
possibilities of a game, we women can do this for ourselves. We can put our
generative capacities to use—not to indulge ourselves, but to bring ourselves into the world, using the love we have reinvested in ourselves in a
maternal project that includes us. We know that to reach this goal, we need
empty spaces and silences where nothing happens, and where we can
decenter our thoughts and let our feelings drift and unexpectedly focus—in
other words, where we can assume an atopic position in relation to the
world and its expectation, but a position that is deeply rooted in a self
founded on its own possibilities of realization.[57]

In a certain sense, Barbara McClintock's capacity to "be alone," not
to distance herself from human society, but to adopt a decentered and
alternative point of view, was decisive. This critical distancing, the questioning of predetermined truths, the suspicion of our own identity, is a
necessary deconstructing movement, but we must combine it with the work
of recovering and constructing the possibilities of the future. The archives
of the female imagination contain elements of our identity; some are
fragmented and some burnt, but they nevertheless can be reclaimed in

thought, reformed in new configurations of thought. However, this can only happen if as women we perform the preliminary gesture of relying upon ourselves—redefining our own gender-specific identities and our own re-ciprocal value by taking even the pre-existing knowledge that opposes us, along with knowledge that stands outside of given disciplinary contexts, and putting it to transgressive uses.

Since the position we assume in relationship to ourselves and the world, and the responsibility we take for our own thought, appear funda-mental in respect to the exercise of our capabilities, we must first ask ourselves whether a mother is an ethical subject, or whether she belongs (as tradition holds) in a private space and in a presymbolic structure that is removed from the exercise of moral virtues.

CHILD REARING AS MORALITY

The Bad Mother: Cultural and Psychoanalytical Views

The equation "mama = goodness" that begins with mother's milk and is confirmed by the rhetoric of social relationships should not deceive us. The figures of the stepmother and the witch have quite another sense in the narrative tradition and the shared imagination. This proclaimed maternal sweetness does not extend beyond the language connected to childhood and the flattery of advertising. On the contrary, the mother is the image upon which shared fears and anxieties are projected, the background where man's most burdensome dictates appear, the promiscuous nature against which the frontiers of law are built. She is nothing taken by herself, having no other subjectivity than that which she derives from her relationship to her child.

In classical culture's model of childhood education (which was only for sons), the mother played a completely marginal role. As long as the little boy was entrusted to female care, he was seen as nothing more than a little animal. The relationship that adults established with him was defined as "raising," or, in the best of cases, "natural education." It was taken for granted that, given his traumatic birth, a long period of intensive care—a prolonged period of gestation of sorts—would be required, in a "transi-tional" space that was outside the mother's body but inside the domestic one. The boy's true birth, the social one, only began when he gained distance from the house and from women, to be entrusted to society and to male training. The processes that took place in the maternal space remained hidden in the shadows. Most importantly, prescriptions for child raising regulated bodily care, mainly in an attempt to limit invasive female affec-tivity, which was felt to be potentially corrupting. This was an age-old conviction, as revealed by the Stoic theory that the hot baths administered to newborns by midwives were the first cause of human corruption—the moment in which evil insinuated itself into original human goodness, through the medium of pleasure.[58] We find this theory intact in the German pedagogy of the late nineteenth century, which justified an education correctly defined as "orthopedic."[59]

Although it has not been further analyzed, the maternal bond is felt to be disturbing because it is the unconscious vehicle of messages that are determinant for the subject's development. As such, it must be limited as quickly as possible. It is confined by the child's access to social language at the end of infancy.[60] What happened earlier remains relegated to a prehistoric past that cannot be recovered through memory. If, in the ancient world, maternal affection was the vehicle for bad morals, for modern culture it is represented as the cause of the "moral illness," the primary cause of psychoses.

Freud was aware that what happens during the later period of childhood is decisive in the constitution of the individual. In plumbing the psychic pathologies of the adult, he moved back to early childhood—retracing to the phase of the mother–child dyad, prior to recognition of the father, the "points of fixation" in psychosis. But Freud limited himself to conceptualizing a pre-Oedipal period that would later be described by his successors, Melanie Klein and David Winnicott in particular. Analyzing childhood games as if they were dreams, Klein rediscovered the lost images of that first mother–child relationship, when the maternal body is for the child the psychic space where the major instinctual impulses toward life and death, toward love and hate, take place. Without reconstructing her "theater of the unconscious,"[61] I would like to emphasize how the drives, which are described as individual dynamics by Freud, are shown to be relational structures—modalities of relating to the object, and first of all to the mother.

The use of psychiatric terms to identify the various positions that the child assumes in relation to the mother ("schizoid," "paranoid," "paranoid–schizophrenic," "depressive") has the effect of making the mother–child relationship appear pathological. In particular, psychoses, which Freud considered impossible to analyze, were instead confronted analytically by his successors, who thus extended to psychoses the theory and method elaborated around the mother–child relationship.[62] Although this outcome was not intended, the mother, the relational object *par excellence*, turns out in this schema to be the first environmental factor to which the psychosis can be traced back.

Harry Stack Sullivan came to the same conclusion through his treatment of adult schizophrenics: The relational failure that is, in the final analysis, the cause of the psychotic condition can be traced back to the child's first relationship to the mother.[63] When she cannot control her anxiety, she is perceived by the child as an evil object that will invade and destroy him or her. In such cases, Sullivan spoke of the "schizophrenogenic mother" a concept that became widespread in psychiatry. It has served the same causal function in the more recent writings of psychoanalysts Heinz Kohut and H. Searles,[64] who have not distinguished between the imagined mother and the real mother. In any case, it has been assumed that the child's psychic development will be optimal if a pathogenic mother does not interfere, "pathogenic" being described in a great variety of ways: "overwhelming," "castrating," "demeaning," "anxiety-producing," "unpredictable," "inadequate," "narcissistic," and/or "depressive." In reply to objections that all of these characteristics may be inevitable reactions to the emotional demands of the maternal task, the authors have responded by calling the cause an excess, either too much or too little. Here we come face to face with mothers who are too giving, too demanding, too distant, or too empathetic—an unlimited causality that can be unified by the statement "All mothers are bad."[65]

After she observed the contradictions of the analytical theories of women, Mitscherlich-Nielsen wrote: "The impossible is demanded of [the mother]. How could a woman possibly succeed in doing what is required today of a mother in terms of love and empathy when she herself was never given love free of ambivalence, as psychoanalytical theory itself attests anyway?"[66] To alleviate the sense of oppression that arises from the heap of accusations directed at the mother, the absent defendant, I often tell this anecdote: "A young woman waiting for her first child went to a very famous psychoanalyst to find out how she should raise her child so that he would grow up to be healthy, happy, and free of complexes. To that question, the psychoanalyst responded solemnly: 'Come back when he's four years old and I'll tell you what you did wrong.'" Many of the excesses of the pathologization of the maternal figure have recently been emended, and the demands for perfection revised—so much so that Winnicott eventually made a point of wishing for "a good enough mother" at best. Bruno Bettelheim has extended this idea to both parents, entitling his book on child raising *The Nearly Perfect Parent.*[67]

Nevertheless, even the most knowledgeable authors may inadvertently have produced a model of maternal psychology that is transferred from that of the child. I am referring to the postulation that the birth of the infantile self takes place on an original substratum of indistinction. Winnicott has spoken of "primary confusion," Maud Khan of "a state of non-integration," and Margaret S. Mahler of "normal autism" followed by a "symbiotic stage."[68] From this stage of symbiotic unity, the child advances to a differentiation of self and to the successive conquest of functional autonomy. In this model, fixation at these early phases of psychic development corresponds to infantile psychoses, in particular to the "autistic syndrome" and the "symbiotic syndrome." The widespread use of these terms, however, allows one to presume that in the symbiotic phase the experiences of mother and child coincide, and that the child's clinging identification with the mother corresponds to an analogous clinging iden‑ tification of the mother with the child. These are terms that describe the protomental indistinction of the nursing child, as can be presumed from observations of the child's behavior and from analytic accounts of psychotic experiences.

Using speculative analogy to extend these same states to the mother is arbitrary, to say the least. It fails to recognize, in any case, that the mother is an adult individual who is part of a complex network of relationships, and that she can only give a small part of herself over to the absolute logic of infantile fantasy. The "dual cavity" takes up all of infantile experience, but it is only a part of maternal experience. If the unconscious channel alone, the umbilical cord of feeling, is given priority, the conscious dimension of the mother's thought—her integration of self and her capacity to reflect on her experience—is disregarded. The very twofold nature of the mother's view of the child, at once imagined and real, prevents a symbiotic union into which it would be possible to introduce later divisions. The mother is an individual, inscribed in a story and life project of her own. Finally, to relegate her to an infantile condition of confusion also means to disregard the incidence of maternal communication, the mother's capacity to trans‑ mit precocious categorical structures. Lorenzer believes that through the practical/gestural codes with which the mother addresses the child, deter‑ mined forms of socialization are reproduced—invisible schemata that pre‑ determine the child's communicative behavior.[69]

To place the mother outside of time and space, in a dimension characterized by the concepts of "early" and "elsewhere," represents sub‑ mission to the mythic imagination and its symbolic determinants. As we know, the script dictates that the male enters onto the scene, bringing difference—order, norm—where confusion, chaos, and anarchy have reigned. Similarly, the Oedipal scheme would have it that the mother–child dyad—the locus of presymbolic communication, of the immediacy of the imaginary realm, of the omnipotence of delirium—be separated as quickly as possible by the intrusion of the father, who is the bearer of the injunction against incest and the very condition of society and of law. Wherever the "name of the father" is not heard, Lacan maintains,[70] the child is subject to maternal desire, obligated to compensate for her castration, and exiled in psychosis and death. Taking the implications of the Freudian model to an extreme (which is characteristic of his intellectual style), Lacan reveals more clearly than anyone else the radical underlying sexual asymmetry, the total negation of the mother's positive aspect in favor of the father's power and will.

In opposition to this model—in which the mother is marginalized and guilt-laden, and in which the moral elements of her behavior are disregarded—I propose to reformulate the mother–child relationship as an "ethical paradigm,"[71] emphasizing its elements of freedom and responsibility.

Ethics of Motherhood: A Reconstruction

To begin with, the original couple constitutes the most universal expression of human interaction. Its communicative codes, which are shared by everybody, are the most sublime known, even if they are exhibited among the most varied social and cultural contexts. Extensive in time and space, the particular intensity of the mother–child relationship corresponds to the conviction that it is absolutely unique and irreplaceable. Whereas the paternal function in generation was long unknown because of the temporal and physical distance between coitus and childbirth, the maternal function was self-evident as a result of its materiality (physicality). "For a long time," writes Franca Basaglia Ongaro, speaking of the origins of humanity, "man didn't connect the sexual act to procreation, so that the woman represented in his eyes the autonomous fullness of a continuous gestation." Out of this perception arose a magical conception of filiation, which anthropological research has tracked to "traditional cultures" of peoples who are our contemporaries.[72]

To the father, procreation represents a gesture that can also be ignored, and filiation a symbolic act that can be denied, whereas for the mother it is a matter of an unforgettable event that involves her completely.[73] A woman cannot reverse or turn back from the choice to have a child—a choice that means she must assume the responsibility for the other, the child, who is experienced as a part of herself but also as a separate object, with his or her own potential capacity for individuation and autonomous growth. As we have seen, staying pregnant is often the conscious or unconscious answer to a maternal call, an archaic and wild appeal in respect to social deadlines, to an instinct for fertilization whose urgency and efficacy are unknown to her. What this requires of the woman is a gesture of obedience to the will of another whose face and voice she does not know.

In any case, whether or not the child is wanted determines a whole series of inescapable behaviors. Once the maternal process is undertaken, it presents itself in terms of necessity. It is up to the woman to reformulate it in terms of desirability. Even if a child is rejected, the cost is still high for the woman: She must root him or her out of her body, and even then the child always remains inscribed in her imagination, alive and unfinished like the figures of the unconscious. As we have noted, the child's sudden appearance on the scene requires a reconstruction of the self, a confrontation between life and death. Biological time inserts itself into biographical time, dramatically revealing the latter's limits. An experience of submission to something that transcends the individual takes the place of the mastery of the self, altering the woman's relationship to nature.

In one of the most intriguing texts ever written on the feminine, Tonka,[74] Robert Musil confronts the incalculable time of gestation, "closer to life (and to death) than to thought"; it seems to him an enigma that imposes an insurmountable barrier to calculative reasoning and its arrogant grasp on reality. Tonka—the obscure girl who loses herself in the impersonality of generation, a body/thing that words cannot reach—seems to mark, for him, the limits of science and the inscrutability of nature.

In recent years, reflections on the relationship between culture and nature have emphasized woman's proximity to life and earth. This position appears to lay the foundations for a more conscious ecological sensibility (so-called "ecofeminism")—an innate consciousness of limits, a spontaneous rejection of domination and exploitation. However, I do not believe that biology gives anybody a privileged position in respect to the world's problems. It will take knowledge, critical awareness, and political passion to transform feeling into wisdom. Rather, the relationship that a mother establishes with her child, and the evolution of that relationship in creative terms as I have analyzed it here, are what constitute a possible ethical paradigm.

We know that the child is expected by a maternal body and by a "maternalized" mind; nevertheless, he or she always arrives unexpectedly. Rather than perceiving the new life as an invasion, the woman reforms the boundaries of her body and her mind to hold the other that is growing within her. Maternity provokes a crisis in the existence of every woman; it requires a destructuring of the pre-existing balances and the elaboration of a different, more complex readaptation. The child represents a new sphere of possibility, but also represents the rejection of other life projects. In this redefinition of self, the woman is relatively alone. Although social injunctions emphasize paternal fertilization, the woman has a virginal concept of her own maternity, as the figure of the Madonna, both virgin and mother, symbolizes. The father, insofar as the original couple is concerned, is an external figure, the guarantor of the social acceptance of the newborn. Fornari points out that the father's function is to take the mother's anxiety into himself and to reduce it.[75] But this happens mostly at the moment of birth, when the man absorbs the specters of death that arise; it is, however, difficult for him to intervene in the elaboration of pregnancy. The quality of the pregnant woman's relationship with her partner is decisive in whether or not she can create a "maternal niche," but the woman elaborates her interior phantasms on her own. Her partner is required to be close—available and ready to listen—but any intrusion will be rejected. Clear regressive dynamics accompany profound evolutive rearrangements. Her swelling belly, which is being filled from within, displaces the anxiety about sterility and inadequacy, and her deformed body corroborates her image as the graces of girlhood never could. Often the man is overcome by envy of the "sumptuous creativity of the woman," who is celebrating the extraordinary rites of maternity.[76]

This female self-sufficiency excludes the man, and the internalization that the woman's energies undergo robs him of her care and affection. Here begins the rivalry with the intruder, the prehistory of the Oedipal conflict. On the other hand, the displacement of her narcissistic libido onto another object does not seem to disturb the mother; she is willing to make the self-sacrifice that this demands of her, because a new love relationship is progressively established. As the expression goes, "a child never asks to be born"; yet the mother feels in her unconscious that her desire for mother-hood was never a solipsistic whim, and that for a child to come into the world, two life projects must correspond.

As studies of immunology show, the mother's biological self, her genetic individuality, does not react toward the embryo as if it were alien; it does not assail the embryo with antigens as it would any other incompat-ible element. In pregnancy, an automatic blocking of the immune system is set off that has no equivalent and that constitutes the condition *a priori* of embryonic development. The suspension of biological aggression is accompanied by an evident dimunition of psychological aggression in respect to the fetus. In spite of the discomfort and illness that come with pregnancy, especially during the final months, the woman endures what she would have never been able to tolerate under other conditions. Any eventual hostile impulses are aimed at the imaginary child, thus protecting the real one from attack. Only at the end of gestation, a whole series of signals—the feelings of heaviness, of suffocation, of the exhaustion of nutritional resources—reactivates aggressive charges in the woman and converges on her in a phantasm of expulsion. We have already seen how childbirth can be an experience characterized by intense feelings of love and hate, and how the birth can transform an experience of happy realiza-tion of self in another.

But after the acceptance of motherhood—the greatest moment of human responsibility—the subsequent generative process, right up until the birth, seems to unfold according to its own intrinsic necessity. Never-theless, what prevails is not an impersonal biological plan, because preg-nancy is an interaction prepared by the fantasies of motherhood. No maternity exists, even potentially speaking, without some preliminary recognition of the other. Procreation is essentially a relationship, and gestation involves a silent dialogue in the shared space of the maternal body. On the other hand, after birth the relationship between mother and newborn is characterized by the transformation of necessity into freedom. The instinctual programming that presides over the rearing of the young is not so predetermined as to remove all margin of intention. The bond between a mother and her newborn is primarily cultural, and as such it presents a wide degree of choice.

If we examine the mother–child relationship as one of many possible human relationships, it appears to be so asymmetrical that it seems the most violent form of domination. In comparison to the baby, the mother possesses more power than any tyrant ever dreamed of exercising. A master's possession of a slave, the mastery of a lord over a servant, the will of a Nazi jailer over a prisoner are all nothing in comparison to the hold that the mother has over her helpless newborn. In the case of interaction between adults, it is always possible for one to preserve a realm of interior freedom— for a part of the self to be withdrawn from the source of oppression, to escape annihilation. For the newborn, on the other hand, there is no possibility of escape except into death, physical or psychic, as Bettelheim's theory of infantile autism demonstrates.[77]

And yet maternal possession never becomes an annihilation of the other, the desire for total subjugation. Instead of occupying a position of power, the mother splits into two: One part contains the immature baby and absorbs his or her regressive tendencies, whereas the other allies herself with the little one's liberating dynamics and with the energies directed toward individuation and separation. The mother's capacity to adapt to the needs of her child is extraordinary, but progressively a complementary capacity for maladjustment and for dissonance emerges. This allows the child to go forward on his or her own, to proceed autonomously by trial and error.

As we have seen, according to psychoanalysis only the father's intervention allows the dyad to diverge, and introduces division where otherwise only a stagnant possessiveness would reign. I believe, though, that the mother holds the desire for distinction within herself and her own generative plan, and that the father affirms and sustains it with his own demand for priority. The omnipotence of the imaginary child and the overwhelming logic of this fantasy make their own irreducible demands in the mother's unconscious, but they are displaced by the wish for freedom—by the mother's desire for her own realization as well as that of her child. This displacement, however, is blocked by a culture that has reactionary attitudes toward maternity, that looks upon the child as the single female accomplishment. In this case, the paternal prohibition against the mother's joining herself to her own generative product, and the external imposition of the incest prohibition, become a necessary antidote to the unifying command.

But when other modes of self-affirmation are offered to the woman as well, the social prohibition loses its former importance, and the father's role as avenger is transformed into that of coauthor in the project of filiation.

The awful image of the father who prevents the unity of mother and child through the threat of castration is replaced by a more tolerant figure who is capable of countering the unconscious fantasies of the self-sufficiency of the original couple. The mother herself attempts to "offer" the child to the father: She tries to get him to recognize the child, to make the child lovable, to introduce him or her into the couple's relationship. In the child's eyes, the real father is the person who is presented as such by the mother. The newborn comes to light as the fruit of the mother's body, but he or she grows up as the child of two parents because the woman has given up a part of her possession over her offspring.

It is told that King Solomon, when called upon to decide the real mother of a child who was being contested, threatened to divide the infant in half "in the name of justice." In the face of this possibility, one of the two women renounced her claim. "This is the real mother," the wise king decreed. In actuality, the "real mother" is both, and as such is characterized by a continual tension that consists of the exercising of her moral subjectivity. Her endless task requires her to move from possessing of the child to allowing for his or her autonomy, from control to trust, from imposition to responsibility.

In this sense, the mother is the only absolute master who limits herself, the only tyrant who loosens the hold that she maintains over her subject. Often she is opposed to love that is bound to rationality and pursues detachment, but maternal love is not irrational and foresees the child's independence as a condition of the realization of both mother and child.[78] Distance, then, does not become abandonment because it does not prevent the mother's responsible involvement, her willingness to take the child in. The image of a mother leaning over a child as the child takes his or her first steps, I think, embodies this two-sided attitude. On one hand, the mother holds the child within the curve of her body and supports his or her fragile arms; on the other, she guides the child's steps away from herself and toward the world. The autonomy and independence that the mother regains by degree do not prevent her from feeling loving and protective toward her child, and the sublimation of her maternal competence does not let the filial bond come untied. Indeed, women who have experienced symbolic maternity enrich biological maternity with value and meaning.

Helene Deutsch concludes her essential study of femininity by asserting that only two alternatives are open to women once they reach maturity: being a grandmother or being a witch.[79] Here, the scientific discourse enacts an absurd threat of blackmail. The preconstituted definitions of femininity represent a trap we must escape, but the homogenization to male definitions are equally off the track. The antinomy between being a passive, marginalized mother consumed in nurturing or an active, socialized woman involved in many things has in fact been overcome, but as a cultural representation it continues to cast a shadow over our identity as women, over the sense that we have of the meaning and value of our sex. To recover motherhood as an intrinsic possibility of being female, independent of its realization, means for many women a rediscovery of a hidden self, the accomplishment of fertile completion.[80] Maternal possibility is an inalienable aspect of female identity that allows a woman to respond with a "yes" or a "no" to its call. Only society sets "mothers" and "nonmothers" in opposition.

There is a discrepancy between our lives and our cultural tradition, between the dominant social representation and the way women see themselves, that leaves us at the mercy of individual strategies and attempts (some more successful than others) at self-realization. Self-realization therefore never becomes a common legacy, a transmissible knowledge. Some women assume important social responsibilities, but independently of or despite the fact that they are women. Glimpsing a creative potential in motherhood and an ethical paradigm in the mother–child relationship can significantly alter the role of women in our society. After all, it is the mother who transforms a mammalian infant into a young citizen, making society and culture possible and allowing their values to be passed on. The opposition between mothers of children and mothers of symbols is therefore arbitrary; both are social and cultural figures.

Only the value of "biological" motherhood remains invisible, canceled out by the presumed inevitability and necessity of the task, and of the private space in which it takes place. We owe this observation to Winnicott, among psychoanalysts, and to Adrienne Rich, among feminists, who have both protested that being "of woman born"[81] has been unjustly misunderstood. "It seems to me," Winnicott wrote, "that something in human society is being lost. Children grow up and become in their turn fathers and mothers, but, on the whole, they don't grow with an awareness of what their mothers did for them at the beginning of life. The reason for that and the role that a mother plays have only recently begun to be noticed."[82] The difficulty of appreciating the mother's devotion and of being grateful to her arises, according to Winnicott, from an inability to admit total dependence upon another human being. This denial provokes fear—of the woman in particular, and of any form of submission in general. Winnicott has glimpsed here a predisposition to dictatorship, in that the dictator gives value to and imposes the subjugation that is feared, thus placating the anxiety-producing fears of his subjects.

Presently, a woman's repression of all dependence would seem to produce the so-called "narcissistic personality," who is closed within herself in a self-sufficient endeavor that renders affective relationships merely instrumental and provisional. However, the mother who represents the opposite—a prevalence of affectivity directed toward the other (whether person or goal)—belies (through her celebration of self and the sublimation of her specific energies) the absolute opposition of narcissism. Narcissism and self-sacrifice are provisional organizations of the libido that only society fixes in roles and in stereotypical attitudes. The reconstruction of the mother–child relationship refutes all illusion of self-sufficiency and forces us to think about ourselves without simplifying matters. Only recently have we begun to look courageously at this central point in our lives. What is too close to us and to our image is difficult to focus upon; self-reflection blurs the lens of thought.

ARTIFICIAL REPRODUCTION: A NEW STRUGGLE FOR GENERATIVE POWER

The advent of artificial insemination, *in vitro* fertilization, and other forms of "artificial reproduction" has distanced fertility from the body and has objectified the reproductive process. This is not so much a matter of scientific discovery, because for two hundred years the possibility was known (moreover, artificial insemination was applied in animal breeding), as much as a cultural event in the broad sense—the emergence of obsolete figures of the imagination. The possibility of fertilizing bodies that would remain sterile in and of themselves modifies a generative sequence that in the entire history of humankind has never known radical variation. Suddenly the time frames, locations, and actors in human procreation have changed; unheard-of modes of selecting and manipulating the generative product have appeared. The observation that most babies are still "made" by traditional methods does not begin to diminish the dizzying implications of the possibilities that face us. In a certain sense, the arena of reproductive technology is nothing more than the latest setting for the centuries-old struggle between the sexes for control over reproductive power. In this setting, the (largely male-dominated) scientific imagination and the feminine imagination are the forces pitted against each other in the quest for generative omnipotence.[83]

The two imaginaries converge in a common phantasm: that of the "child of the night," which is articulated for the woman in the desire for a child "no matter what the cost," and for the doctor in the desire for a child "no matter what the method." The omnipotence that dominates both desires is concealed behind the therapeutic concept of new reproductive technologies. Although sterile individuals remain so even when they are induced to procreate, the fertility intervention comes to be compared with the healing of sick bodies. Research on the causes and possible prevention of sterility is replaced by the more remunerative research aimed at discovering a way to "bypass" the interrupted procreative process. The acceptance of the technology of cure not only hides the desire for power that animates it, but hinders us from assuming critical attitudes and socially responsible reactions—which becomes particularly difficult, given the profound complicity that has been established between the "discoveries" of medicine and the unconscious psychic economy, which is extremely intolerant of any limitation.

Even when sterility is associated with the husband, it is always the woman who is subjected to the most invasive procedures of artificial fertilization. Among these are the suppression of the natural hormonal cycle and its replacement with a more predictable artificial cycle that is pharmacologically induced. The physiological clock of the female is thus abused by the artificial clock of (the medical) cure. The cure in question is a sporadic intervention that nevertheless appears to be extremely significant—significant in that it completes a process that began with the distant loss of estrus and the consequent domestication of the female body, subjected to an internal regulation that anticipates the replacement of its reproductive function by a technological apparatus.

Although the male project of total control over filiation seems rather close to being realized, its connection to the unconscious imagination, with its narcissistic and omnipotent desire, has not been acknowledged. This is tru of women's requests for artificial insemination as well. The possibility of turning to an anonymous donor for semen seems to fulfill the illusion of parthenogenesis, of procreative autonomy, that characterizes the way young girls think about the enigma of birth. Furthermore, the loss of the sexual partner, who is replaced by the doctor who carries out the fertilization, seems to satisfy the remote fantasy of receiving a child from the father without arousing the Oedipal prohibition. In a certain sense, the seed that is released uncontrollably, the ovum that is offered for unforeseen fertilization, the uterus that accepts the fetus of another—all of these form the image of a fragmented body, sectioned off in the partiality of its separate components and functions, just as we find in the most precocious infantile fantasies that precede the acquisition of identity and that reappear in the most disturbed regressions of psychotic delirium.

Perhaps the quintessential moment of artificial reproduction, the synthesis of its interventions, occurs during *in vitro* fertilization when the sperm and ovum meet in a test tube. This extracorporeal occurrence is completely removed in time and space from the organisms that, at a given moment in their history, have produced those generative elements. The praxis of the laboratory is substituted for the sexual encounter, casting a shadow over the creators of a procreation that never knows the heat of affectivity or the violence of drive. Thus, a new life begins—in the absence of the subjective intentionality that, as we have seen, has characterized the scientific model of biology since Aristotle.

The birth of a "test-tube baby," which can take place far from the bodies of the biological parents and even many years after they are dead, infringes upon the autobiographical coordinates of filiation—the proximity that has always been required by consanguinity, at least until now. The gap between the individual's time and the impersonal time of reproductive cells allows us to see that double register of life whose presence Freud glimpsed in us and identified as the eternity of the species. And for the "child of science," cut off from any kind of historically pre-established genealogy, it is legitimate to elaborate a "family novel" around the mystery of his or her origins, written wholly by desire—to imagine giving birth to himself or herself, just like the narcissistic personalities who characterize our time.

Without these hidden analogies between the scientific imagination and the individual unconscious, we cannot explain the ease with which our society accepts the most unforeseen modes of filiation, and the indifference with which we accept the most unheard-of forms of kinship in a family system that has always been based on the ties of consanguinity and on the priority of the "name of the father." The desire for procreation is certainly legitimate, even when it comes up against the boundaries of sterility, but the medical control of fertility cannot limit itself to eradicating sterility. We cannot forget that the unconscious, which is absolutely egocentric and egotistic, is utterly indifferent to the consequences of its actions and to the relational aspects of its goals. The indifference is all the greater in the case of the scientific imagination, because the myriad of figures involved in every new generative process remains hidden by the impersonality of technology and the self-justifying logic of scientific progress.

But technologically supported fertilization and gestation are only the beginnings of biological manipulation. Beyond them we can glimpse the advent of genetic engineering, with its threatening potential to give shape to the desire for an ideal offspring, for an "ideal filiation." The "child of the night" thus risks connecting the individual imagination to the power of science without hope of mediation, enacting the theatre of dreams in our society. If this occurs, it will take us by surprise; we will be unable to recognize the residue of the past and the determinations of the unconscious, and unable to connect them with the deadlines awaiting us.

The fanciful events that emerge from medical laboratories from time to time undermine our most sacred points of reference, but they fail to provide us with substitutes in the meantime. Paradoxically, as the future invades our lives, it seems to drag the relics of the past into the lacuna of the present. In this lacuna, women appear, once again, to be containers of a generative process that somehow escapes their responsibility and their management. Often the desire for motherhood is experienced in solitude and can only be expressed as a request for therapy, which is prompted by the medical establishment itself in its offer of advanced cures. But, as we know, the need to be a mother can be a metaphor for other things and can find alternative expression, if the definition of human reproduction is not given over to gynecology.

In the face of the uncontrollable advance of reproductive technologies and the questions that they pose, perhaps it is not too late to rethink motherhood, to remove it from the stereotypes that waste its wealth of resources. To give voice to the silence of motherhood, to reclaim the complexity of the maternal endeavor and the morality inherent in its exercise of limits—this would appear to be the final act in the age-old dispute over who holds the power to engender. And it may also be women's last chance to alter the final outcome of an age-old defeat, which we can trace to the origins of humanity, though it still casts a shadow upon our incomplete identity.

Notes

CHAPTER 1

1. On this point Freud wrote, "The Emperor and Empress (or the King and Queen) as a rule really represent the dreamer's parents; and a Prince or Princess represents the dreamer himself or herself." "The Interpretation of Dreams" (1899), in J. Strachey (Ed. and Trans.), *The Standard Edition of the Complete Psychological Works of Sigmund Freud* (hereafter *SE*) (London: Hogarth Press, 19; original work published 1923), Vol. 5, p. 353.
2. Trevi, "Per una valutazione critica dell'opera di C. G. Jung," *Aut aut*, no. 229–230 (Jan.–Apr. 1989), p. 29.
3. Plato, *Symposium*, 180 e. Freud commented upon this myth in "Beyond the Pleasure Principle" (1920). In a note, he referred to one of the most ancient Indian myths, which describes how the universe originated from the *Atman* (the subject or ego); "But he [the Atman] felt no delight. Therefore a man who is lonely feels no delight. He wished for a second. He was so large as man and wife together. He then made his Self to fall in two, and then arose husband and wife. Therefore Yagñavalkya said: 'We two are thus (each of us) like half a shell.' Therefore the void which was there, is filled by the wife." *SE*, Vol. 18, p. 58n. On the hermaphrodite, see also C. G. Jung, "The Psychology of the Transference," in *Collected Works* (Princeton, NJ: Princeton University Press, 1954), Vol. 16.
4. Artemidorous, *The Book of Dreams*, V, p. 12.
5. S. Freud, "Three Essays on the Theory of Sexuality" (1905), *SE*, Vol. 7, p. 193, and "The Sexual Enlightenment of Children" (1907), *SE*, Vol. 9, p. 136. The priority of the question on origins will subsequently be reserved only for men. See "Some Psychical Consequences of the Anatomical Distinction between the Sexes" (1925), *SE*, Vol. 19, p. 252, n. 2.

In the myth of Oedipus, taken up again in Sophocles's tragedy, the Sphinx, who stands guard at the gates of Thebes, puts this riddle to him: "What animal walks on four legs in the morning, on two at noon, and on three at night?"

"Man," Oedipus answers, "the baby who crawls, the adult who walks, and the old man who advances with a cane." Oedipus's experience represents the prohibition against incest that is in opposition to the infantile desire to love the parent of the opposite sex, becoming the rival of the parent of the same sex.

6. S. Freud, "The Theme of the Three Caskets" (1913), *SE*, Vol. 12.
7. J. Lacan, *Le Séminaire*, Book 2, *Le Moi dans la théorie de Freud et dans la technique de la psychoanalyse* (Paris: Seuil, 1978), p. 189.
8. B. Bettelheim, *Symbolic Wounds: Puberty Rites and the Envious Male*. (Glencoe, IL: Free Press, 1954).
9. J. Chevalier & A. Gheerbrant, *Dictionary of Symbols*, 2 Vols. (1969).
10. Freud discusses this problem in "The Dissolution of the Oedipus Complex" (1924), *SE*, Vol. 19.
11. The expression is inspired by the portion of the bas-relief in the Gradiva, analyzed by Freud in "Delusions and Dreams in Jensen's *Gradiva*" (1907 [1906]), *SE*, Vol. 9, and by the sentence that he quotes in "Analysis Terminable and Interminable" (1937), according to which "Every step forward is only half as big as it looks at first." *SE*, Vol. 23, p. 228. On this point, see also *Tra nostalgia e trasformazione*, Centro Documentazione Donna di Firenze, Quaderno di Lavoro n. 2, March–May 1986.
12. Plotinus, VI, 7.34. This theme winds through the last book of E. Fachinelli, *La mente estatica* (Milan: Adelphi, 1989).
13. I am referring here to the work of E. Fachinelli, *La freccia ferma: tre tentativi di annullare il tempo* (Milan: L'Erba Voglio, 1979).
14. S. Freud, "Three Essays on the Theory of Sexuality," op. cit., p. 151.
15. J. P. Vernant & P. Vidal-Naquet, *Myth and Tragedy*, Vols. 1 & 2, trans. Janet Lloyd (New York: Zone Books, 1987).
16. Freud discusses the symbolic equation of the foot–phallus repeatedly, particularly in "Three Essays on the Theory of Sexuality," p. 154; "Delusions and Dreams in Jensen's *Gradiva*," pp. 45–47; "Leonardo da Vinci and a Memory of His Childhood" (1910), *SE*, Vol. 11, p. 102.
17. S. Freud, "Hysterical Phantasies and Their Relation to Bisexuality," *SE*, Vol. 9, p. 164.
18. On this point J. Breuer writes, "the clonic movements of struggling and of shaking the legs, remain for all of life the forms of reaction for cases of maximum excitement of the brain." J. Breuer and S. Freud, "Studies in Hysteria" (1892–1895), *SE*, Vol. 2.
19. Freud wrote, "[I have a] suspicion that this phase of attachment to the mother is especially intimately related to the aetiology of hysteria, which is not surprising when we reflect that both the phase and the neurosis are characteristically feminine, and further, that in this dependence on the mother we have the germ of later paranoia in women." "Female Sexuality" (1931), *SE*, Vol. 21, p. 227.
20. L. Boella, "Pensare liberamente pensare il mondo," in Diotima, *Mettere al mondo il mondo* (Milan: La Tartaruga, 1990), p. 184.
21. S. Freud, *The Complete Letters of Sigmund Freud to Wilhelm Fliess, 1887–1904*, J. M. Masson (Ed. & Trans.). Cambridge, MA: Harvard University Press, 1985.

22. F. Papi, "Verità e racconti d'infanzia," in M. Nardini & M. Rossi Monti (Eds.), *Psicopatologia e teoria della conoscenza* (Rome: Athena Editrice, 1989), pp. 131–146.
23. S. Freud, "Female Sexuality," op. cit., p. 254.
24. Ibid.
25. S. Freud, "Psycho-Analytic Notes on an Autobiographical Account of a Case of Paranoia (Dementia Paranoides)" (1910), *SE*, Vol. 12, p. 13.
26. Freud advanced a series of extraordinarily interesting interpretations of the figure of the kite or vulture in "Leonardo da Vinci and a Memory of His Childhood." Among these is the idea that the bird represents virginal motherhood.
27. On these themes see M. Vegetti, *Il coltello e lo stilo* (Milan: Il Saggiatore, 1987), pp. 116f.; and S. Campese, P. Manuli, & G. Sissa, *Madre materia: sociologia e biologia della donna greca* (Turin: Boringhieri, 1983).
28. The author of the Hippocratic treatise *De glandulis* compares the female body to woolen fabric (16, LVIII 5727).
29. S. Freud, "Analysis Terminable and Interminable," p. 251.
30. On the opposition of brain–body in ancient thought, see P. Manuli & M. Vegetti, *Cuore sangue e cervello: biologia e antropologia nel pensiero antico* (Milan: Episteme Editrice, 1977), pp. 9–10.
31. M. Klein, "Envy and Gratitude," in *Envy and Gratitude and Other Works, 1946–1963* (New York: Free Press, 1975), pp. 176–235.
32. J. Piaget & R. Garcia, *Psychogenesis and History of the Sciences*, trans. Helga Feider (New York: Columbia University Press, 1989).
33. M. Foucault, *The Will to Know, Vol. 1: An Introduction*, trans. Robert Hurley (New York: Pantheon, 1978–1986).
34. S. Freud, " 'Civilized' Sexual Morality and Modern Nervousness" (1908), *SE*, Vol. 9, pp. 188–189. Emphasis in original.
35. C. G. Jung, "Psychological Aspects of the Kore," in *Collected Works*, Vol. 9, 1959.
36. "The behavior with regard to jealousy differs in general from that towards envy. . . . The reason for this distinction must be found in the widely held conviction that the assassination of a rival implies love for the unfaithful person. That means . . . that the love for the 'good' object exists and the beloved object is not damaged or ruined as he would be in the case of envy," M. Klein, "Envy and Gratitude," in *Envy and Gratitude and Other Works 1946–1963* (New York: The Free Press, 1975).
37. The discussion of the categorical or phenomenological nature of the primary scene is analytically developed by Freud in "From the History of an Infantile Neurosis" [clinical case of the Wolf-Man] (1914, 1918), *SE*, Vol. 17. J. Laplanche & J. B. Pontalis, *Fantasme originaire: fantasme des origines, origines du fantasme* (Paris: Hachette, 1985). See also the philosophical essay by E. Paci, "Per una fenomenologia dell'eros," in *Aut aut*, no. 214–215 (July–Oct. 1986), pp. 3–20; commentary by M. Pogatschnig, "La trascendenza dell'eros nel pensiero di Enzo Paci," ibid., pp. 111–128.
38. Freud wrote on this point, "Indeed, we have to reckon with the possibility that a number of women remain arrested in their original attachment to their

mother and never achieve a true change-over towards men." "Female Sexuality," p. 226.

39. Cf. S. Freud, "Some Reflections on Schoolboy Psychology" (1914), SE, Vol. 13.

40. S. Freud, "New Introductory Lectures on Psycho-Analysis: Lecture 31" (1933 [1932]), SE, Vol. 22, p. 76.

41. This is a reference to the musical compositions, quite popular at that time, composed by young Chileans who were exiled by the Pinochet dictatorship.

42. On this point see S. Vecchio (Ed.), *Nostalgia: scritti psicoanalitici* (Bergamo: Pierluigi Lubrina Editore, 1989).

43. Freud wrote, "What in adult life is described as 'perverse' differs from the normal in these respects: first, by disregarding the barrier of species (the gulf between men and animals), secondly, by overstepping the barrier against disgust, thirdly that against incest (the prohibition against seeking sexual satisfaction from near blood-relations), fourthly that against members of one's own sex and fifthly the transferring of the part played by the genitals to other organs and areas of the body. None of these barriers existed from the beginning; they were only gradually erected in the course of development and education. Small children are free from them." "Introductory Lectures on Psycho-Analysis, Lecture 13" (1916–1917 [1915–1917]), SE, Vol. 15, p. 209.

44. On this point see W. Burkett, *Homo necans: interpretationen altgriechischer opferriten und mythen* (Amsterdam: De Gruyter, 1972).

45. R. Girard, *Violence and the Sacred*, trans. Patrick Gregory (Baltimore: Johns Hopkins University Press, 1972).

46. N. Loraux, *Tragic Ways of Killing a Woman* (Cambridge, MA: Harvard University Press, 1987).

47. Ibid.

48. Cf. M. Vegetti, *L'etica degli antichi* (Bari: Laterza, 1989), pp. 99–100.

49. B. Bettelheim, *Symbolic Wounds: Puberty Rites and the Envious Male* (Glencoe, IL: The Free Press, 1962).

50. Aristotle, *Generation of Animals*, Loeb Classical Library, No. 366 (Cambridge, MA: Harvard University Press, 1943), I, 20.

51. An exhaustive review of the contributions made by the first women psychoanalysts can be found in J. Chasseguet-Smirgel (Ed.), *Female sexuality* (Ann Arbor: University of Michigan Press, 1970). See also C. Zanardi, *Essential Papers on the Psychology of Women* (New York: New York University Press, 1990), and S. Vegetti Finzi (Ed.), *Psicoanalisi al femminile* (Rome-Bari: Laterza, 1992).

52. The significance of the displacement of symptoms from the lower to the upper body is considered by Freud, mainly in "Fragment of an Analysis of a Case of Hysteria" [clinical case of Dora] (1905 [1901]), SE, Vol. 7, p. 28f., 82n.

53. See on this point, S. Freud, "On Transformations of Instinct as Exemplified by Anal Eroticism" (1917), SE, Vol. 17, and "Some Psychical Consequences of the Anatomical Distinction between the Sexes."

54. G. Bompiani, *L'attesa* (Milan: Feltrinelli, 1988), p. 41.

55. On this point, see S. Freud, "The Taboo of Virginity (Contributions to the Psychology of Love, III)" (1918 [1917]), SE, Vol. 11.

56. S. Freud, "On Transformations of Instinct as Exemplified by Anal Eroticism," (1917), *SE*, Vol. 17, p. 130.
57. S. Freud, "Three Essays on the Theory of Sexuality," (1905), *SE*, Vol. 7, p. 197.
58. See on this point, E. Funari (Ed.), *Il doppio tra patologia e necessità* (Milan: Cortina Editore, 1986).
59. D. W. Winnicott, *The Maturational Processes and the Facilitating Environment. Studies in the Theory of Emotional Development* (London: The Hogarth Press and the Institute of Psycho-analysis, 1965).
60. E. Shorter, *History of Women's Bodies* (New York: Basic Books, 1982). See also G. Bock & G. Nobili (Eds.), *Il corpo delle donne* (Ancona-Bologna: Transeuropa, 1988), and S. Vegetti Finzi, "The Female Animal," in S. Kemp and P. Bono (Eds.), *Lonely Mirror: Italian Perspectives on Feminist Theory* (London, New York: Routledge, 1993).
61. Compare: R. Schérer & G. Hocquenghem, *Co-ire: album systémetique de l'enfance* (Paris: Recherches, 1976), and G. Botteri, "Il bambino e la marionetta: Le avventure di Pinocchio," *Aut aut*, no. 191–192 (Sept.–Dec. 1982).
62. The unconscious always derives a sense of victory in passing from passivity to activity. "Female Sexuality," op. cit., p. 235.
63. According to Freud, a trauma of seduction (real or imaginary) is always at the source of hysterical disturbance, and generally speaking, begins the process that leads to the narcissistic closure to relationships. See "Studies in Hysteria." See also S. Vegetti Finzi, "Un quesito freudiano: Il bambino è nell'infanzia?" *Aut aut*, no. 191–192 (Sept.–Dec. 1981), and A. Saraval (Ed.), *La seduzione: saggi psicoanalitici* (Milan: Cortina Editore, 1989).
64. The asymmetry of the position of the male and female in relation to the mother is pivotal to N. Chodorow's theoretical position in *The Reproduction of Mothering* (Berkeley and Los Angeles: University of California Press, 1978).
65. For a man, it is a question of the impossibility of submitting to another man, for the woman of renouncing her claims to virility, as Freud demonstrates in "Analysis Terminable and Interminable."

CHAPTER 2

1. E. Paci, "Per una fenomenologia dell'eros." *Aut aut*, no. 214–215 (July–Oct. 1986), pp. 3–20. Also see M. Pogatschnig, "La trascendenza dell'eros nel pensiero di Enzo Paci," ibid., pp. 111–128.
2. R. Barthes, "L'ancienne rhétorique. Aide-mémoire," in *L'aventure sémiologique* (Paris: Éditions du Seuil, 1958), p. 163.
3. S. Freud, "Five Lectures on Psycho-Analysis" (1910 [1909]), *SE*, Vol. 11, p. 36.
4. On this point, see "Il vuoto e il pieno," minutes of the conference entitled: *Psichiatria e psicoanalisi di fronte al disagio femminile* (6–7 November 1982), Centro Documentazione Donna di Firenze, Quaderno di lavoro n. 1. See also E. Fachinelli, *La mente estatica* (Milan: Adelphi, 1989).
5. For a theoretical exploration of this concept, see the program entitled "L'am-

biguo materno: Ipotesi di ricerca," Virginia Woolf Women's University of Rome, 1981–1982.

6. "Transitional object" is used here in the sense proposed by D. W. Winnicott in *Playing and Reality* (New York: Basic Books, 1971).

7. S. Freud, "On the History of the Psycho-Analytic Movement" (1914), *SE*, Vol. 14, p. 18.

8. S. Freud, "Three Essays on the Theory of Sexuality" (1905), *SE*, Vol. 7, p. 180.

9. S. Freud, "Instincts and Their Vicissitudes" (1915), *SE*, Vol. 14, p. 128.

10. S. Freud, "Some General Remarks on Hysterical Attacks" (1909 [1908]), *SE*, Vol. 9, p. 232.

11. S. Freud, "Hysterical Phantasies and Their Relationship to Bisexuality" (1908), *SE*, Vol. 9, p. 160.

12. S. Freud, "Female Sexuality" (1931), *SE*, Vol. 21, p. 237.

13. S. Freud, "Minuta LI" (1892–1897), *SE*, Vol. 1, p. 230.

14. S. Freud, "Introductory Lectures on Psychoanalysis (1915–1917)," Lecture 23, *SE*, Vol. 16, p. 370.

15. On this point, see H. A. Frankfort, J. A. Wilson, T. Jacobsen, W. A. Irvin, *Philosophy before Greece* and L. Cagni, *Crestomazia accadica: la creazione e il destino dell'huomo* (Instituto di Studi del Vicino Oriente, Università degli Studi di Roma, 1971), pp. 133–137. On the Orphic theogonies see M. West, *Orphic poems* (Oxford: 1983); G. Colli, *La sapienza greca*, I (Milan: Adelphi, 1977).

16. This is probably on the horizon of the fantastic anthropology of J. J. Bachofen, "The Matriarchy" (1861), in *Myth, Religion, and Mother Right: Selected Writings of J. J. Bachofen*, trans. Ralph Mannheim (Princeton, NJ: Princeton University Press, 1967).

17. On these themes, refer to A. Rich, *Of Woman Born: Motherhood as Experience and Institution* (New York: Norton, 1976); M. Stone, *When God Was a Woman* (New York: Harbrace, 1978).

18. C. Kerényi, *Die Mythologie der Griechen* (Zurich: Rhein Verlag, 1951). Ital. trans. *Gli dei e gli eros della Grecia, Vol. I, 1951* (Milan: Il Saggiatore, 1963), pp. 26–27.

19. Ibid. According to Karl Albert, "Chaos means 'fissure,' 'cavity,' and is connected to the Greek verb 'Chao,' that in its derivative forms is also used in the sense of a mouth that opens, a wound that heals, a cavern that opens in a mountain," quoted in E. Modena, "E. B. L'uomo incinto," *Psicoterapia e Scienze umane* 1 (1990), p. 91.

20. The polarity male-active–female-passive appears in many Freudian writings. The most exhaustive definition, however, appears, I think, in the notes added in 1914 to "Three Essays on the Theory of Sexuality," p. 219. In this regard, see also my original essay: "Topologia della sessualità e cancellazione del femminile," *Aut aut*, no. 177–178 (May–Aug. 1980).

21. L. Brisson, "Les théogonies orphiques et le papyrus de Derveni" in *Revue Histoire des Réligions* (1985), pp. 389–420.

22. S. Weil, *The Notebooks of Simone Weil*, trans. Arthur Wills, Vol. 2 (New York: Putnam, 1956).

23. See, in this regard, the essay by W. Tommasi, "Simone Weil: Dare corpo al

pensiero" in Diotima, *Mettere al mondo il mondo* (Milan: La Tartaruga, 1990), pp. 77–91.

24. Hesiod, *Theogony*, M. L. West (Ed.) (Oxford: Oxford University Press, 1966).

25. Following the ancient debate, it was not until the end of the 1700s that a model was put forth acknowledging the equal contribution of both sexes of generative material.

26. C. Kerényi, op. cit., Ital. trans., p. 103.

27. On the ambiguous power of lettuce, the food of cadavers, and the cause of male impotence, see M. Detienne, "Potagerie de femmes ou comment engendrer seule" in *L'écriture d'Orpheé* (Paris: Gallimard, 1988).

28. Ibid., p. 76.

29. A. Sami, *L'espace imaginaire* (Paris: Gallimard, 1974).

30. Freud wrote, " 'Having' and 'being' in children. Children like expressing an object-relation by an identification: 'I am the object.' 'Having' is the latter of the two; after loss of the object it relapses into 'being.' " "Findings, Ideas, Problems" (1941 [1938]), *SE*, Vol. 23, p. 299.

31. S. Freud, "Beyond the Pleasure Principle" (1920), *SE*, Vol. 18, pp. 14–17.

32. See, in this regard, N. Fusini, *La luminosa: genealogia di fedra* (Milan: Feltrinelli, 1990).

33. See, in this regard, S. Vegetti Finzi, Topologia della sussualità e cancellazione del femminile, pp. 27–58.

34. C. Kerényi, op. cit., p. 209.

35. S. Freud, "A Child Is Being Beaten: A Contribution to the Study of the Origin of Sexual Perversions" (1919), *SE*, Vol. 17, pp. 187–188.

36. M. Detienne, *Dionysos mis à mort* (Paris: Gallimard, 1977), pp. 172 and 210, n. 20. See also the suggestive short story written by T. Villani in *Demetra* (Milan: Mimesis, 1987).

37. C. Kerényi, op. cit., p. 210.

38. Ibid., p. 213.

39. This impersonal formulation relates to another phantasm studied by Freud in "A Child Is Being Beaten: A Contribution to the Study of the Origin of Sexual Perversions."

40. See, in this regard, C. Kerényi, op. cit., p. 215.

41. This episode is told in a tragedy by Euripides, *The Bacchae*.

42. C. Kerényi, op. cit., pp. 224–225.

43. I. Matte Blanco, *The Unconscious as Infinite Sets: An Essay in Bi-Logic* (London: Duckworth, 1975).

44. J. Piaget, *The Child's Conception of the World*, trans. Joan and Andrew Tomlinson (New York: Harcourt, Brace, 1929).

45. The major theoretician of this project is E. Fox Keller, whose works include: "Feminism and Science," *Signs, 3*, Spring 1982, 589–602; "A Feminist Critique of Science: A Forward or a Backward Move?" *Fundamento Scientiae, 1*, 1980, 341–349; *A Feeling for the Organism* (New York: Freeman, 1983); *Reflections on Gender and Science* (New Haven, CT: Yale University Press, 1985).

46. M. Vegetti, *L'etica degli antichi* (Bari: Laterza, 1989).

47. S. Freud, "Three Essays on the Theory of Sexuality," p. 219, n. 1. This position

was be taken up critically by Freud himself ten years later in "Instincts and Their Vicissitudes," p. 134.

48. *De morbis mulierum* (I 17, L) (VIII 56) (I 8, L) (VIII 34); *De genitura:* quotations taken from P. Manuli, "Donne mascoline, femmine sterili, vergini perpetue," in S. Campese, P. Manuli & G. Sissa, *Madre materia: sociologia e biologia della donna greca,* (Turin: Boringhieri, 1983), p. 163.

49. Aristotle, *Generation of Animals,* op. cit., 741, 9, 6–9.

50. Aristotle, *Research on Animals (Historia animalium),* V, 1 (Ed. M. Vegetti). In *Opere biologiche* (Turin: Utet, 1971).

51. His model of animal reproduction assumes that normally it is the sexual act that determines not only fertilization but also the production of the egg.

52. P. Manuli, "L'elogio della castità: La ginecologia di Sorano," in *I corpi possibili, Memoria,* 3 March 1982.

53. Aristotle, *Generation of Animals,* op. cit., I, 2.

54. M. Detienne, "Miti greci e analisi strutturale," in *Il mito greco* (Bari: Laterza, 1973).

55. P. Dubois, *Sowing the Body: Psychoanalysis and Ancient Representations of Women* (Chicago: University of Chicago Press, 1988).

56. Aristotle, *Generation of Animals,* IV, 767 b 18.

57. S. Campese, "Madre materia: Donna, casa, città nell'antropologia di Aristotele," in S. Campese, P. Manuli, & G. Sissa, *Madre materia,* op. cit., p. 48.

58. Aristotle, *Physics,* op. cit., *192a,* 21–25.

59. S. Campese, P. Manuli, & G. Sissa, *Madre materia,* op. cit., p. 88.

60. Plato, "Timaeus," in *Timaeus and Critias,* trans. H. D. P. Lee (Baltimore: Penguin, 1972).

61. G. Sissa, *Le corps virginal,* Librairie Philosophique (Paris: J. Vrin, 1987), p. 69.

62. S. Campese, P. Manuli, & G. Sissa, *Madre materia,* p. 166.

63. L. Irigaray, *Speculum of the Other Woman* (Ithaca, NY: Cornell University Press, 1985).

64. S. Campese, P. Manuli, & G. Sissa, *Madre materia,* op. cit., p. 48.

65. Aristotle, *Historia animalium,* VII 581 b.

66. Ibid., VII 582 a.

67. D. Lanza, "La struttura della teoria genetica in De generatione animalium," in Aristotle, *Opere biologiche,* p. 815.

68. Aristotle, *Generation of Animals,* op. cit., IV 767 b.

69. Ibid., IV 775 b 25, 776 b 14.

70. P. Manuli, "Donne mascoline, femmine sterili, vergine perpetue," in S. Campese, P. Manuli, & G. Sissa, *Madre materia,* op. cit., p. 169.

71. Aristotle, *Politics,* I, 13, 1260 a. The line from Sophocles is Ajax, 293.

72. Aristotle, *Nicomachean Ethics,* VII, 6.

73. P. Vidal Naquet, "Esclavage et gynécocratie dans la tradition, le mythe, l'utopie," in *Recherches sur les structures sociales dans l'antiquité classique* (Paris: 1970), pp. 63–80. On this theme, see also W. Lederer, *The Fear of Women* (New York: Grune & Stratton, 1968).

74. E. Cantarella, *L'ambiguo malanno* (Rome: Editori Riuniti, 1983[2]), pp. 45f.

75. Plato, *Laws*, VI 781 C–D.
76. M. Vegetti, *Il coltello e lo stilo* (Milan: Il Saggiatore, 1987), p. 123.
77. The quote from Simonides's poem is taken from E. Cantarella, *L'ambiguo malanno*, op. cit., pp. 46–49.
78. On this point, see N. Fusini, *La Luminosa*, op. cit.
79. Aristotle, *Politics*, I, 5–9. On this point, see also S. Campese & S. Gastaldi, *La donna e i filosofi* (Bologna: Zanichelli, 1977); D. Lanza, *Il tiranno e il suo pubblico* (Turin: Einaudi, 1977); D. Lanza & M. Vegetti, *L'ideologia della città* (Naples: Liguori, 1977); beyond this, S. Campese, P. Manuli, & G. Sissa, *Madre materia*, op. cit.
80. Plato, *Timaeus*, op. cit., 90e. On this point, see also E. Cantarella, *L'ambiguo malanno*, pp. 75–78.
81. Essential, on this point, is L. Irigaray, *Speculum of the Other Woman*.
82. G. Wajeman, *Le maître et l'hysterique* (Paris: Navarin, Seuil, 1982).
83. C. Kerényi, op. cit., pp. 101–102.
84. B. This (Ed.), *Cantiques lacaniens de la sexuation (Lacan l'amour)* (Paris: Le Coq-Heron, pre-print). (Lacan's Emphasis)
85. Aristophanes, *Lysistrata*, verses 638–645; this translation by C. T. Murphy, from "Lysistrata," in L. R. Lind (Ed.), *Ten Greek Plays in Contemporary Translations* (Boston: Houghton-Mifflin, 1975). On the educational functions of rites, see W. Burkert, "Kekropidensage und Arrephoria. Vom Initiations ritus zum Panathenäenfst," *Hermes*, XCIV, 1966, pp. 1–25; S. Campese, & S. Gastaldi, "La festa e l'educazione del cittadino," in E. Becchi (Ed.), *Storia dell'educazione* (Firenze: La Nuova Italia, 1987); especially, by the same authors, "Immagini e pratiche educative della città antica," in *Per un una storia del costume educativo (età classica e medio evo)*, Fondazione Giangiacomo Feltrinelli, n. 23 (1983).
86. S. Campese & S. Gastaldi, "La festa e l'educazione del cittadino," op. cit., p. 22.
87. C. Kerényi, op. cit., p. 209f.
88. S. Guettle Cole, "Ragazzi e ragazze ad Atene: Koureion e Arkteia," in G. Arrigoni (Ed.), *Le donne in Grecia* (Bari: Laterza, 1985).
89. S. Campese & S. A. Gastaldi, "Immagini e pratiche educative della città antica," op. cit., p. 25. Also essential on this question is M. Detienne, "Violent Eugeneis," in M. Detienne & J. P. Vernant, *The Cuisine of Sacrifice among the Greeks* (Chicago: University of Chicago Press, 1989).
90. On this point, see M. Detienne, *The Gardens of Adonis: Spices in Greek Mythology*, trans. Janet Lloyd (Atlantic Highlands, NJ: Humanities Press, 1976); and S. Vegetti Finzi, "La maternità negata: Alle origini dell'immaginario femminile," in *Memoria*, 7 Sept. 1983.
91. Plato, *Phaedrus*, 276 b.
92. C. Kerényi, op. cit., pp. 202–203; see also G. Devereux, *Baubo: la vulve mythique* (Paris: Godefroy, 1983). Freud wrote of this in "A Mythological Parallel to a Visual Obsession" (1916), *SE*, Vol. 14, pp. 337–338.
93. On this point, see S. Freud, "The Interpretation of Dreams" (1900), *SE*, Vol. 4 , and "Jokes and Their Relation to the Unconscious" (1905), *SE*, Vol. 8.

CHAPTER 3

1. F. Grazzini, "Un centro imprendibile," in *Lapis: percorsi della riflessione femminile*, 7 March 1990, p. 33f.
2. As the book from the Diotima philosophy collective clearly indicates: *Mettere al mondo il mondo* (Milan: La Tartaruga, 1990).
3. On the function of imitation as a precursor of identification, see E. Gaddini, "Sulla imitazione" (1969), in *Scritti 1953–1985* (Milan: Cortina, 1989).
4. S. F. Ferraro & A. Nunziante Cesaro take concave space to be the original fact of femininity, *Lo spazio cavo e il corpo saturato* (Milan: Angeli, 1985).
5. S. Maiello Hunziker, "Corpo femminile, contenimento e creatività," in *Il vuoto e il pieno*, Centro Documentazione Donna di Firenze, Quaderno di Lavorno n. 1, November, 1982.
6. G. J. Lacan, *Le seminaire livre XV encore* (Paris: Seuil, 1975).
7. F. Pizzini (Ed.), *Sulla scena del parto: luoghi, figure, pratiche* (Milan: Angeli, 1981).
8. S. Freud, "Mourning and Melancholia" (1917 [1915]), *SE*, Vol. 14, p. 246.
9. Ibid., p. 249.
10. P. DuBois, *Sowing the Body: Psychoanalysis and Ancient Representations of Women* (Chicago: University of Chicago Press, 1988).
11. Research on this very issue is being carried out at the Philosophy department at Pavia University.
12. I am referring here to Freud's observation that man denies his animal nature because this carries with it a "narcissistic wound." S. Freud, "A Difficulty in the Path of Psycho-Analysis" (1916), *SE*, Vol. 17, p. 137.
13. Pliny, *Natural history*, II, 171, 2.
14. D. Symons, *The Evolution of Human Sexuality* (Oxford: Oxford University Press, 1979).
15. Ibid.
16. Ibid.
17. D. Morris, *The Naked Ape: A Zoologist's Study of the Human Animal* (New York: McGraw-Hill, 1969).
18. M. Davis Caufield, "Che cos'è naturale nel sesso?," *Memoria* 15, 3, 1985, pp. 23–24
19. D. Johanson & M. Edey, *Lucy: The Beginnings of Human Kind* (New York: Warner, 1982).
20. S. Hrdy, *The Woman That Never Evolved* (Cambridge, MA: Harvard University Press, 1981).
21. The theories of N. Tanner and A. Zihlman have been introduced by D. Haraway, "Animal Sociology and a Natural Economy of the Body Politic," *Signs* 4, 1978.
22. As Margaret Mead's anthropological studies demonstrate: *Male and Female: A Study of the Sexes in a Changing World* (Greenwood, 1949); *Sex and Temperament in Three Primitive Societies* (Morrow, 1963).
23. See, in particular, N. Makepeace Tanner, *On Becoming Human* (New York: Cambridge University Press, 1981).
24. J. J. Bachofen, *Myth, Religion, and Mother Right: Selected Writings of Johann Jakob*

Bachofen, trans. Ralph Mannheim (Princeton, NJ: Princeton University Press, 1967).

25. F. Engels, *The Origin of the Family, Private Property and the State* (New York: International Publishers, 1972).

26. C. Lévi-Strauss, *Race et histoire: suivi de l'ouvre de Claude Lévi-Strauss* (Paris: Editions Gonthier, 1961).

27. F. Héritier, "Famiglia," entry in the *Enciclopedia* (Turin: Einaudi, 1979), Vol. 6, p. 7.

28. On this point, see P. Tabet, "Fertilité naturelle, reproduction forcée," in N. C. Mathieu (Ed.), *L'arraisonnement des femmes: essais en anthropologie des sexes*, Collection of Cahiers de l'homme (Paris: Ecole des Hautes Etudes en Sciences Sociales), which I have referred to throughout.

29. F. Basaglia Ongaro, *Una voce* (Milan: Il Saggiatore, 1982), p. 10.

30. S. Vegetti Finzi (Ed.), *Le culture del parto*, (Milan: Feltrinelli, 1985); E. Shorter, *The History of Women's Bodies* (New York: Basic Books, 1982).

31. The medical and hospital management of childbirth is inscribed in a much broader social regulation; on this, see M. Foucault, *Madness and Civilization: A History of Insanity in the Age of Reason*, trans. Richard Howard (New York: Pantheon); *The Birth of the Clinic: An Archaeology of Medical Perception*, trans. A. M. Sheridan (New York: Pantheon, 1973). In particular, I draw your attention to G. Colombo, F. Pizzini, & A. Regalia, *Mettere al mondo: la produzione del parto* (Milan: Angeli, 1984).

32. E. Badinter, *Mother Love: Myth and Reality. Motherhood in Modern History* (New York: Macmillan, 1981).

32a. In many of his works, Freud discusses *coitus interruptus* as a cause of anxiety neurosis, in particular in "Minute teoriche per Wilhelm Fleiss" (1892–1897); "Justification for the Separation of Neurasthenia into Precise Complex Symptoms in Anxiety Neurosis" (1894); "Proposition for a Critique of Anxiety Neurosis" (1895); and "Sexuality in the Aetiology of the Neuroses" (1898), SE, Vol. 3, pp. 263–285.

33. Demosthenes, *Adversus Neeram*, 122.

34. M. Detienne, *The Gardens of Adonis: Spices in Greek Mythology*, trans. Janet Lloyd (Atlantic Highlands, NJ: Humanities Press, 1976).

35. E. C. Keuls, *The Reign of the Phallus: Sexual Politics in Ancient Athens* (New York: Harper & Row, 1985).

36. E. Shorter, *The History of Women's Bodies* (New York: Basic Books, 1982).

37. F. Dolto, *Sexualité féminine: libido, érotisme, frigidité* (Paris: Scarabée et Compagnie, 1982).

38. C. Saraceno, *Sociologia della famiglia* (Bologna: Il Mulino, 1988). See also S. Vegetti Finzi, "Female Identity between Sexuality and Maternity."

39. F. Héritier, "Famiglia," op. cit., p. 3.

40. M. Langer, *Motherhood and Sexuality*, trans. Nancy Caro Hollander (New York: The Guilford Press, 1992).

41. M. Gauchet & G. Swain, *La pratique de l'ésprit humain* Paris: Gallimard, (1984).

42. J. D. T. de Bienville, *Nymphomania or the Uterine Fury* (1771).

43. Dr. Tissot (1760), *L'onanisme: dissertation sur les maladies produites par la masturbation* (Paris: Le sycomore, 1980).
44. J. Breuer, "Theoretical considerations," in (with S. Freud) "Studies on Hysteria" (1893–1895), *SE*, Vol. 2, p. 246. (emphasis added).
45. Ibid. (emphasis in original).
46. Given the impossibility of citing a complete bibliography on the subject, I cite the following: J. Chasseguet-Smirgel, *Female Sexuality*; Y. Mitchell, *Psychoanalysis and Feminism*; S. Vegetti Finzi (Ed.), *Psicoanalisi al femminile*, op. cit.
47. Essential in this regard is L. Irigaray, *Speculum of the Other Woman*, op. cit.
48. R. Siebert, "É Femmine peró é Bella," in *Tre generasioni di donne al sud* (Turin: Rosenberg & Pellier, 1991); C. Saraceno, *Pluralità e mutamento* (Milan: Angeli, 1987).
49. S. Freud, "The Psychopathology of Everyday Life" (1901), *SE*, Vol. 6.
50. S. Freud, "On Narcissism: An Introduction" (1914), *SE*, Vol. 14, pp. 78ff.; "Beyond the Pleasure Principle" (1920), *SE*, Vol. 18, pp. 45ff.
51. S. Freud, "On Narcissism: An Introduction," op. cit., p. 78.
52. Ibid., p. 91.
53. On the subject of abortion see E. Quintavalla & E. Raimondi (Eds.), *Aborto perche?* (Milan: Feltrinelli, 1989); R. Carini & I. Finzi, *Aborto volontario ripetuto e desiderio di gravidanza* (Milan: F. Angeli, 1987).
54. S. Freud, Preface to "Reik's Ritual: Psycho-Analytic Studies" (1919), *SE*, Vol. 17, p. 260.

CHAPTER 4

1. T. de Lauretis, *Alice Doesn't: Feminism, Semiotics, Cinema* (Bloomington, Indiana University Press, 1986).
2. As is demonstrated in Diotima, *Mettere al mondo il mondo* (Milan: La Tartaruga, 1990).
3. On these points, see M. L. Boccia, *L'Io in rivolta: vissuto e pensiero de Carlo Lonzi* (Milan: La Tartaruga, 1990).
4. P. Violi, "Genere, soggettività, linguaggio," in G. Bock & S. James (Eds.), *Beyond Equality and Difference: Citizenship, Feminist Politics and Female Subjectivity* (London, New York: Routledge, 1992).
5. The quotation is a collage of three different passages from Freud, found, respectively, in "Civilization and Its Discontents" (1930 [1929]), *SE*, Vol. 21, p. 91; "The 'Uncanny,' " (1919), *SE*, Vol. 17, p. 245; and "The Interpretation of Dreams" (1899), *SE*, Vol. 5, 398.
6. Artemidorous, *The Book of Dreams*, I, 79.
7. S. Freud, "The Interpretation of Dreams," p. 577.
8. C. G. Jung, "Psychological Aspects of the Archetype of the Mother" (1938/1954).
9. S. Freud, "The Theme of the Three Caskets" (1913) *SE*, Vol. 12.
10. C. Merchant, *The Death of Nature: Women, Ecology and the Scientific Revolution. Feminist Reappraisal of the Scientific Revolution* (San Francisco: Harper & Row, 1980).

11. C. Pancino, *Il bambino e l'acqua sporca: storia dell'assistenza al parto dalle mammane alle ostetriche (secoli XVI–XIX)* (Milan: Angeli, 1984), p. 17.
12. On this point, see A. W. Meyer, *An Analysis of the "De generatione animalium" of William Harvey* (Stanford, CA: Stanford University Press, 1963), pp. 131 and 153.
13. Ibid., p. 202.
14. G. Pomata, *In scienza e coscienza: Donne e potere nella società borghese* (Firenze: La Nuova Italia, 1979); F. Pizzini (Ed.), *Asimmetrie comunicative* (Milan: Angeli, 1990).
15. B. Constantino, "Travail, travaglio," *Tematiche femminili* (Turin: Il Segnalibro, 1988), p. 143.
16. Among the many others, see the view theorized by L. Irigaray, "La doppia soglia," in G. Buzzatti et al., *Verso il luago delle origini* (Milan: Le Tartaruga, 1992); and "Women, the Sacred, and Money," in *Sexes and Genealogies*, trans. Gillian C. Gill (New York: Columbia University Press, 1993).
17. On this point, see the entry "Lavoro" by S. Borutti in *Dizionario Marx Engels* (general editor, F. Papi) (Bologna: Zanichelli, 1983).
18. P. Tapet, "Fertilité naturelle, reproduction forcée," op. cit.
19. Plato, *Laws*, 780a–781d, trans. R. G. Bury (Cambridge, MA: Harvard University Press, 1926). See also, S. Campese & S. Gastaldi (Eds.), *La donna e i filosofi: archeologia di un'immagine culturale* (Bologna: Zanichelli, 1977), p. 45.
19a. Thucydides, III, 104.
20. Plato, *Symposium*, 206–207c, trans. Benjamin Jowett (Indianapolis: Bobbs-Merrill, 1956).
21. See L. Irigaray, *An Ethics of Sexual Difference*, trans. Carolyn Burke & Gillian C. Gill (Ithaca, NY: Cornell University Press, 1993).
22. M. Vegetti, *L'etica degli antichi*, (Bari: Laterza, 1989), pp. 137–138.
23. Plato, *Symposium*, 207b–c.
24. Ibid., 209 a–d.
25. Quotation taken from M. Fumagalli Beonio Brocchieri, "Ildegarda la professa," in *Medivo al femminile* (Roma-Bari: Laterza, 1989), p. 156.
26. On this point, see T. Perlini, "Spunti per un'auto-riflessione critica all'interno delle scienze umane," in *Psicoterapia e scienze umane*, 20, no. 3 (1986).
27. S. Moravia, *L'enigma della mente* (Bari: Laterza, 1986).
28. Thanks to the author, I had access to this important research on maternal desires, to which I refer here, while it was still in manuscript form: C. Pancino, "L'assistenza al parto dalla pratica femminile all'intervento medico," in *Sulla scena del parto: luoghi, figure, pratiche* (Milan: Angeli, 1981), p. 62.
29. M. Foucault, *The Birth of the Clinic: An Archaeology of Medical Perception*, trans. A. M. Sheridan (New York: Pantheon, 1973).
30. M. Scipione, *La comare o raccoglitrice* (Venice, 1601).
31. L. Muratori, *Della forza della fantasia umana* (Firenze, 1745), pp. 93, 94.
32. Quotation taken from C. Pancino, op. cit.
33. An interesting take on this subject can be found in H. Ellis, op. cit., *Psychology of Maternity*, in *Studies on the Psychology of Sex* (New York: Random House, 1937).
34. H. Rutgers Marshall, in *British Medical Journal*, July 29, 1905.

35. M. Mancia, "Vita prenatale e organizzazione della mente," in M. Ammaniti (Ed.), *La nascita del Sé* (Roma-Bari: Laterza, 1989).
36. On this point, see W. Bion, "Learning from Experience," in *Seven Servants: Four Works* (New York: Basic Books, 1961).
37. J. Michelet, *L'amour* (1858).
38. C. Lispector, *The Passion According to G. H.* (Minneapolis: University of Minnesota Press, 1988).
39. On this point, see A. Miller, *The Drama of the Gifted Child*, trans. Ruth Ward (New York: Basic Books, 1981).
40. M. Klein, "Envy and Gratitude," in *Envy and Gratitude and Other Works, 1946–1963* (New York: Free Press, 1975), pp. 176–235.
41. J. Habermas, "The Claim of the Universality of Hermeneutics," in *Critical Culture* (1970).
42. See W. Tommasi, "Simone Weil: Dare corpo al pensiero," in Diotima, *Mettere al mondo il mondo*.
43. I am referring to what Spitz calls "precursors." See *The First Year of the Life of the Baby* (1958). On this point, I also cite S. Vegetti Finzi (with A. M. Battistini), *A piccoli passi psicologie del bambino dall' attesa ai cinque anni* (Milan: Mondadori, 1994).
44. J. Chasseguet-Smirgel, *Creativity and Perversion* (New York: Norton, 1984).
45. The spiritual sublimation of the maternal body is particularly evident in the works of Saint Catherine and Saint Teresa of Avila.
46. L. A. Salomé, *Die Erotik*, Ital. trans. *L'erotiquo* (Milan: La Tartaruga, 1985), p. 92.
47. Cf. L. Balbo (Ed.), *Time to Care* (Milan: Angeli, 1987).
48. S. Freud, "On Narcissism: An Introduction" (1914), *SE*, Vol. 14, p. 89.
49. Ibid., p. 88.
50. S. Freud, "Femininity," in "New Introductory Lectures on Psycho-Analysis," *SE*, Vol. 22, p. 133.
51. Ibid.
52. Cf. L. Wahl Rabine, "Una politica di non identità," in *Memoria*, 25, 1, 1989.
53. This competence is explored philosophically in, Diotima, *Mettere al mondo il mondo*.
54. E. Fox Keller, *A Feeling for the Organism: The Life and Work of Barbara McClintock* (San Francisco: W. H. Freeman, 1983).
55. Ibid.
56. See E. Donini, "Soggetto donna/oggetto scienza: Gli interrogativi dell'identità di genere," in R. Alicchio and C. Pezzoli (Eds.), *Donne di scienza: esperienze e riflessioni* (Turin: Rosenberg & Seller, 1988).
57. See H. Arendt, *Rahel Varnhagen: The Life of a Jewish Woman*, trans. Richard & Clara Winston (New York: Harcourt, Brace, Jovanovich, 1974); and A. Caverero, "Dire la nascita," in Diotima, *Mettere al mondo il mondo*.
58. M. Vegetti, "Passioni e bagni caldi: Il problema del bambino cattivo nell'antropologia stoica," in *Tra Edipo e Euclide* (Milan: Il Saggiatore, 1983).
59. D. G. M. Schreber, *The New Gymnastics for Men, Women, and Children*, trans. D. Lewis (Boston: Tichnor & Fields, 1864 [Microfilm: New Haven, CT: Research Publication, Inc., 1975]).

60. On this point, see M. T. Maiocchi, *In-fans? la costruzione scientifica dell'infanzia e la psicoanalisi* (Milan: Angeli, 1985); and S. Vegetti Finzi, "Un quesito freudiano: Il bambino è nell'infanzia?" in *Aut aut*, no. 191–192 (Sept.–Dec. 1982).

61. An exhaustive review of Kleinian thought can be found in G. De Simone Gaburri & B. Fornari, "Melanie Klein e la Scuola inglese," in *Trattato di psicoanalisi*, Vol. 1 (Milan: Cortina, 1988). Also see S. Vegetti Finzi, "Il teatro dell'inconscio," in *Storia della psicoanalisi* (Milan: Mondadori, 1990).

62. M. Arrigoni Scortecci, "La costruzione di modelli psicoanalitici nelle psicosi," in *Trattato di Psicoanalisi*, Vol. 2.

63. H. S. Sullivan, in *The Interpersonal Theory of Psychiatry*, Helen Swick & Mary Ladd Garvel (Eds.) (New York: Norton, 1953).

64. H. Kohut, *The Analysis of the Self: A Systematic Approach to the Psychoanalytic Treatment of Narcissistic Personality Disorders* (New York: International Universities Press, 1971); H. F. Searles, *Selected Papers on Schizophrenia and Related Subjects* (London: The Hogarth Press and the Institute of Psycho-analysis, 1965).

65. I am referring to A. Zambelli Fabbrichesi, "Tutte le mamme sono cattive," in *Gli Argonauti*, 20, VI, 84.

66. M. Mitscherlich-Nielsen, "Psicoanalisi della femminilità," in *Psicoterapia e Scienze umane* 16, no. 3 (1982).

67. B. Bettelheim, *A Good Enough Parent* (New York: Knopf, 1987).

68. M. S. Mahler, *The Psychological Birth of the Human Infant: Symbiosis and Individuation* (New York: Basic Books, 1975).

69. A. Lorenzer, *Zur Begründung einer Materialistichen Sozialisationstheorie* (Frankfurt: Suhrkamp Verlag, 1972); *Sprachzerstörung and Rekonstruktion* (Frankfurt: Suhrkamp Verlag, 1970).

70. J. Lacan, *Écrits* (Paris: Editions du Seuil, 1966).

71. By "moral" I mean the sum of values and behaviors shared by a group, while the term "ethical" stresses the reflection upon the moral, its explicit generalization. For a discussion of a specifically feminine morality, see L. Irigaray, *An Ethics of Sexual Difference*, trans. Carolyn Burke & Gillian C. Gill (Ithaca, NY: Cornell University Press, 1993); C. Gilligan, *In a Different Voice: Psychological Theory and Women's Development* (Cambridge, MA: Harvard University Press, 1982); "Questioni di etica," in *Memoria*, 26, 2, 1989.

72. See J. J. Goux, "Materia, differenza dei sessi," in *Vel. Materia e pulsione di morte* (Venice: Marsilio, 1975); and F. Basaglia Ongaro, *Una voce* (Milan: Il Saggiatore, 1982), p. 9.

73. On this point, see C. Ventimiglia, "La filiazione tra simbolico e pricipio di realtà," *Politica del diritto* 19 no. 2 (June 1988).

74. R. Musil, *Five Women*, trans. Eithne Wilkins & Ernst Kaiser (Boston: D. R. Gondine, 1966).

75. F. Fornari, *Il codice vivente* (Turin: Boringhieri, 1981).

76. G. Pitetropolli Charmet, "L'invidia del padre," in *L'invidia: aspetti sociali e culturali* (Milan: Scheiwiller, 1990).

77. B. Bettelheim, *The Empty Fortress: Infantile Autism and the Birth of the Self* (New York: Free Press, 1967).

78. I am referring here to the provocative thesis proposed by C. Contini in *Non di solo amore* (Milan: Longanesi, 1990).

79. H. Deutsch, *Psychoanalysis of the Sexual Functions of Women*, ed. Paul Roazen, trans. Eric Mosbacher (London and New York: Karnak, 1991); and *The Psychology of Women: A Psychoanalytic Interpretation* (New York: Grune & Stratton, 1944–1945).

80. See M. Masud R. Khan, *The Hidden Selves: Between Theory and Practice in Psychoanalysis* (London: Hogarth Press, 1983).

81. This is the title of Adrienne Rich's best-known work, *Of Woman Born: Motherhood as Experience and Institution* (New York: Norton, 1976).

82. D. W. Winnicott, *Home Is Where We Start From: Essays of a Psychoanalyst*, Clare Winnicott, Ray Shepherd, & Madeleine Davis (Eds.) (New York: Norton, 1986). On this point, see also A. Salvo, "L'essere una e tre delle donne: Dialogando con Winnicott," in *Reti* 1 (Jan.–Feb. 1989).

83. See A. Di Meo & C. Mancina (Eds.), *Bioetica* (Roma-Bari; Laterza, 1989); and C. Ventimiglia (Ed.), *La famiglia moltiplicata* (Milan: Angeli, 1987).